The Handbook to Wills, Funerals, and Probate

Third Edition

How to Protect Yourself and Your Survivors

THEODORE E. HUGHES
AND DAVID KLEIN

Facts On File
An imprint of Infobase Publishing

The Handbook to Wills, Funerals, and Probate:
How to Protect Yourself and Your Survivors

Copyright © 2007, 2001, 1987, 1983 by Theodore E. Hughes and David Klein

Text new to this edition
Copyright © 2007 by Theodore E. Hughes

Facts On File, Inc.
An imprint of Infobase Publishing
132 West 31st Street
New York NY 10001

ISBN-10: 0-8160-6669-8   ISBN-13: 978-0-8160-6669-8

Library of Congress Cataloging-in-Publication Data

Hughes, Theodore E.
The handbook to wills, funerals, and probate : how to protect yourself and
your survivors / Theodore E. Hughes. — 3rd ed.
p. cm.
Rev. ed. of: The family guide to wills, funerals, and probate / Theodore E. Hughes
and David Klein. 2nd ed. 2001.
ISBN 0-8160-6669-8 (hc : alk. paper)
1. Wills—United States—Popular works. 2. Probate law and practice—United States—
Popular works. 3. Undertakers and underaking—United States.
I. Klein, David, 1919–2001 II. Hughes, Theodore E. Family guide to wills, funerals,
and probate III. Title.
KF755.Z9 H84 2007
346.7305'2—dc22   2006026726

Text design and layout by Erika K. Arroyo
Cover design by Cathy Rincon

Printed in the United States of America

MP FOF 10 9 8 7 6 5 4 3 2 1

This book is printed on acid-free paper.

CONTENTS

Part II
COPING WITH A DEATH IN THE FAMILY

DOCUMENTS

TABLES

INTRODUCTION

. . . in this world nothing is certain but death and taxes.
—Benjamin Franklin, 1789

Few of us want to think about death, even fewer feel comfortable talking about it, and fewer still are willing to plan for it. In fact, in an age when life has generally become easier and "sensitive" topics are discussed more openly, death has become increasingly difficult to face, and it has outstripped sex as *the* taboo topic of our times.

This is not to say that people of any period faced death with equanimity. But there are several reasons why the prospect of death is more frightening to us than it was to our parents and grandparents.

To begin with, death is far less familiar today. In our parents' day, almost everyone over the age of thirty had experienced the death of a parent, a sibling, or a close friend. Thus, death was an expected part of daily life, and people learned to accept and cope with it. But in our times the dramatic increase in life expectancy has made our encounters with death far less frequent, and when they occur, we have little experience to help us deal with them.

Our unfamiliarity with death is increased by the fact that most people today die not in their own beds, surrounded by their families, but in hospitals, nursing homes, or hospices attended by impersonal professionals during the last hours of their lives and the first hours of their deaths. These strangers often make "professional" decisions that may serve their own interests or reflect their own values rather than those of the dying person or the survivors.

The decrease in family size and the weakening of family bonds have created further problems. No longer can we expect our survivors to find emotional comfort and economic shelter among members of a large, extended family on the family farm or in the family business. Instead, we must make formal, often complex, and legalistic arrangements to ensure that our assets will be safely and swiftly transferred to our survivors, that our minor children will be taken care of, that whatever business was interrupted by our death will be brought to an orderly close, and that our final medical care will be consistent with our wishes.

Lastly, in the case of almost every death, the normal process of our survivors' grief and bereavement is interrupted by their need to deal with a number of bureaucracies—banks and brokers, probate courts, federal and state tax authorities, and other government agencies—many of which did not exist or played no part in deaths that occurred a few decades ago.

Perhaps all this explains why many people acknowledge that their deepest anxieties about death center not on their own fate but on what will happen—emotionally, socially, and financially—to those they leave behind. And psychologists who have studied bereavement conclude that the survivors, no matter how intense their love for the deceased, may actually be grieving more acutely about their own plight—emotional, social, and financial.

Our purpose in this book, then, is to relieve to some extent your anxieties about your survivors and to ease their distress about their own situation, at least in its material aspects. To the extent that we succeed, your concern with your death can focus on your emotional relationships with your survivors, and their grief for you will center on the loss of your companionship and not on "the mess we've been left in."

Planning for your own incapacity and death involves three areas that are only slightly related to each other: (1) making end-of-life health care decisions, (2) managing the transfer of your assets to your survivors as efficiently as possible, and (3) dealing with your bodily remains in a way that you and your survivors feel is appropriate.

The problem of health-care decisions can be substantially alleviated by the preparation of a medical power of attorney—a document that we deal with at length in chapter 8.

The "assets" issue we can deal with objectively and precisely. Assuming that you prefer to leave as much as possible of your estate to your survivors and as little as possible to tax collectors, creditors, courts, and lawyers, we can show you the right and wrong ways to achieve this end.

Disposing of your remains and preserving your memory are such personal matters that obviously there can be no right or wrong procedure. Whether you prefer an elaborate funeral service and an impressive mausoleum or a minimal-cost "direct disposal" arrangement with a simple memorial service, we have no wish to influence your choice. Yet, whatever your preference, we will note more efficient and less efficient ways of having it carried out.

The easiest way to deal with an unpleasant prospect is by procrastination. And this is probably why most Americans die without a will, without an advance directive, and without any plans for the disposition of their bodies or their property. Given a life expectancy of some seventy years, most young adults apparently believe that making a will, planning their estate, preparing for incapacity, and doing anything else that forces them to recognize their own mortality can safely be put off until their late sixties.

But those who take comfort from mortality tables overlook a fact that appears daily on the obituary pages: people die at all ages. The most common cause of death before the age of forty is accidents. And because accidents sometimes kill husband and wife simultaneously, designating a guardian for your minor or disabled children and planning for the management of their inheritance are absolutely essential, even for parents who have not reached the midpoint of their statistical life expectancies.

Planning for your survivors should begin as soon as you have acquired assets that give you even a modest net worth or as soon as you become legally responsible for minor children, through birth or through adoption. Moreover, it should proceed continuously as your net worth and your kinship network change—as you accumulate wealth, as you gain or lose relatives and friends by birth, marriage, divorce, estrangement, or death, and whenever you change your state of residence. This does not mean that you need to devote an inordinate amount of time to planning your estate or contemplating your death or that you ought to revise your will every time you get into an argument at a family reunion. It does mean that you ought to devote perhaps half a day each year to calculating your net worth and reviewing your will, your estate plan, your financial and medical powers of attorney, and your funeral arrangements in the light of any recent changes.

The Handbook is intended to make all this easier for you by suggesting a systematic course of action. Chapters 1–10 deal with matters that you can and should attend to immediately, no matter what your age. The more effectively you deal with them, the less you will have to do when age or illness makes disability or death seem imminent. What to do when death seems close at hand is dealt with in chapter 11. Again, the more effectively you cope with last-minute problems, the less difficult will be the problems faced by your survivors—problems dealt with in chapters 12 through 16.

If at this point you have not set this book aside, you obviously are willing to face the possibility of your incapacity or the inevitability of your own death. If you can share its contents with your family and perhaps a close friend and use it to formulate plans that are both satisfying and practicable, what is inevitable will be less painful for all of you.

Part I

MAKING LIFE EASIER FOR YOUR SURVIVORS

✥ **1** ✥

YOUR WILL AND
ITS FUNCTIONS

For most people, preparing a will is their first confrontation with their own mortality. This is probably why they tend to procrastinate—and why three out of every four Americans die without one. Yet a will, thoughtfully prepared, can do much to alleviate your fears about death because it enables you to provide for the welfare of your survivors after you are gone and because it assures you that whatever estate you leave behind will be distributed as you would like it to be.

Basically a will has three functions: to designate a guardian for your minor children in the event that you and your spouse die simultaneously, to specify precisely who is to inherit how much of your estate and with what strings attached, and to name a personal representative (formerly called an executor) who will see to it that your estate is distributed according to the terms of your will. These functions will all be carried out whether you leave a will or not, but if you die intestate—that is, without a will—the decisions will be made by the local probate court in compliance with state law—and with consequences that you would probably find quite unacceptable.

If, for example, you and your spouse die simultaneously, the probate court will appoint a guardian for your minor children. But in such circumstances the court is likely to appoint a relative— perhaps a sister whose values and life-style are very different from yours—whereas you might prefer a close friend as the person most likely to rear the children according to your own values.

This loss of control applies also to whatever assets you leave. If you die without a will (dying "intestate"), these assets will be distributed to your creditors and your "heirs at law" by the probate court. Although the intestacy laws vary slightly from one state to another, their common underlying premise is that "blood is thicker than water"—that kinship is the fundamental principle governing

TABLE 1.1

Intestate Succession Under the Uniform Probate Code

If Deceased Is Survived[1] by	Deceased's Probate Estate Distributed as Follows
I (a) Spouse and descendants[2] (Born to deceased and spouse)	a) Spouse takes 1st $150,000 plus half of balance[5] b) Descendants share half of balance
I (b) Spouse and descendants[2] (Born to deceased alone)	a) Spouse takes 1st $100,000 plus half of balance[5] b) Issue share half of balance
II Spouse and Parents (No descendants)	a) Spouse takes 1st $200,000 plus three-fourths of balance b) Parents share half of balance
III Spouse only (No descendants)	Spouse takes all
IV Descendants only (No spouse)	Descendants take all
V Parents (No spouse or descendants)	Parents take all
VI Parents' descendants[3] (No spouse, descendants or parents)	Parents' descendants take all
VII Grandparents or their descendants[4] (No spouse, descendants, parents, siblings)	a) Paternal grandparents or their descendants share half b) Maternal Grandparents or their descendants share half
VIII None of the above survive.	State takes all[6]

[1] By at least 120 hours.

[2] Children, grandchildren, great-grandchildren, etc.

[3] Deceased's brothers, sisters, nephews, nieces, grandnephews, grandnieces, etc.

[4] Deceased's uncles, aunts, first cousins, first cousins once removed.

[5] In addition, the spouse takes all of the deceased's community property.

[6] When the deceased is not survived by any persons in categories I through VII, his or her intestate probate estate escheats to the deceased's state of domicile.

Source: Uniform Probate Code

the distribution of your estate. Thus, if you die without leaving a will, some state laws specify that up to three-fourths of your estate must go to your spouse, the balance to be equally divided among your children or grandchildren. If you leave a spouse but no children, half may go to your parents. If both your spouse and your parents are dead and you leave no children or grandchildren, everything will go to your brothers and sisters or nieces and nephews. And if you leave neither spouse nor kin, your entire estate goes to the state. If you leave no will, then friends, lifetime partners, stepchildren, or charities get nothing.

It's conceivable that this state-specified plan coincides exactly with your own preferences—in which case you may have no need for a will. But it's more likely that one or more of its provisions will be totally unacceptable. For example, do you want your children to get half your estate (which you could have willed to your spouse)—especially if they are minors, self-sufficient, or alienated from you. If you do want your children to inherit, do you want them to share equally if one of them is a minor or is disabled, retarded, or indigent and the others are adults, healthy, or well off? And, lastly, do you have some nonkin—friends, stepchildren, a lifetime partner, employees, your alma mater, or some charitable institution—to whom you'd like to leave a special gift or a sum of money?

A personal representative appointed by the court in the absence of a will is entitled to a fee and must pay an annual bonding premium, both of which will be charged against your estate. Would you prefer to make your own choice in a way that can keep the fee in the family and save the cost of a bond premium?

Since any of these questions may lead you to make a will, why is it that most Americans die without one? As we have noted, the real reason may be that making a will requires one to acknowledge the prospect of one's own death, but since admitting to a fear of death makes most people uncomfortable, other excuses are commonly offered. Here are some of them, along with counterarguments:

"Why think about it now? There's plenty of time."

Usually presented by young and middle-aged people, this argument overlooks two points. First, death, especially by accident, can come at any time. Perhaps more important, it is people in the younger age groups who are most likely to leave minor or dependent children, and since many accidents kill husband and wife simultaneously, only a will can ensure that the person they choose will be appointed as guardian of the children.

"My net worth isn't high enough to justify the trouble and expense."

Actually, the lower your net worth, the more important it is that you have a will—to ensure that the probate court does not automatically deprive your spouse of half your estate or reduce your estate by the fees of a court-appointed personal representative. And, of course, the question of the guardianship of your minor children becomes more important if the value of your estate is small.

In fact, however, most people underestimate their net worth, not realizing what inflation has done to the value of their real estate, their automobiles, their investments, their stamp collections, and other possessions that have accumulated over a lifetime. Moreover, there is no way for you to estimate accurately what your net worth will be at the time of your death—or even afterward. You may die holding a winning lottery ticket for a million-dollar prize. Or you may die in an accident that results in a successful $500,000 lawsuit for damages arising from your death through another's negligence. Or one of your stocks, whose value has been negligible for years, may suddenly "take off."

"All my property is held jointly with my spouse; thus it will pass automatically to her [him] when I die."

Joint ownership, as we shall see, makes good sense in many marital situations, but despite your intentions, it almost never covers all your possessions and assets. Are your cars owned jointly? What about your collection of guns or clocks? Does the bill of sale for that antique Chippendale table list both of you as owners? Are there some securities that you or your broker neglected to register in joint ownership or with a transfer-on-death beneficiary? Even the most carefully planned estate is likely to include some property that is yours and yours alone. Unless such property is willed to a specific beneficiary, it will be distributed by the probate court in accordance with state intestacy laws.

Perhaps more important, even if absolutely everything is owned jointly, you need to be concerned with what happens to your property if you and your spouse or other joint owner are killed simultaneously or if one of you survives but dies sometime later without having made a will.

WHAT A WILL CAN DO

It would seem, then, that every adult who owns anything of worth or who has a spouse, children, or friends should make a will to ensure that his or her estate will be disposed of according to personal preferences rather than state law. Here, in summary, are some of the issues that a will can settle:

It can name an executor (sometimes called a personal representative) who will be required by law to manage your estate until it is finally distributed. Although an executor appointed by the probate court must be bonded (with the bonding premium paid by your estate) and is limited in his authority, your will can specify that the bond requirement is to be waived and that an executor's authority be far broader than what state law permits.

It can name a guardian and an alternate guardian for your minor children and a conservator (also sometimes called a guardian) to manage their inherited assets until they reach the age of majority. Some states, however, permit a guardian for minors to be nominated by a writing separate from a will.

It can designate your primary and contingent beneficiaries: "I give $5,000 to A if he survives my death; otherwise to B."

It can specify charitable gifts—to churches, educational institutions, and philanthropic organizations, for example.

It can make conditional gifts: "I give $1,000 to my nephew Steven Cort if he has earned his undergraduate degree by the time of my death."

It can forgive a debt. If, for example, A owes you $5,000, your will can specify that your estate forgive the balance outstanding at the time of your death.

It can establish a trust and name a trustee for minor children or aged or disabled persons so that they get the benefit of part of your estate but do not have the responsibility for managing it. Such a "testamentary" (will-created) trust can be used to postpone ultimate distribution of an inheritance to children beyond the age of majority, say, to age twenty-five, when they are more mature and less likely to be parted from their money. Without a trust, a child will have complete access to his total inheritance, no matter its size, upon reaching the age of majority, which is eighteen in most states. Similarly, a will can transfer some or all of your estate to a custodial account for a minor, or to a living trust that you may have established during your lifetime.

It can establish the order of survivorship in cases where spouses die simultaneously in an accident, by stating:

> In the event that my wife (husband) and I die simultaneously or under circumstances where it cannot be determined who died first, then it shall be presumed that my wife (husband) survived me, and all provisions of my will shall be construed based on such presumption.

This distinction can be important because in some states, if the two deaths are simultaneous, all jointly owned assets are divided in half, each half requiring separate probate administration. If, on the other hand, one joint owner is regarded as having died later than the other, he or she is deemed to have acquired the entire joint estate and is thus able to pass it on intact to his or her survivors without necessitating double probate.

It can, in some states, include a clause authorizing you, by use of a separate document, to later make an informal list of gifts of specific items of personal property. For example, your later list, which could take the form of a handwritten and unwitnessed letter or an informal note, can make gifts of heirlooms, keepsakes, or other personal items to family and friends—and can be used subsequently to amend such a list, all without the formalities of visiting your lawyer, amending your will, or making a new will.

It can disinherit survivors other than a spouse, who normally has a right to override a will that disinherits him or her.

It can revoke all previous wills.

WHAT A WILL CAN'T— OR SHOULDN'T—DO

Because most people have learned what they know about wills from news stories, movies, novels, or television shows, it's not surprising that they have picked up a good deal of misinformation. There are some provisions that should not be included in a will, either because they are clearly illegal and will not be enforced by the courts or because they are simply inadvisable. Here are some examples:

Although a will can transfer "probate assets" (assets in your name alone at death), a will cannot supersede transfers that occur automatically to beneficiaries named in a living trust, pay-on-death bank accounts, transfer-on-death securities accounts, transfer-on-death real estate deeds, and transfer-on-death vehicle titles, property owned jointly with someone who survives you, or life insurance proceeds and retirement account funds where you have designated a beneficiary who survives you.

A will may not place a condition on a gift if the condition is generally seen as contrary to sound public policy. Thus, if you leave $5,000 to one of your daughters "provided she divorce the man to whom she is married," the court would hold that the disruption of marriage is against public policy and thus the condition would be unenforceable. Similarly, will provisions that bequeath gifts to illegal organizations, such as terrorist groups, may be successfully contested.

Although it can limit a spouse's share of the estate to the minimum specified by law, a will may not disinherit a spouse entirely. If your surviving spouse is dissatisfied with the provisions in your will, most state laws allow him or her to elect to "take against" the will, which will almost certainly result in the spouse receiving part of your estate. A will may disinherit a child, but the child should be named specifically. Otherwise the child may successfully claim that he or she was omitted unintentionally and is hence entitled to an amount equal to what he would have inherited had the parent died without leaving a will.

A will may not force a gift on an indifferent or unwilling recipient. A beneficiary is under no obligation to accept anything left to him by the will and may disclaim any bequest.

A will may not impose penalties on anyone who chooses to contest its provisions. A condition such as "I give my son Jonathan $5,000, but if he contests my will, I direct that he shall receive nothing" will not be upheld if the court feels that the son's lawsuit contesting the will has some merit. Similarly, a will cannot successfully require that anyone contesting the will must pay all litigation costs, including those incurred by the estate.

It is both unnecessary and unwise to disinherit anyone by bequeathing to him or her the sum of one dollar. All beneficiaries must sign receipts for their inheritances before the estate can be closed, and if the beneficiary thus insulted refuses to cooperate, a problem may be created for the personal representative.

There is no restriction against specifying funeral or burial arrangements or anatomical gifts in a will, but both may become irrelevant if the will is not located and read immediately upon your death. (Chapter 10 suggests a more effective technique for making such wishes known.)

Although a will may specify that some of your possessions are to be given to designated beneficiaries, it should not contain a complete inventory of your assets, since any change in these would necessitate a revision of your will. Assets should be inventoried not in your will but in a letter of instruction (see chapter 10).

You may, if you wish, include in your will whatever statement of your philosophy or "message to the world" you choose, but it is unwise to use your will as a vehicle for venting your displeasure with or animosity against any named individuals. Once the will is probated, it becomes a public document, and any scurrilous attacks it contains will, at best, embarrass your survivors and, at worst, involve your estate in the expensive defense of a libel suit brought by the defamed party.

In disposing of your property, a will must express clear, unambiguous instructions, not mere wishes or hopes. Thus, "I wish my friend John to receive my clock" is an unclear and possibly unenforceable version of "I give John Howard my Chauncey Jerome banjo clock."

WHO SHOULD PREPARE THE WILL?

The foregoing list of dos and don'ts is not intended to encourage you to embark on a do-it-yourself will. On the contrary, it illustrates that a very large number of details, many of them seemingly petty, can render invalid in whole or in part a will prepared without competent professional advice.

Once again, thanks to the mass media, a good deal of misinformation abounds. Is it possible, for example, to make a will simply by writing out your instructions in longhand and then adding your signature? Aside from the technical errors it may contain, such a will—known as a holographic (in your handwriting) will—has no legal standing whatever in about half the states, but in some circumstances it is better than no will at all (see table 1.2). Oral wills, such as deathbed statements, are even less widely accepted.

Must you, then, pay for the professional services of a lawyer, or can you make your own will by following the instructions or using the forms provided in a number of "how to make a will" books and

TABLE 1.2
Requirements Governing Wills, by State

	Minimum Age to Make a Will	Number of Required Witnesses	Recognizes Holographic Wills	Recognizes Oral Wills	Conditions Imposed on Oral Wills*
Alabama	18	2	No	No	
Alaska	18	2	Yes	Yes	6, 8, 17, 18
Arizona	18	2	Yes	No	
Arkansas	18	2	Yes	No	
California	18	2	Yes	No	
Colorado	18	2	Yes	No	
Connecticut	18	2	No[21]	No	
Delaware	18	2	No	No	
District of Columbia	18	2	No	Yes	6, 7, 8, 12, 16
Florida	18	2	No	No	
Georgia	14	2	No	No	
Hawaii	18	2	Yes	No	
Idaho	18	2	Yes	No	
Illinois	18	2	No	No	
Indiana	18	2	No	Yes	3, 4, 6, 9, 11, 12, 17, 18, 20
Iowa	18	2	No	No	
Kansas	18	2	No	Yes	6, 7, 12, 17, 21
Kentucky	18	2	Yes	No	
Louisiana	16	2	Yes	No	
Maine	18	2	Yes	No	
Maryland	18	2	No[22]	No	
Massachusetts	18	2	No	Yes	6, 8
Michigan	18	2	Yes	No	
Minnesota	18	2	No	No	
Mississippi	18	2	Yes	Yes	7, 10, 12, 18

TABLE 1.2
Requirements Governing Wills, by State (continued)

	Minimum Age to Make a Will	Number of Required Witnesses	Recognizes Holographic Wills	Recognizes Oral Wills	Conditions Imposed on Oral Wills*
Missouri	18	2	No	Yes	2, 6, 11, 12, 17, 19, 20
Montana	18	2	Yes	No	
Nebraska	18	2	Yes	No	
Nevada	18	2	Yes	No	
New Hampshire	18	2	No	Yes	7, 10, 13, 15, 18
New Jersey	18	2	Yes	No	
New Mexico	18	2	No	No	
New York	18	2	Yes	Yes	9, 19
North Carolina	18	2	Yes	Yes	7, 12
North Dakota	18	2	Yes	No	
Ohio	18	2	No	Yes	7, 12, 14, 16, 18
Oklahoma	18	2	Yes	Yes	3, 8, 11, 12
Oregon	18	2	No	No	
Pennsylvania	18	2	Yes	No	
Rhode Island	18	2	No	No	
South Carolina	18	2	No	No	
South Dakota	18	2	Yes	No	
Tennessee	18	2	Yes	Yes	3, 6, 11, 12, 17, 18, 21
Texas	18	2	Yes	Yes	7, 10, 13, 19
Utah	18	2	Yes	No	
Vermont	18	3	No	Yes	1, 6, 15, 18
Virginia	18	2	Yes	Yes	6, 8
Washington	18	2	No[21]	Yes	3, 5, 6, 7, 12, 17, 18
West Virginia	18	2	Yes	Yes	6, 8
Wisconsin	18	2	No[21]	No	
Wyoming	18	2	Yes	No	

* Key to Conditions Imposed on Oral Wills
  1. Limited to $200.
  2. Limited to $500.
  3. Limited to $1,000.
  4. Limited to $10,000.

5. Unlimited if testator is in military service.
6. Limited to only personal property.
7. Available only during last illness.
8. Testator must be in military service.
9. Testator must be in military service during wartime.
10. Testator must be at home or other place of death.
11. Testator must be in contemplation or fear of death.
12. Requires two witnesses.
13. Requires three witnesses.
14. Witnesses must not be beneficiaries of will.
15. Must be reduced to writing within 6 days.
16. Must be reduced to writing within 10 days.
17. Must be reduced to writing within 30 days.
18. Must be probated within 6 months following death.
19. Expires 1 year after testator's discharge from service.
20. Cannot be used to revoke a written will.
21. Holographic will properly executed outside state is valid.
22. Holographic will valid if made outside United States by person in military but void 1 year after discharge.

computer software programs? Unfortunately, there is no unequivocal answer to this question. Many practicing lawyers would caution you against the do-it-yourself alternative—just as most of them are unenthusiastic about the simplified do-it-yourself divorce procedure—but one can hardly assume that their advice is entirely disinterested. The make-your-own-will books and computer software programs are, after all, written by lawyers at least as competent as the general practitioner who has not specialized in estate planning.

On the other hand, many lawyers point out that problems arise not because the do-it-yourself will kits are defective but because readers are careless in following the instructions or unable to apply the general instructions to some exceptional situations. As of this writing, four states (California, Maine, Michigan, and Wisconsin) have adopted "statutory will" forms that comply with the state laws governing wills. Free copies are available from members of the state legislature and state bar associations.

Our advice is that *if* your assets are not large and varied, *if* the provisions you intend in your will are fairly conventional, and *if* you have the time and patience to read and follow sometimes complicated instructions, you may safely write your own will, using a book or software on the subject or perhaps following the form shown in figure 1.1, below. But these are rather significant *ifs*, and you may decide that the relatively modest cost of professional preparation is a bargain in terms of the sense of security it can provide.

Figure 1.1

WILL

LAST WILL AND TESTAMENT OF JOHN J. JONES

I, JOHN J. JONES domiciled in Lansing, Michigan, declare this to be my last will, hereby revoking all previous wills and codicils.

FIRST

1.1 *Payments of Debts and Taxes*: I direct my Executor to pay all of my legally enforceable debts, expenses of last illness, funeral and burial expenses, and expenses of administering my estate. I direct my Executor to pay all taxes imposed by reason of my death upon any transfer of property includable in my estate, as an expense of administration, unless voluntarily paid by some party.

SECOND

2.1 *Specific Bequest*: I give and bequeath my stamp collection to my son, WILLIAM B. JONES, if he survives me; otherwise this gift shall lapse.

2.2 *Disposition of Residue*: I give, devise, and bequeath all of the rest, residue, and remainder of my estate, real, personal or mixed, wherever situate and whether acquired before or after the execution of this will, to MARY K. JONES (hereafter "my wife"), if she survives me.

2.3 *Alternative disposition—Residue*: If my wife does not survive me, then I give, devise, and bequeath all of the said remainder of my estate to my children surviving me, in equal shares, provided, however, the issue of a deceased child surviving me shall take and share equally the share that their parent would have taken had he or she survived me. If my issue do not agree to this division among them, the decision of my Executor shall be in all respects binding upon my issue.

THIRD

3.1 *Survivorship Defined*: In the event that my wife and I die under circumstances where it cannot be established who died first, then it shall be presumed that my wife survived me and this will and the dispositions hereunder shall be construed on that presumption. No person other than my wife shall be deemed to have survived me or to be living at my death if he or she shall die within ninety (90) days after my death.

FOURTH

4.1 *Executor*: I nominate my wife as my Executor, to serve without bond. If my wife predeceases me, declines to act, or having qualified, resigns, dies, or is removed, I nominate Capitol Bank and Trust Company, Lansing, Michigan, as my Executor.

4.2 *Powers*: I give my Executor all powers of administration granted to independent personal representatives as set forth in the laws of this state at the time of execution of this will, including the power to sell any real or personal property, and for that purpose I hereby incorporate those powers by reference.

Figure 1.1

WILL *(continued)*

4.3 *Guardian and Conservator*: In the event that my wife fails to survive me, I nominate and appoint my brother and his wife, Richard A. Jones and Elizabeth Jones, Cleveland, Ohio, as Guardians of the person and Capitol Bank and Trust Company, Lansing, Michigan, as Conservator of the estate, of any of my children who is a minor at the time of my death.

_____

John. J. Jones

On _____, the above testator signed the foregoing instrument (typewritten on two [2] sheets of paper, upon the bottom of each of which he/she also signed) and declared that he/she signed it freely and voluntarily as his/her Last Will; we witnessed the signing in the presence of said testator, and we now, on the same day, sign as witnesses in the presence of said testator and of each other; to the best of our knowledge, said testator is now 18 or more years of age, of sound mind, and under no constraint or undue influence.

Witnesses: Addresses:

_____   _____

Roberta Roe   Lansing, Michigan

_____   _____

Belinda Blue   Lansing, Michigan

SELF-PROVING AFFIDAVIT

STATE OF _____

COUNTY OF _____

Each of the undersigned, Roberta Roe and Belinda Blue, both on oath, says that:

The attached will was signed by John J. Jones, the testator named in the will, on _____, at Lansing, Michigan.

When he signed the will, John J. Jones declared the instrument to be his last will.

Each of us then signed his or her name as a witness at the end of this will at the request of John J. Jones and in his presence and sight and in the presence and sight of each other.

Figure 1.1

WILL *(continued)*

John J. Jones was, at the time of executing this will, over the age of eighteen years and, in our opinions, of sound mind, memory, and understanding and not under any duress or in any respect incompetent to make a will.

In our opinions, John J. Jones could read, write, and speak in English and was suffering from no physical or mental impairment that would affect his capacity to make a valid will. The will was executed as single original instrument, and was not executed in counterparts.

Each of us was acquainted with John J. Jones when the will was executed and makes this affidavit at his request.

Witnesses: Addresses:

_____   _____

Roberta Roe   Lansing, Michigan

_____   _____

Belinda Blue   Lansing, Michigan

_____ (signature and official seal)
Notary Public

WHAT YOUR LAWYER NEEDS TO KNOW

Although fees for the preparation of simple wills don't vary widely from one lawyer to another, all lawyers earn a living by selling their time. Your bill may be smaller, therefore, if you come prepared with all the information your lawyer is likely to need. A complete listing of your assets, for example, will not only shortcut a long question-and-answer session but will avoid omissions and oversights that require subsequent visits, correspondence, or telephone calls. You may, when you enter the lawyer's office, have only a vague idea of what a "contingent beneficiary" is, but you ought to have clearly in mind all the individuals to whom you intend to leave something. Here is some of the information that your lawyer is likely to need for preparation of even the simplest will. A listing of the personal and property information needed by your lawyer is set forth in figure 1.2.

YOUR EXECUTOR

Be prepared to name a person (or a bank) who will, on your death, see to it that your assets are collected and inventoried, your legitimate debts paid, your assets distributed according to your wishes, and your estate closed. If your estate is large and complex, you may prefer an executor with considerable experience in estate management—a bank or a trust company. But bear in mind that the executor is entitled to a fee ranging from 1 to 5 percent of the value of the estate, that any individual executor must be bonded (to protect your estate from his possible fraud, embezzlement, or negligence), and that both the fee and the bonding premium are paid with funds from your estate.

The term *executor* refers to the person or entity named in your will as the person responsible for settling your estate. The term *administrator* refers to the person or entity appointed by the probate court to probate your estate if you died intestate, that is, leaving no will. Some states instead use the term *personal representative*, popularized by the Uniform Probate Code, to describe both executors and administrators. For simplicity, we will use the term *executor*, whether the deceased left a will or died intestate.

If your estate is relatively simple, you may prefer to choose a trusted friend or a member of the family—even one of your beneficiaries if you foresee no conflict of interest with the other beneficiaries. Such a person should be younger—or at least no older—than you and possess good judgment and reasonable competence in ordinary business transactions. Some states require that the executor be an adult resident of your state. See Table 1.3.

Friends or relatives may choose to waive the executor's fee, and your will can stipulate that they need not be bonded—unless you feel that bonding will protect your estate against their possible negligence. In addition, if you choose a trusted and competent person, you can give that person, through your will, considerably more authority to settle your affairs than is granted to the executor by the laws of most states. Obviously, you should obtain the person's consent before naming him or her in your will. And if you choose an individual rather than a bank, be prepared to name an alternate, since the first-named executor may not outlive you or may for other reasons be unable or unwilling to assume the responsibility. Banks, on the other hand, are "immortal" and hence dependable, but banks may not be the best possible executor for small or simple estates; because their fees are often based on the size of the estate, they may not be motivated to work as quickly or efficiently as they would for a large one.

TABLE 1.3
Eligibility of Nonresident Executors, by State

Alabama	Nonresident eligible, but only when acting as executor for the same estate by appointment of some other state.
Alaska	Nonresident eligible without restrictions.
Arizona	Nonresident eligible without restrictions.
Arkansas	Nonresident eligible, but must appoint resident agent to accept service of papers.
California	Nonresident eligible, but must be resident of United States.
Colorado	Nonresident eligible without restrictions.
Connecticut	Nonresident eligible without restrictions.
Delaware	Nonresident eligible, but must appoint register of wills as agent to accept service of papers.
District of Columbia	Nonresident eligible, but must appoint register of wills as agent to accept service of papers.
Florida	Nonresident eligible only if related to testator by blood, marriage, or adoption.
Georgia	Nonresident eligible without restrictions.
Hawaii	Nonresident eligible without restrictions.
Idaho	Nonresident eligible without restrictions.
Illinois	Nonresident eligible, but must appoint resident agent to accept service of papers.
Indiana	Nonresident eligible, but must appoint resident agent to accept service of papers.
Iowa	Nonresident eligible without restrictions.
Kansas	Nonresident eligible, but must appoint resident agent to accept service of papers.
Kentucky	Nonresident eligible only if related to testator by blood, marriage, or adoption, or be a spouse of a person so related. Also nonresident must appoint resident of county of probate as agent to accept service of papers.
Louisiana	Nonresident eligible, but must appoint resident agent to accept service of papers.
Maine	Nonresident eligible without restrictions.
Maryland	Nonresident eligible, but must appoint resident agent to accept service of papers.
Massachusetts	Nonresident eligible, but must appoint resident agent to accept service of papers.

TABLE 1.3

Eligibility of Nonresident Executors, by State *(continued)*

Michigan	Nonresident eligible without restrictions.
Minnesota	Nonresident eligible without restrictions.
Mississippi	Nonresident eligible without restrictions.
Missouri	Nonresident eligible, but must appoint resident agent to accept service of papers.
Montana	Nonresident eligible without restrictions.
Nebraska	Nonresident eligible without restrictions.
Nevada	Nonresident eligible, but only if he/she associates as co-executor with resident appointed as executor.
New Hampshire	Nonresident eligible, but must appoint resident agent to accept service of papers.
New Jersey	Nonresident eligible, but must post bond unless will provides otherwise.
New Mexico	Nonresident eligible without restrictions.
New York	Nonresident eligible without restrictions.
North Carolina	Nonresident eligible, but must appoint resident agent to accept service of legal papers.
North Dakota	Nonresident eligible without restrictions.
Ohio	Nonresident eligible only if related to testator by blood or marriage or is resident of state that allows nonresident executors.
Oklahoma	Nonresident eligible, but must appoint resident agent of county of probate as agent to accept service of papers.
Oregon	Nonresident eligible without restrictions.
Pennsylvania	Nonresident eligible, but only if permitted by register of wills.
Rhode Island	Nonresident eligible, but must appoint resident agent to accept service of papers.
South Carolina	Nonresident eligible without restrictions.
South Dakota	Nonresident eligible without restrictions.
Tennessee	Nonresident eligible if related by blood or marriage to testator, if a resident is appointed co-executor, or if approved by the court. Nonresident executor must appoint resident agent to accept service of papers.
Texas	Nonresident eligible, but must appoint resident agent to accept service of papers.
Utah	Nonresident eligible without restrictions.
Vermont	Nonresident eligible, but only in the court's discretion, and if approved, must appoint resident agent to accept service of papers.

TABLE 1.3

Eligibility of Nonresident Executors, by State (continued)

Virginia	Nonresident eligible, but must appoint resident agent to accept service of papers.
Washington	Nonresident eligible, but must appoint resident of county of probate as agent to accept service of papers.
West Virginia	Nonresident eligible, but only if named in decedent's will as executor.
Wisconsin	Nonresident eligible, but must appoint resident agent to accept service of papers. Nonresidency may be sufficient cause for nonappointment, or removal, in court's discretion.
Wyoming	Nonresident eligible, but must appoint resident agent to accept service of papers.

GUARDIAN AND CONSERVATOR FOR MINOR CHILDREN

If you have minor children, your will should name a guardian for them—someone who will take over your role as parent until each child reaches the age of eighteen. Some states permit parents to name a guardian in a writing separate from a will. You may have read novels or seen movies in which the twelve-year-old daughter heroically undertakes the rearing of her younger siblings, but the fact is that your minor children cannot legally be enrolled in school or consent to medical treatment, among other things, except through an adult guardian authorized by the court to act in their behalf. This is why the probate court will select a guardian of its choosing if your will fails to nominate one.

Here your choice is entirely unlimited, and the guardian, unlike the personal representative, need not be a resident of your state. You may choose a relative or perhaps a close friend. Parents of teenage children sometimes list three or four persons as acceptable guardians and permit the children to make the final choice. Some parents choose an adult child as guardian for their minor children, but this can be risky; even if the current sibling relationship is very sound, the sudden increase in authority endowed by the guardianship can threaten it. In all states a child, upon reaching fourteen, has the right to veto the parents' choice of guardian and to nominate a substitute; if the probate court judge agrees that the proposed substitution is in the best interests of your child, your original nomination may be overruled.

Your principal criteria in choosing a guardian are likely to include the prospective guardian's personality, ethical values, and

Figure 1.2

ESTATE PLANNING QUESTIONNAIRE

CONFIDENTIAL INFORMATION FOR ESTATE PLANNING

Date _____

Individual	Husband	Wife
Name	_____	_____
Also known as	_____	_____
Social Security no.	_____	_____
Birth date	_____	_____
U.S. citizen	❑ Y ❑ N	❑ Y ❑ N
Living parents	_____	_____
Former spouse	_____	_____
Business address	_____	_____
Telephone number	_____	_____
Fax number	_____	_____
E-mail address	_____	_____
Home address	_____	_____
County of residence	_____	_____
Date of marriage	_____	_____

Children

Living children (indicate children from a prior marriage and adopted children)

Name	Birth date	Social Security No.	No. of children
_____	_____	_____	_____
_____	_____	_____	_____
_____	_____	_____	_____
_____	_____	_____	_____
_____	_____	_____	_____

Deceased children _____

Living children of deceased child _____
Note: If there are no living children or grandchildren, list the brothers and sisters (living and deceased) of the husband and the wife.

Agents and brokers

Safe-deposit box	❑ Y ❑ N	Location _____
Accountant	❑ Y ❑ N	Name _____
Insurance agent	❑ Y ❑ N	Name _____
Stockbroker	❑ Y ❑ N	Name _____

Figure 1.2

ESTATE PLANNING QUESTIONNAIRE *(continued)*

CONFIDENTIAL INFORMATION FOR ESTATE PLANNING

Date _____

Real estate (including land contracts)
Description

(include owner: H-husband, W-wife, J-joint)	Mortgage balance	Market value
_____	$ _____	$ _____
_____	$ _____	$ _____
_____	$ _____	$ _____
_____	$ _____	$ _____

Cash (checking, savings, CD, money market, credit union) Location of account
(include owner: H, W, J)   Amount

_____ $ _____
_____ $ _____
_____ $ _____
_____ $ _____

Stocks and bonds (if in a brokerage account, list firm name)
Listed securities (H) _____
Listed securities (W) _____
Listed securities (J) _____
Closely held (family) securities _____

Life insurance (include insured, insurance company, insurance type, owner,
and beneficiary)   Face amount

_____ $ _____
_____ $ _____
_____ $ _____
_____ $ _____

Retirement benefits (list company)
IRA (list location, type (Roth, non-Roth), and amount)_____
_____

Miscellaneous
Household furnishings, autos, collections _____
Money owed by others to you _____ $_____
Miscellaneous (trusts, etc.) _____ $_____
Expected inheritances _____ $_____
List all gifts made by you over $3,000 in value (date and beneficiary)
_____

Any gift tax return filed   ❏ Y ❏ N   Years filed _____
List significant debts or obligations other than mortgages listed above
_____

child-rearing style as well as his or her current relationship with your children. But financial stability cannot be entirely disregarded. Guardians are entitled to reimbursement from the child's inheritance for all reasonable costs incurred in maintaining and educating the child and providing medical and other services, but since the cost of rearing a child from infancy through college is currently estimated at about $190,000, anyone undertaking a guardianship takes on a substantial financial burden. This burden should be lightened as much as possible by life insurance and other assets, especially since a guardian is not entitled to compensation. Needless to say, you will want to obtain in advance the consent of anyone you plan to nominate.

If, on the other hand, you are providing very amply for your children, the question arises as to who should control their inheritance—not only to oversee disbursement for current expenses but also to conserve or increase it through effective investment strategy. The person you select to take this responsibility is called a conservator. You may, if you wish, choose the same person to serve both as guardian and conservator (or, for that matter, as personal representative), but since skill in child rearing is not necessarily related to financial acumen, you may prefer to appoint a separate person: perhaps a bank if the inheritance is a large one. The conservator, like the personal representative, is entitled to a fee for managing the child's estate.

The responsibility of the conservator, like that of the guardian, terminates when the child reaches maturity—the age of eighteen in most states. If you have left your children a substantial amount of money and if you think that, at age eighteen, the child is not likely to be mature enough to use it wisely, you can, in your will, set up a trust for each child, specifying that the child not have access to the trust assets until whatever age you choose. In the interim, the trust's assets will be managed by a trustee of your choice, who thus fulfills the function of a conservator but without the time limits, probate court oversight, and other restrictions imposed on a conservator.

BENEFICIARIES

Although you undoubtedly know whom you intend to make your *primary* beneficiaries (presumably your spouse and children, perhaps a favorite niece or nephew), it is important to have in mind also several *contingent* beneficiaries—that is, beneficiaries who will be "next in line" should a primary beneficiary die before you do. If you are married or have a lifetime partner, then perhaps the most obvious contingent beneficiaries are your children. Even if they are primary beneficiaries, as well, your will can specify that whatever part of your estate you have willed to your spouse is to go to your children (though not necessarily in equal shares) should your spouse predecease you.

But what if a married daughter—even though she is thirty years younger than you—should predecease you? Do you want her share to go to her surviving spouse or to a trust for your daughter's children, with someone else appointed as trustee? All of these specifics should be clearly spelled out in your will.

Estate planning lawyers are not congenital pessimists, but they are trained to identify and plan for contingencies, no matter how improbable. Although it is highly unlikely—short of a catastrophe at a family reunion—that most of your primary beneficiaries will die before you do, you ought to provide your lawyer with a least one level of contingency for each separate gift. For example, "I give $10,000 to A, provided he survives me; otherwise to B."

Given the decreasing size of families, the dispersal of the extended family, and the prevalence of divorce and unmarried cohabitation, you may find yourself running out of relatives before you have exhausted all possible contingencies. But bear in mind that if all your reasonable contingencies do become exhausted and if you do not have any surviving relatives who step forward to claim your probate estate, the residue of your estate is forfeited to the state through what is called escheat procedures. This may not strike you as an unmitigated disaster, but if you prefer to avoid it, you can always add as contingent beneficiaries various friends, charities, or other organizations.

SPECIFYING MONEY BEQUESTS

Because you may not die for fifty years or more after making your will, you have no way of estimating the ultimate value of your estate. This is of little consequence if you have only two or three primary beneficiaries, because in such circumstances you are likely to specify your bequests in terms of percentages or fractions of the total estate: "75 percent to my wife, Mary, the remaining 25 percent to be divided equally between my son, John, and my daughter, Helen."

If, however, you make a number of small bequests, you need to decide whether to express them in dollars or in percentages. If, for example, you'd like to leave a favorite nephew $1,000, which now represents 1 percent of your current net worth, should you describe the bequest as "$1,000" or as "1 percent of my estate?" If, fifty years from now, $1,000 shrinks to one-fifth of its current value, the gift will be insultingly small; on the other hand, 1 percent of your total estate may at that time represent an amount much larger than you intended. There is no general answer to this dollars-versus-percentage issue, but it needs to be considered for each of your smaller bequests and reconsidered each time you revise your will.

SPECIFIC PROPERTY GIFTS

Aside from gifts of money, real estate, or securities, you may want to give certain of your possessions, large or small, to specific people, whether or not they are beneficiaries of other gifts. Your gun collection, for example, may be given to a fellow member of your gun club; your grandmother's gold brooch may be given to your daughter rather than to your son. If, before you die, any of these things pass from your possession—through loss or theft, for example—you need not revise your will; the gift "fails" and the intended recipient will have no claim against your estate.

LIST OF ASSETS

Although a complete inventory of your assets has no place in a will (because it is likely to change significantly before you die), it's useful to show one to your lawyer before he draws up your will. (The form shown in figure 1.2 can be used for this purpose.) To begin with, the inventory will give him a general idea of how complex your will needs to be. Perhaps more important, if your estate is a large one, he may have a number of useful suggestions for avoiding taxes and other problems by reducing the size of your estate—a subject dealt with in chapter 2.

If you feel uncomfortable about disclosing to your lawyer the full extent of your assets because you suspect he will not keep the information confidential, you ought to find yourself another lawyer. Making an estate plan, including a will, is a "moment of truth," and concealing any relevant information can only frustrate your plan and jeopardize the interests of your beneficiaries.

Your lawyer and almost certainly your spouse or partner should be included in your "circle of confidentiality" with respect to your will, but whom else to include is a matter for careful judgment. You may want to elicit specific preferences from your children about some of your possessions, or you may want to discuss with your alma mater the exact terms of a proposed bequest, but generally speaking, a will should be considered a very personal affair. It is not uncommon for elderly persons to use the provisions of their will as threats or rewards in their dealings with their likely beneficiaries, but such behavior benefits nobody.

SIGNING AND
PROTECTING THE WILL

Armed with the information described in the preceding pages, you should be able to answer expeditiously whatever questions your lawyer asks. The technical details of compliance with state law can be left to him, and your next step is to read the draft of the will (at home, relaxed, and probably in consultation with your spouse) to make certain that it specifies precisely each of your directions. The signing of the will is best done in the lawyer's office, because he is familiar with the state requirements for signing and witnessing. There is no need for the witnesses to read the will; they are witnessing your signature only, although they must understand that what you are signing is your will.

Some lawyers draft wills naming themselves as the executor or as the lawyer who will be employed to probate the will. There is, however, no reason for you to commit your estate or your survivors to employing a specific lawyer. You may move from the community or change lawyers for other reasons, and a specific commitment would then require revision of the will.

By statute in many states, a will may be written so that it is "self-proved," by means of an affidavit that may be an integral part of the will (see figure 1.1) or a separate affidavit attached to a previously signed will. The affidavit serves to preserve the sworn testimony of the witnesses, taken at the time of signing, which creates a presumption that the will was properly signed. This makes it possible to dispense with live witness testimony later to prove the validity of the will in a probate proceeding following the death of the person who made the will.

Although you will receive copies of the will, you should sign only the original, to avoid problems of retrieving and destroying several signed copies if you later decide to revise or revoke it.

The signed original should be kept where it is (1) safe against fire, theft, or other loss; (2) readily retrievable by you; (3) confidential; (4) likely to be located after your death by your survivors. The storage location that probably best meets these criteria is the will depository maintained by most county probate courts. For a small one-time filing fee, you can file the will for safekeeping until it is probated or revoked. During your lifetime, only you have access to it. On your death, however, copies become available to your survivors for use in the probate process.

Storing a will in a safety deposit box is a common practice, but it has one disadvantage: on hearing of your death, the bank is sometimes required by law to seal the box until a representative of the state treasury can inventory its contents. In such circumstances, your survivors may need to apply for a court order permitting them to open the box to search for and retrieve the will.

Storing the will at home, along with other important papers, is a common practice, but a desk drawer or filing cabinet may provide insufficient privacy or protection against fire and theft. And storing it in your lawyer's office, as some lawyers recommend, may place you under an obligation that you may find awkward if you move or establish a relationship with a different lawyer. Moreover, if the lawyer has possession of your will, your survivors may, upon your death, feel some obligation to hire that lawyer when, in fact, they would prefer to use another.

AMENDING OR REVOKING YOUR WILL

As we have noted, it is important to make a will early in life because death can occur at any time. But the statistical probability is that you will live for many years after signing your will and that many of the circumstances on which you based your original will may change. The value and complexity of your assets, for example, may increase. A beneficiary may die; a beneficiary's needs may increase or diminish; your feelings toward a beneficiary may change drastically. You may divorce your current spouse, or separate from your unwed partner, or you may adopt a child, or you may want (or need) to change your will's designations of personal representative, guardian, conservator, or trustee. It is also possible that you will move to another state and that your will may need revision to comply with the new state's laws since not all states recognize the validity of a will you executed when you lived elsewhere. Obviously, then, a will is not something that you can sign and then put away with a sigh of relief. It requires periodic review, and each review may lead to minor changes or major revisions.

Like the original will, changes and revisions should be executed promptly and not be put off on the grounds that you are in good health at the moment. Bear in mind that a will can be executed or amended only when you are mentally competent and that mental incompetence—as a consequence of senility, mental illness, or coma caused by accidental injury, for example—can precede your death by many years. In such a situation, a guardian or a conservator may be appointed to handle your business affairs, but neither representative has the authority to amend or revoke your will.

CODICILS

If your will requires only a minor amendment—for example, a change in the amount you've bequeathed to a specific beneficiary, the addition of a gift to a charitable institution, or a change in the designation of the guardian—you can make the change by means of a codicil. A codicil (see figure 1.3) is simply an amendment to the original will. Like the will, it must comply with state law regarding witnessing and other formalities, and, after death, it will be probated together with the will.

Although there is no limit to the number of changes that can be embodied in a codicil or, indeed, to the number of codicils that can accompany a will, the presence of a large number of codicils can complicate the probate process and possibly invite a will contest. There comes a point at which it is more efficient and no more expensive to rewrite the entire will—a procedure that is essentially the same as the preparation of the original will.

REVOCATION

There are several ways in which your current will can be revoked. You can, at any time, simply destroy it (or instruct someone to destroy it in your presence), but this leaves you without a will. Or you can sign a new will that states specifically that it revokes all previous wills. It is also possible that some portions of your will may be automatically revoked by law. If, for example, you have left

Figure 1.3

CODICIL

FIRST CODICIL TO LAST WILL OF JOHN J. JONES

I, JOHN J. JONES declare this to be the First Codicil to my Last Will dated

_____.

FIRST

I hereby revoke in their entirety Items 2.1 and 4.3 of my Last Will dated _____, and substitute in lieu thereof new Items with the same numbers, which Items shall read as follows:

2.1 *Specific Bequest*: I give and bequeath my stamp collection to my daughter, SALLY L. JONES, if she survives me; otherwise this gift shall lapse.

4.3 *Guardian and Conservator*: In the event that my wife fails to survive me, I nominate and appoint my friend, and his wife, Alfred R. Miller and Susan T. Miller, Detroit, Michigan, as Guardians of the person and Liberty Federal Bank, Lansing, Michigan, as Conservator of the estate of any of my children who is a minor at the time of my death.

SECOND

I republish and reaffirm my said Last Will as herein modified, amended, and supplemented by this First Codicil as if the same were set out here in full and do incorporate the same by this reference thereto.

_____

John J. Jones

On _____, the above person signed the foregoing instrument (typewritten on one [1] sheet of paper) and declared that he/she signed it freely and voluntarily as the First Codicil to his/her Last Will; we witnessed the signing in the presence of said person, and we now, on the same day, sign as witnesses in the presence of said person and of each other; to the best of our knowledge, said person is now 18 or more years of age, of sound mind, and under no constraint or undue influence.

WITNESSETH

Witnesses:	Addresses:
_____	_____
Roberta Roe	Lansing, Michigan
_____	_____
Belinda Blue	Lansing, Michigan

Figure 1.3
CODICIL *(continued)*

SELF-PROVING AFFIDAVIT

STATE OF _____

COUNTY OF _____

Each of the undersigned, Roberta Roe and Belinda Blue, both on oath, says that:

The attached codicil was signed by John J. Jones, the testator named in the codicil, on _____, at Lansing, Michigan.

When he signed the codicil, John J. Jones declared the instrument to be a codicil to his last will.

Each of us then signed his or her name as a witness at the end of this codicil at the request of John J. Jones and in his presence and sight and in the presence and sight of each other.

John J. Jones was, at the time of executing this codicil, over the age of eighteen years and, in our opinions, of sound mind, memory, and understanding and not under any duress or in any respect incompetent to make a codicil.

In our opinions, John J. Jones could read, write, and speak in English and was suffering from no physical or mental impairment that would affect his capacity to make a valid codicil. The codicil was executed as single original instrument, and was not executed in counterparts.

Each of us was acquainted with John J. Jones when the codicil was executed and makes this affidavit at his request.

Witnesses: Addresses:

_____   _____
Roberta Roe   Lansing, Michigan

_____   _____
Belinda Blue   Lansing, Michigan

_____ (signature and official seal)
Notary Public

everything to your spouse and you divorce and die before revising your will, the laws of many states provide that a divorce automatically revokes gifts to your former spouse unless your will specified that your estate is to go to your spouse even after divorce.

Obviously, the most efficient and orderly way for you to manage your affairs is to update your will periodically, by signing a codicil or a new will. If you do this conscientiously, your will should accurately reflect your most recently expressed wishes.

LOOKING AHEAD TO PROBATE

Although the preparation of your will may strike you as a generally grim process, the review of your assets it requires you to make may lighten your spirits considerably. Many people who are forced into this inventory of their accumulated possessions experience pleasure and pride because their net worth turns out to be more substantial than they had anticipated.

But this justifiable satisfaction should be tempered by one important consideration: the higher the total value of the assets that you intend to bequeath by means of your will, the more complex and expensive will be the process of probate administration after your death. This means that your beneficiaries will have some of their inheritance eroded by legal fees and court costs, and that several months, or sometimes years, may lapse before they actually have their inheritances in hand.

If the prospect of probate-court expense and delay concerns you, your best strategy is to reexamine the inventory of your assets with a view to transferring them to your surviving beneficiaries *by some means other than your will* and thus avoid the need for probate administration. Bear in mind that your will can transfer only those assets that are in your name at the time of death. Thus, if you transfer the bulk of your assets into joint ownership or the trustee of a revocable trust, you retain control of them while you are alive, but they will not be yours to bequeath by will when you die. If you do this effectively, it may be that upon your death you own nothing that is in your name alone—in which case your will, no matter what it specifies, will not require probate. Or you may own so little in probate assets that the remaining assets are eligible for transfer by an informal "small estate" probate process that is both swifter and cheaper than full probate administration. The next chapter discusses the various ways by which you can reduce the size of your probatable estate.

~ 2 ~

PROBATE ADMINISTRATION AND HOW TO AVOID IT

The probating of your estate is not your responsibility, because it cannot take place before your death. Since it will be taken care of by your survivors, it is explained in detail in chapters 12 through 16. But the way in which you manage your assets and the form in which you own them from now until the time of your death will determine whether or not your estate will require probate administration, and how complex the probate process is likely to be. This is why making a will discharges only one of your responsibilities to your survivors. Another—at least as important—is to arrange your assets, by forms of ownership and beneficiary designations, in ways that reduce the difficulties your survivors will have to face in order to inherit them.

THE PROBLEMS OF PROBATE

Briefly, probate court administration of your estate is the legal procedure by which the state ensures that after your death your creditors will collect their lawful debts, the state and federal governments will collect the taxes due them, your rightful beneficiaries will be identified, and the balance of your probate estate will be distributed according to the terms of your will or, if you did not leave a will, according to state intestacy laws. The entire procedure is supervised by a county court, usually called a probate court but in some states referred to as a surrogate, orphans', or chancery court.

Formal probate administration is always time-consuming, usually expensive, and often enormously frustrating. To begin proceedings, the probate judge must appoint an executor who will manage, liquidate, and eventually settle your estate. The executor will have to be compensated and, unless your will specifies otherwise, bonded, the costs of which, in addition to court costs, will have to be paid by your estate. The executor is required to notify your creditors and invite them to submit their claims, and the costs of this notification (by mail and by newspaper advertisement) are also borne by your estate.

If the executor needs the help of accountants, lawyers, or realtors in managing and selling your probate assets, their professional fees will be added to the cost of the probate procedure. And since the entire process will take not less than six months and may continue for several years, there is a possibility that your survivors may have to wait a long time for their inheritance.

In addition to the considerable costs in money and time, probate administration has other disadvantages. For one thing, because the probate process is a matter of public record, anyone can find out what you owned, what your debts were, and who inherited how much of your assets. This information may encourage claims, illegitimate as well as legitimate, against your estate, and it may expose your beneficiaries to annoying solicitation by charities and other "worthy causes" or by schemers of various kinds. Moreover, your personal representative, no matter how conscientious, may not handle your assets wisely without the benefit of your guidance, especially if your probate estate includes a flourishing business or securities with which he is unfamiliar. All these considerations make the avoidance of probate highly desirable, and the enormous success of Norman Dacey's *How to Avoid Probate* substantiates this.

The requirement that an estate be probated is not directly related to its value. A multimillion-dollar estate may, if it is properly planned, avoid probate, while an estate worth only $5,000 may have to undergo full probate administration. In trying to avoid probate, therefore, you must bear in mind that probate administration involves basically those assets *solely owned by you at the moment of your death*. This means that anything you give away, place in joint ownership, hold in a pay-on-death bank account or transfer-on-death securities account, or transfer to a trust or custodial account is not a *probate asset* because it is not in your sole name at the moment of death. Thus, in order to avoid probate, you should consider rearranging legal ownership of as much of your assets as possible without at the same time giving up control over them or the income that they may be producing.

It's rarely practical, of course, to rid yourself of all your possessions simply to avoid probate, and this isn't really necessary. Most states provide simple, inexpensive, and quick procedures for the settlement of so-called "small estates" without lengthy probate administration. Thus, you may be able to avoid the expense, delay, and other problems of probate by now retitling or changing beneficiary designations on some of your highly valuable assets but retaining in your own name those whose value does not exceed the $3,000–$200,000 limits that various states impose on the use of "small estate" transfer procedures (see chapter 16 and tables 16.1 and 16.2). In this chapter we describe the various transfer options that can be used to avoid probate.

REDUCING YOUR PROBATE ASSETS

Depending on your state of residence, your estate may require probate administration even if the value of your probate assets is no more than a few thousand dollars. For this reason, we will here describe the various strategies that can effectively reduce your probate assets—preferably without depriving you of control or income. The tax implications of each of these will also be discussed.

GIVING IT AWAY

Since your probate assets consist only of those assets that you own at the time of death, a simple way to eliminate them from your probate estate is to give some of them away while you are still alive. In a sense, of course, even a trivial gift, such as a $25 birthday check to a child or grandchild, reduces your probate assets, but there may be good reasons for making larger gifts. If an adult child of yours is in financial difficulties or has an opportunity to make a business investment, for example, giving him or her the money while you are alive instead of willing it at death gets it to the recipient in time of need and allows you to experience his or her gratitude and to witness the results of your benevolence.

Giving away a major part of your assets, however, is a strategy that few of us can afford until death seems imminent. For this reason, we shall deal with it in chapter 11.

JOINT OWNERSHIP

Probably the most widely used tactic for avoiding probate is to transfer assets into joint ownership, because upon the death of one joint owner the assets pass automatically to the surviving joint owner or owners without probate and regardless of any contrary instructions in the deceased's will. Joint ownership can apply to any type of property—real estate, household contents, bank and money market accounts, securities, motor vehicles, collectibles, etc.—and it may exist between any two or more persons, whether or not they are related. Joint ownership is, moreover, simple and inexpensive to establish. For a bank account, it requires only the signing of a new signature card; for real estate, simply the preparation and recording of a new deed; for securities, a cost-free change in registration of the certificates or the brokerage account; for household contents, heirlooms, keepsakes, and the like, the signing of an assignment of personal property.

Because joint ownership is so easy to establish and because it performs many of the functions of a will but avoids probate, it has been called "the poor man's will." But although you may derive advantages from establishing joint ownership of your house and your securities with your spouse, or bank accounts with one or more of your children, you need to be aware that this form of ownership has some inherent and unavoidable disadvantages as a probate-avoidance technique.

To begin with, joint ownership can jeopardize your control over the assets, because a transfer of assets into joint ownership is irrevocable and cannot be "unwound" without the consent of all joint owners. Thus, if you establish joint ownership of assets with your spouse or partner and you ultimately divorce or separate, complications are almost inevitable. If you place real estate or securities in joint ownership with a minor child, they may not be sellable until the child reaches majority, because a minor is legally incapable of making this kind of transaction. If you place assets in joint ownership with a second spouse, you automatically cut off any children born to you and your first spouse (unless, of course, you survive the second spouse).

Joint ownership, moreover, is inflexible. Once it is established, not only can you not change your mind—as you can with a will—but you may have problems in shifting the assets into more attractive investments, transferring them to a trust, or liquidating them, because such changes may require the consent of all the joint owners.

Perhaps more important, complications may arise from the fact that the sequence of deaths of the joint owners is unpredictable. For example, you may deed your house into joint ownership among yourself and your two adult daughters, intending that they and their children share the ultimate proceeds equally, after your death, which you assumed would occur before those of your children. If one of the daughters predeceases you, however, ownership upon your death passes entirely to the surviving daughter, who is under no legal obligation to share half the proceeds with the children of your daughter who died.

If you and your spouse own assets jointly and die simultaneously, the assets become subject to probate administration. On the other hand, if your spouse survives you, but not long enough to have made a will or to make further changes in ownership, the assets will pass, if you are childless, to his or her next of kin and not to yours.

In view of all this, before you create joint ownership of a substantial portion of your assets, you need to assess the soundness of your relationships with any other prospective joint owners as well as your need to retain control and flexibility. A prudent plan may be to transfer some of your assets into joint ownership and retain a comfortable balance that you can convert to joint ownership when death seems more imminent than it does at the moment, meanwhile considering some of the less problematic probate-avoidance alternatives described later in this chapter. For more information on joint ownership, including its tax implications, see chapter 3.

PAY-ON-DEATH BANK ACCOUNTS

One way of achieving the advantages of joint ownership while avoiding its disadvantages is to establish a pay-on-death (POD) bank account. This account, available at no cost from banks, savings and loan associations, and credit unions, permits the owner to retain complete control over the account balance (and responsibility for taxes on its earnings). But on the death of the original owner, the account balance automatically passes to the named beneficiary without probate administration. Should the owner need the money in the account or change his mind about the POD beneficiary, he is free to spend the money or change the beneficiary. To claim the account balance on the owner's death, the named beneficiary need only visit the financial institution, identify herself, and withdraw the account balance.

Choosing Beneficiaries

Residents of community property states who name someone other than their spouse as a POD beneficiary should inform the spouse. In these states, a spouse who is dissatisfied with her inheritance may be able to claim a specified percentage of the deceased spouse's property. But since most spouses receive more than their entitled "spousal" share, a court challenge is unlikely. And in some states POD accounts are not subject to a spouse's claim.

Although there are few restrictions on the choice of beneficiaries, some aspects warrant consideration. It is legal, for example, to name a minor as a POD beneficiary, but if the account is worth more than a few thousand dollars, and if the child is still a minor and unmarried at the time of your death, it is wiser to arrange for an adult to manage the money. If this is not done, one of two results may occur. (1) If the amount is small—generally about five thousand dollars, depending on state law—the bank may turn it over to the child or the child's parents. (2) If the amount is substantial, the parents must go to court to petition for a guardian or conservator to collect and hold the money until the minor reaches maturity—usually age 18. (If the parents are dead, a guardian or conservator presumably will have been appointed for the minor.) The delay and expense of a court proceeding can easily be avoided by naming, as the POD beneficiary, an adult as custodian for the child under the Uniform Transfers to Minors Act (see p. 48).

More than one POD beneficiary can be named on an account simply by listing their names on the account but, unless it is otherwise specified, each beneficiary will inherit an equal share of the balance. If state law does not permit differentiating among beneficiaries, the owner can, of course, establish a separate POD bank account for each beneficiary.

An alternate or contingent beneficiary—that is, someone to receive the account balance should your first choice not survive you—is not permitted on a POD bank account. It is widely believed that if three beneficiaries are named and if Number 1 predeceases the owner, then Number 2 inherits Number 1's share. But in fact Number 1's share will be divided equally among the surviving beneficiaries. If this is not the owner's intent, he should immediately name a new beneficiary to replace the one that predeceased him.

Advantages

Aside from the ease of establishing it, one advantage of the POD bank account is that Federal Deposit Insurance Commission coverage, which normally protects only the original owner of the bank account up to $100,000, is automatically extended to protect the beneficiaries if they are a close relative—a spouse, sibling, grandchild, or parent of the deceased. In addition, if the account restricts early withdrawals—a certificate of deposit, for example—the early withdrawal penalty will probably be waived should the owner die before the penalty expires.

Disadvantages

One disadvantage of a POD account is that it is limited to bank products, which almost invariably offer a lower yield than other investments. Depending on the state of the economy and the stock market, you may instead prefer to use a transfer-on-death (TOD) securities registration, which is nearly as easy to establish but is used to transfer securities rather than bank products (see p. 40).

Some types of bank accounts cannot be automatically transformed into POD bank accounts. If, for example, a joint bank account specifies "right of survivorship," one of the owners may name a POD beneficiary, but the surviving owner retains the right to change or eliminate the designation. In a community property state, of course, half of the account balance already belongs to the spouse, and a POD beneficiary can be named for the other half.

Perhaps a more serious shortcoming of a POD bank account is that the owner may not impose any conditions for the beneficiary to meet before receiving the money, as is possible with a revocable living trust (see below). If this limitation is not important to the owner, the POD bank account is a far less expensive way to achieve probate avoidance.

TRANSFER-ON-DEATH SECURITIES REGISTRATION

Transfer-on-death (TOD) securities registration, similar in many respects to the POD account for bank products, is used for stocks and bonds held in a brokerage account. It is available in all states except New York, North Carolina, and Texas. As in the case with the POD bank account, TOD securities registration is set up by naming a beneficiary or beneficiaries on the brokerage account preceded by the phrase "Transfer on death to . . . "

Like the POD bank account, the TOD securities registration may have multiple beneficiaries, but unlike the POD account, it may name alternate or contingent beneficiaries if allowed by the brokerage firm.

It is possible, of course, to keep one's securities at home or in a safe deposit box rather than in the broker's street account, but if several securities are involved, registering them with TOD beneficiary designations would require dealing with the corporate transfer agents for each security. Keeping the securities in a broker's street account reduces the effort substantially.

In addition to the advantages offered by the POD bank account, TOD securities registration has the additional advantage of prompting the owner to keep his investments in the broker's "street" account rather than in a bank safe deposit box or a desk drawer. This means that when income tax is due, the broker will provide the owner with a comprehensive Form 1099 to submit with his tax return, sparing him the laborious task of compiling one that includes his every investment. It also means that selling a security does not involve the sometimes frantic task of finding the security certificate and mailing it to the broker within the relatively short time limit for settling security transactions.

TRANSFER-ON-DEATH DEED OF REAL ESTATE

A relatively new tool for transferring real property at death and outside of probate is called the *transfer-on-death* (TOD) deed, currently available in six states (Arizona, Colorado, Kansas, Missouri, New Mexico, and Ohio) and being considered in several other states.

Under a TOD deed, the owner or joint owners of real property may sign a deed naming a successor owner (the "grantee-beneficiary"), effective at the death of the current owner. For joint owners, the beneficiary only takes title to the property upon the death of the last surviving joint owner. A most useful feature of this transfer technique is that the named grantee-beneficiary has no vested interest in the property until the death of the current owner—who remains free to change the grantee-beneficiary's name at any time before his or her death by simply signing and recording a new deed, all without the signature, consent, or even knowledge of the original grantee-beneficiary.

When properly signed and recorded, the TOD deed becomes effective upon the death of the original owner, at which time the grantee-beneficiary simply records the owner's death certificate. By doing so, the named grantee-beneficiary immediately acquires ownership of the property, all without the necessity of probate administration. To ensure that the TOD deed is not used to avoid claims of the deceased owner's creditors, state enabling laws typically permit creditors' claims to be filed against the decedent's probate estate *and* against any real property transferred by a TOD deed.

To further ensure that the TOD deed is not misused, state laws authorizing its use require specific language to be prominently displayed on the TOD deed reciting that the property does not pass to the named grantee-beneficiary until the death of the current owner. These state laws also require that the right to revoke the TOD designation and the requirement to record the deed also be prominently noted on the deed.

ENHANCED LIFE ESTATE DEED OF REAL ESTATE

Another little-known tool for transferring real property at death and outside of probate is called a *Ladybird deed*, more accurately called an *enhanced life estate deed*. These deeds, although available in just a few states (including Florida, Michigan, and Texas), got their colorful name because President Johnson reportedly used this type of deed to transfer some Texas land to his wife, Lady Bird.

A "life estate" is an ownership arrangement for land designed to accomplish two things: (1) it allows the owner to retain the use of the real estate (for example, a house) during his or her lifetime, and (2) it transfers title to the property upon the original owner's death without the need for probate administration. In a regular life estate deed, the owner reserves the "life estate" and conveys a "remainder interest" to someone who will inherit the property. The current owner continues to occupy and use the property and is entitled to all money that may come from the property. The owner, however, cannot sell the property without the agreement and participation by the holder of the remainder interest.

The use of a "Ladybird" enhanced life estate deed adds one significant feature: the owner retains the right to sell or give away the property without the remainderman's consent or participation. Essentially, the owner has the unilateral right to cancel the remainder interest.

If the arrangement under the Ladybird deed is not cancelled, then when the owner dies the life estate expires automatically. The remainder interest matures into full unrestricted ownership in the remainderman . . . all without the necessity of probate administration.

TRANSFER-ON-DEATH REGISTRATION OF VEHICLES

In five states (California, Connecticut, Kansas, Missouri, and Ohio), motor vehicle owners have the option of naming on their vehicle's certificate of title a *transfer-on-death* beneficiary to inherit the vehicle after they die. If you live in one of the states allowing this procedure and if you name a TOD beneficiary on your car's title, the TOD beneficiary has no rights in the car while you remain alive. You are free to borrow money on the car, sell it, give it away, or name a different person on the title as TOD beneficiary—all without the signature, consent, or even knowledge of the present TOD beneficiary.

To name a TOD beneficiary on a vehicle in those states where permitted, simply visit your state's motor vehicle registration office and apply for a new certificate of title in "beneficiary form." When you receive your new title, it will identify you as the vehicle's owner and also whoever you have named as your TOD beneficiary. Upon your death, the TOD beneficiary automatically acquires ownership of your vehicle, without the necessity of probate administration.

DESIGNATING BENEFICIARIES ON
IRA, 401(K) AND OTHER RETIREMENT ACCOUNTS

Your retirement accounts may (and usually do) contain substantial funds—often a significant part of your estate. As with life insurance, if you fail to designate a beneficiary on your retirement accounts, or worse yet, designate "my estate" or "my executor" as the account beneficiary, these funds will, upon your death, become a part of your probate estate, and consequently, will require probate admin-istration in order to pass the funds to your survivors. A far better strategy is to name on the account a beneficiary and contingent beneficiary for your IRA or 401(k) account, profit-sharing plan, or other individual retirement account. And if you have any vested rights in a pension plan, you may also be able to designate a benefi-ciary to inherit your pension rights.

Naming Your Spouse as Beneficiary

Many people name their spouse as the beneficiary on their retire-ment accounts. Indeed, if you have a 401(k) plan, you must name your spouse as the account beneficiary unless your spouse signs a written waiver. For individual retirement plans (IRAs and SEPs), you can name as the account beneficiary anyone you choose. But in community property states, your spouse has a legal interest in any funds that the other spouse has earned, unless he or she signs a release giving up such interest. Spouses, as retirement plan ben-eficiaries, enjoy several advantages that other beneficiaries do not receive. A surviving spouse who inherits funds as the beneficiary of an individual retirement plan can elect to have the money paid out over the same period of time he or she would have had if he or she had created the plan him/herself. Another break given only to a surviving spouse is the choice of rolling over a deceased spouse's retirement funds into his or her own retirement plan—thus further deferring income tax on the money.

Naming Others as Beneficiary

Some retirement account owners choose to name a non-spouse (a child or some other person) as the account beneficiary, and this is perfectly legal. These nonspousal beneficiaries may have different options on how they receive the funds over time, but these choices are subject to rather complex rules. Sometimes the nonspousal beneficiary can elect to receive the account funds in a lump sum or, alternatively, in payments distributed over several years. Other beneficiaries may be required to take installment payments based on life expectancy tables.

Owners of retirement funds should always designate an account beneficiary. But before deciding on a spouse, a nonspouse, or a trust as your retirement account beneficiary, consider consulting with an estate planning lawyer or a tax expert.

U.S. SAVINGS BONDS REGISTERED IN BENEFICIARY FORM

A U.S. savings bond may be registered in *beneficiary form* rather than co-ownership form. Suppose that Mary with her separate funds purchases a bond in the form "Mary, payable on death to Joseph." The federal regulations state that "[a] savings bond registered in beneficiary form will be paid to the registered owner during his or her lifetime upon surrender with an appropriate request. Upon payment . . . , the beneficiary will cease to have any interest in the bond." 31 C.F.R. § 315.38. Furthermore, "[i]f the owner of a bond registered in beneficiary form has died and is survived by the beneficiary, upon proof of death of the owner, the beneficiary will be recognized as the sole and absolute owner of the bond." 31 C.F.R. § 31.70(c)(1).

A U.S. savings bond registered in beneficiary form serves substantially the same purpose as one registered in *co-ownership form*, because, upon death of one co-owner, the survivor is entitled to payment or reissue. Registration in co-ownership would be "Mary and Joseph," in which case either Mary or Joseph could immediately redeem the bond. But the two forms are not identical. If Mary purchases a bond in the form "Mary, payable on death to Joseph," then Joseph is not entitled to redeem the bond, receive interest, or reissue it during Mary's lifetime.

THE REVOCABLE LIVING TRUST

A probate-avoidance device that is far more flexible than joint ownership is the revocable living trust, which is coming into wider use as increasing numbers of people recognize its advantages. A revocable trust is a legal entity ("The Roger J. Smith Trust") to which you can transfer assets in any amount and of any kind: real estate, motor vehicles, bank and brokerage accounts, securities, household contents, heirlooms, collectibles, etc. Because the assets thus transferred are no longer owned by you individually, they are not subject to probate; instead, upon your death they remain in the name of the trustee or the successor trustee named in the trust, who must distribute them to the trust's beneficiaries according to the terms of the trust agreement.

During your lifetime, however, you retain full control over the trust assets and their income—you can sell them, remove them from trust ownership, add new assets to the trust, and use any income produced by the trust. In addition, you have the right to change the beneficiaries, the share of trust assets that each is to receive, or the conditions under which they will receive their shares. These changes, made by amending the trust agreement, are at least as easy to make as changes in your will.

A typical trust agreement names one or more trustees and one or more successor trustees who assume responsibility when the original trustees die, become incapacitated, or simply wish to retire. You may, if you wish, designate yourself as the original trustee and the principal beneficiaries of the trust (your spouse and children) as successor trustees. If, however, you have a disabled child or a spouse who is inexperienced in managing assets, you may prefer to designate, either as trustee or successor trustee, a bank, a trust company, or even a trusted friend who possesses sound business judgment.

The trust agreement should also specify the length of the trust's life (its "term"), the rate of compensation (if any) for the trustees, the range of discretion the trustees are to have over the trust's assets, and the timeframe and conditions under which the trust's assets are to be distributed to its beneficiaries. You may specify, for example, that some or all of the beneficiaries must attain the age of thirty before receiving their share or that the share of one of them must be used in whole or in part for a specified purpose, such as college tuition or payment of medical expenses or the purchase of a new home.

Assets not currently held in the trust can be "poured over" into the trust on your death. You can, for example, designate the trustee or successor trustee of your trust as the beneficiary of your life insurance policies or IRA, Keogh, SEP, and 401(k) accounts, in which case the proceeds will be paid out, without probate, to the trustee for distribution to the beneficiaries along with the other trust assets. If, in addition, you designate the trust as your sole beneficiary in your will by the use of a "pour over" clause, the trust will receive any probate assets you may own at the time of your death—after, of course the expense and delay of probate administration. In such a situation, the trust agreement serves, for all intents and purposes, most of the functions of a will.

Although it is generally effective for avoiding probate administration of your estate, the typical revocable living trust does not avoid income or estate taxes. Because you have control of the trust's assets and the use of their earnings, you remain liable for all income tax. You do not pay gift tax on assets you transfer to the trust, but all trust assets are included as part of your taxable estate for federal estate tax purposes. Beneficiaries of a revocable trust normally must pay any applicable state inheritance and estate taxes.

In addition, the revocable living trust offers you no protection against creditors' claims. If, for example, an automobile accident in which you are found negligent results in a judgment against you that exceeds your auto liability insurance coverage, assets owned by the trust can be reached to satisfy the excess liability. Although in some states creditors cannot make claims against trust-held assets, in general a trust does not offer you the "limitation of liability" that a corporation provides for its shareholders. As "Roger J. Smith, Trustee of the Roger J. Smith Trust," you remain liable for any claims made against either the trust or yourself as a private person.

As you may have concluded at this point, the revocable living trust offers you many of the same advantages as joint ownership: primarily the avoidance of probate. Why, then, go to the trouble and expense of setting up a trust? The answer is that a trust offers you several advantages not available through joint ownership. First, it enables you to retain full control over your assets, including the right to change beneficiaries at any time. Second, the trust does not expose your assets to claims of a joint owner's creditors. Third, the trust enables you to designate a disinterested trustee to manage your assets in case you become disabled. Moreover, the trust avoids all the disadvantages and limitations of joint ownership.

Setting up a trust is not a do-it-yourself project, because a trust agreement should be custom tailored to your specific needs and assets. The process is, however, relatively standard for a modest estate, and a lawyer should not charge you for more than three to six hours of his time for preparing the documents. As an understanding of the advantages of the revocable living trust has proliferated, so, too, has the number of firms advertising, in print and on the Internet, their services in preparing such trusts. Although some of these firms are undoubtedly reputable, an increasing number have come to the attention of state and federal consumer protection agencies for various negligent or fraudulent actions, among them deceptive fee schedules, failure to transfer assets into trust ownership, using "one size fits all" boilerplate provisions instead of an individually prepared document, and negligence in monitoring changes in trust holdings.

If you are considering whether this type of trust is best for you, we recommend you discuss it with an attorney skilled in estate planning. For more on trusts, see chapter 4.

THE IRREVOCABLE LIVING TRUST

Like the revocable living trust, the irrevocable living trust is an effective means of probate avoidance. In addition, it can reduce both income and death taxes. Its basic (and for most people insuperable) disadvantage, however, is reflected in its name: transfers of your property to it are irrevocable. You can never change your mind or, in fact, exercise any significant control over assets in an irrevocable trust. In a very real sense, you have given them away forever.

Irrevocable trusts have traditionally been used by the rich to reduce their income taxes while still keeping certain assets in the family. When assets are transferred into an irrevocable trust, tax on the income they produce is payable either by the trust itself or by family members in lower tax brackets who derive income from the trust. Transfers of assets worth more than $12,000 / $24,000 annually are taxable as gifts, but if you do not exceed this annual gift-tax exclusion, or, more significantly the current lifetime gift tax exclusion of $1 million, you can build up the trust assets substantially over a period of years without paying any federal gift tax. Because the trust is irrevocable, its assets are not counted as part of your estate in calculating possible estate taxes. And, here again, the beneficiaries pay no inheritance taxes, as they would had they inherited the same assets through your will.

The reason why people of modest means do not use this type of trust is that in order to enjoy the income tax relief it affords, they must not use either assets or income from the trust personally or to support anyone (such as a child) whom they are legally required to support, to pay life insurance premiums or any other obligations, or to accumulate income for later use. In short, the tax advantage requires that they part forever with assets that they may need for their own current support and eventual retirement.

If you are considering the establishment of a trust to care for a disabled child or to protect a surviving spouse against financial inexperience, bear in mind that the revocable living trust automatically becomes irrevocable on your death and hence may serve the same purpose without the lifetime disadvantages of irrevocability. The "price" you pay for revocability is essentially a matter of income tax and possible federal estate tax, and the flexibility you get in return for this price may well be worth it.

CUSTODIAL ACCOUNTS FOR MINORS

Just as the POD bank account trust serves as a "miniature" revocable living trust for people of moderate means, so, too, there exists a "miniature" irrevocable trust: the custodial account authorized by the Uniform Gifts to Minors Act or the Uniform Transfers to Minors Act, one of which laws has been adopted by every state. This type of account, which is available for bank accounts, securities, and, in some states, all types of real and personal property, permits you to play the role of benevolent parent or grandparent and, at the same time, reduce your income and estate taxes as well as avoid probate.

Under the Uniform Gifts to Minors Act, for example, you can set up an account in a financial institution (or register securities) in the name of an adult who serves as custodian of your gift to the minor. Gifts of less than $12,000 / $24,000 a year per beneficiary are not subject to federal gift tax, and the account is not included in your taxable estate if you do not serve as its custodian.

No matter who makes the gift to your child, income tax on the first $1,400 of the account's earnings is payable by the child—at a rate presumably lower than yours—but the rest is payable at his parents' highest tax rate until the child reaches the age of fourteen. At that time, tax on the entire income from the account is payable at the child's rate. Because $28,000 at 5% will not generate over $1,400 annually, in the custodial account, most parents can realize a tax saving on the account without concern that its yield will add to their own tax burden.

Of course, since such accounts are considered completed gifts to the minor, neither you nor any custodian may use either the interest or the principal for your own purposes. The account's assets may be used to pay for certain extraordinary expenses of the minor—summer camp fees, music lessons, college tuition—but not for food, clothing, medical expenses, or other items that parents are normally required to provide for minor children.

A custodial account can, of course, be added to at any time. If, for example, you are currently accumulating a nest egg for a child's college education, converting it into a custodial account accomplishes the identical purpose but relieves you of liability for income tax on the earnings. On the other hand, the account's assets become available to the minor child when he or she reaches age 18 (21 in some states), whether you are alive or not, at which time there is no safeguard against irresponsible dissipation of the money, as there can be in a formally established trust.

LIFE INSURANCE

Although life insurance is usually bought to protect your survivors in the event of your untimely death (see chapter 5), it also offers a way to avoid probate of sizable sums, because the proceeds of a life insurance policy pass directly to the beneficiary designated in the policy and are not considered probate assets, unless of course you have (unwisely) designated your own estate or its executor as the policy beneficiary.

Although not considered part of your probate estate, life insurance proceeds *are* considered part of your taxable estate for federal estate tax purposes. You can avoid this exposure to tax by transferring ownership of the policy while you are still alive to one of your survivors—presumably a beneficiary named in the policy. After the transfer, you may continue to pay the premiums, but the new owner must possess what the IRS terms all "incidents of ownership," which include the right to change beneficiaries and even to cancel the policy. To transfer ownership of a policy, you need only ask your agent or the company for an assignment form, sign it, and return it to the company, keeping a copy for your records. But this may not be a concern for you, given the exemption of $2 million for years 2006–2008, and increasing to $3.5 million in 2009. See chapter 6.

The gift of a life insurance policy is governed by some limitations. First, like any other gift, it will be subject to federal gift tax if its cash surrender value exceeds the $12,000 annual exclusion. (Term policies, of course, have no cash surrender value at any time.) Premiums that you continue to pay on policies that you have transferred are also considered gifts, but they are not likely to exceed the $12,000 annual exclusion. Moreover, if the policy is transferred within three years of your death, it will be presumed by the Internal Revenue Service to have been made "in contemplation of death," and the full death benefit will be included as part of your taxable estate. But the gift tax may be of no concern to you, given the current lifetime gift tax exclusion of $1 million.

TABLE 2.1
Legal Consequences of Various Forms of Ownership

Form of Ownership	Subject to Probate	Subject to Federal Estate Tax	Control During Your Lifetime	Bequeath-able by Will	Subject to Creditors' Claims Before Death	Subject to Creditors' Claims After Death	Availability to Beneficiaries
Asset solely owned	Yes	All	Full	Yes	Yes	Yes	Delayed
Asset owned jointly with spouse	No (1)	One-half	Divided	No (1)	Yes	No (2)	Immediate (1)
Asset owned jointly with non-spouse	No (1)	All (3)	Divided	No (1)	Yes	No (1)	Immediate (1)
Assets in pay-on-death bank account	No	All	Full	No	Yes	No	Immediate
Assets in custodial account for minors	No	None (4)	None (4)	No	No	No	Immediate
Life insurance owned by insured	No (8)	All	Full	No (8)	No	No (8)	Immediate
Life insurance owned by other than insured	No (8)	None (9)	None	No	No	No (8)	Immediate
Life insurance payable to insured's estate or personal representative	Yes	All	Full	Yes	Yes (10)	Yes	Delayed

Securities in transfer-on-death securities account (5)	No	All	Full	No	Yes	No	Immediate
Real estate subject to transfer-on-death deed (6)	No	All	Full	No	Yes	No	Immediate
Auto subject to transfer-on-death title (6)	No	All	Full	No	Yes	No	Immediate
Assets in a revocable living trust	No	All	Full	No	Yes	Possibly (11)	Immediate (12)
Assets in an irrevocable living trust	No	None	None	No	No	No	Immediate (12)

1. Provided that you are survived by a joint owner.
2. Unless debt was incurred by both joint owners.
3. Except to the extent your estate can prove that a surviving joint owner contributed to the acquisition or improvement of the asset.
4. Unless you are a custodian as well as a donor.
5. Not available in New York, North Carolina, or Texas.
6. Available only in Arizona, Kansas, Missouri, New Mexico, and Ohio.
7. Available only in California, Connecticut, Kansas, Missouri, and Ohio.
8. Provided that you are survived by a beneficiary designated in the insurance policy. Otherwise the proceeds become a part of your probatable estate.
9. Unless you assigned the policy to another within three years of the date of your death.
10. Limited to the cash surrender value of the policy.
11. Several states expose the assets in a revocable living trust to creditors' claims.
12. Subject, however, to all of the terms of the trust, which may include a provision postponing distribution of the property.

51

If you do not give away your insurance policies, it is important that you keep the designation of beneficiaries up to date, because if all designated beneficiaries die before you, the insurance proceeds will be paid to your estate and thus become probatable and, where applicable, subject to state estate or inheritance tax. If you have set up a revocable living trust, you might consider naming the trust as sole beneficiary of all your life insurance, so that upon your death the proceeds pass, via the trust, to its beneficiaries, thus avoiding both probate administration and state estate or inheritance taxes, if any. This tactic will not, however, avoid federal estate tax unless the assets pass to your surviving spouse, who has the benefit of the unlimited marital deduction.

If your life insurance proceeds constitute the major part of your assets and if you do not otherwise plan to establish a trust, you might consider establishing a revocable life insurance trust to serve as the beneficiary of all your policies. Such a trust is useful for the care of a disabled child or the protection of a financially inexperienced spouse. Moreover, because it is revocable, you can terminate or modify it at any time prior to your death.

For more information on life insurance, see chapter 5.

LOOKING AHEAD

As you consider the various strategies described in this chapter and summarized in table 2.1, you may decide that some of them are immediately practicable for you, some are worth considering in later years when the value of your assets is likely to have increased and the needs of your dependents are likely to have changed, and some are simply irrelevant to your financial or family circumstances.

Obviously, those that are immediately suitable and very simple to implement—transferring some assets into joint ownership, for example, or perhaps transferring ownership of or changing beneficiaries on one or more of your life insurance policies—should be done immediately because, after all, you may die tomorrow. On the other hand, there is no reason to postpone certain other actions merely because you cannot take full advantage of them now. Most of them are not all-or-nothing arrangements. You can, for example, set up a custodial bank account under the Uniform Transfers to Minors Act with an initial deposit of $25 or less and have it available for much larger deposits later on. Similarly, if you set up a revocable living trust now—even if you transfer only a single bank or broker-age account—it will be ready and waiting for the transfer of all your other assets, even if you do this in thirty years, only a few hours before your death.

As we shall see in chapter 11, many of the strategies that are impractical for you today will become highly practical when death seems imminent. But the extent to which you can take advantage of them at that time may depend largely on the plans you make today.

⁓ 3 ⁓
JOINT OWNERSHIP AND ITS PROS AND CONS

Sharing the ownership of property with one or more other persons may strike you as a good deal less desirable than owning it all by yourself—and if the property was acquired through your own efforts and hence really "belongs" to you, sharing its ownership may strike you as downright irrational. Yet joint ownership of all sorts of real and personal property—not only homes but also bank accounts, securities, and other items of value—is quite common. Most joint owners are married couples, but many are not. Frequently ownership is shared by parents and children, grandparents and grandchildren, siblings, other relatives, friends or unmarried cohabitants.

Obviously, then, joint ownership offers—or at least promises—some very significant advantages over sole ownership. But some of these advantages are more apparent than real, some depend on the specific form of co-ownership, and many are coupled with limitations or distinct disadvantages, which may not be immediately apparent.

There are three basic forms of co-ownership: *joint ownership* (sometimes called *joint tenancy*), *tenancy by the entirety*, and *tenancy in common*, and they differ significantly from one another. We shall deal first with joint ownership, because its simplicity, versatility, and other advantages combine to make it by far the most popular form of co-ownership. The other two forms, discussed later in this chapter, also deserve mention, because you may find them appropriate either for your personal situation or for some of your property. Bear in mind that co-ownership is not an all-or-nothing matter: You may decide to use different forms at different times in your life or for different assets; you may also decide to retain some assets in sole ownership.

If you live in a community property state, bear in mind that the conditions of co-ownership may be significantly affected by the laws of those states.

JOINT OWNERSHIP

Under joint ownership—usually abbreviated on stock certificates and bank records as JT TEN (joint tenants) or JT WROS (joint tenants with rights of survivorship)—two or more persons can share the legal ownership of any kind of property: a house, cottage, office, acreage or other real estate, bank accounts and securities, motor vehicles, household contents, antiques, or virtually anything of value. Because each joint owner has what is known as an "undivided interest" in the jointly owned property, either or any one of them is entitled to full use of the property and to his or her *share* of any income it may yield, regardless of which of them acquired it initially. The share of each owner is automatically determined by the number of persons involved in the joint ownership. If there are two joint owners, each is entitled to one-half; if three, one-third; and so on.

The most significant characteristic of joint ownership is that it includes *rights of survivorship*. That is, upon the death of any one joint owner, his or her interest passes automatically, by operation of law, to the surviving owner or owners. Because property held in joint ownership is not considered part of the deceased owner's probate estate, it passes to the surviving owners without the delay and expense of probate administration.

THE ATTRACTIONS OF JOINT TENANCY

Symbolic Significance

For couples who have just married—and, indeed, for some cohabitants who have dispensed with the formality of marriage—joint ownership may have considerable symbolic value because it reflects, in a sense, compliance with the "with all my worldly goods I thee endow" stipulation of the Protestant marriage service. The partners may see the merging of their individual assets into joint ownership as somehow reinforcing their merger into a social and emotional partnership. And the element of automatic inheritability reflects each partner's concern for the other's future welfare. Given the current divorce rate and the difficulty of terminating a joint ownership, this view may not be altogether rational, but it is quite common.

Convenience

Aside from its symbolic value, however, joint ownership offers some very practical advantages, among them convenience. In many circumstances one joint owner can act on behalf of the other(s) whenever they are unavailable. If, for example, you are traveling abroad, or are hospitalized or otherwise unavailable or incapacitated, a joint owner can buy or sell jointly owned securities, pay bills from a joint checking account, retrieve an urgently needed document from a jointly leased safe deposit box, and in general take care of many financial concerns.

Protection Against Creditors

Joint ownership, in addition, may offer some protection against your creditors' claims after your death. Since your jointly owned property passes automatically to your surviving joint owner(s) and therefore is no longer yours, and since no person—not even your spouse—is normally responsible for your debts (unless you incurred them jointly), the jointly owned assets need not be used to satisfy any of your debts that are outstanding at the time of your death.

Protection against creditors' claims during your lifetime, however, is a different matter. If, for example, you declare bankruptcy, or if you are found liable in an automobile accident and the damage award exceeds your liability insurance coverage, joint ownership does not offer you complete immunity.

In such circumstances the jointly held assets' vulnerability to creditors depends on the nature of the asset and the laws of your state, but generally speaking the share of the jointly held asset that you originally contributed is likely to be exposed to creditors' claims. Thus, if you hold a bank account in joint ownership with your spouse but in fact all deposits came from your earnings, your creditors may have the right to attach all of it. If, on the other hand, 50% of the house which you hold in joint ownership was paid for by your joint owner, only half its value would be available to satisfy your creditors' claims.

Creditors seeking to attach jointly held assets must first file suit and obtain a judgment against you, a process that may discourage them from trying to collect relatively small debts. Against major debts and damage claims, however, joint ownership offers far less protection than another form of co-ownership, tenancy by the entirety, discussed later in this chapter.

Tax Advantages

As we shall see, joint tenancy may offer certain tax advantages, but mainly with respect to death taxes—the federal gift and estate tax and the various state inheritance and estate taxes. With respect to federal and state income taxes, the advantages are probably more limited than many people believe.

Inheritability

One indisputable advantage of joint ownership undoubtedly accounts for its popularity with spouses, other family members, and occasionally close friends. That is the automatic inheritability of the jointly held property by the surviving joint owner(s). This simple and inexpensive tactic for avoiding the expense and delay of probate administration is so widely appreciated that some people transfer almost everything they own into joint ownership with spouses, children, and others whom they expect to survive them. With the bulk of their assets in joint ownership, they anticipate that the value of the few assets remaining in sole ownership upon their death will be low enough to qualify for the various types of small estate transfer procedures that avoid full probate administration (see chapter 2). This is why joint ownership has been called "the poor man's will."

Although there is no doubt that joint ownership, carefully planned, can avoid probate or reduce its costs, it does not, as we shall see shortly, relieve you of the need to make a will or to devote further thought to other forms of ownership, to estate planning, or possibly to tax planning.

SOME DISADVANTAGES OF JOINT OWNERSHIP

Seduced by its obvious advantages, many people precipitately place many of their assets in joint ownership without an awareness of its limitations. Some of these may strike you as insignificant or irrelevant to your personal situation, but others can give rise to serious problems, either immediately or in the future.

Risk

In order to gain the advantage of convenience, both (or all) joint owners must have unrestricted access to some types of jointly held assets; they must be able to sign checks, liquidate securities or other assets, and remove the contents of a jointly-leased bank safe deposit box. But with such access, there is nothing to prevent a joint owner from liquidating and absconding with the assets at any time. This means that you should not consider as a joint owner anyone with whom you do not anticipate a very stable relationship for the expected duration of the joint ownership. Considering the fact, however, that some divorces occur between spouses in their fifties, that some children become alienated from their parents on reaching adulthood, and that some close friendships terminate unexpectedly, it is inevitable that joint ownership involves some degree of risk.

In addition to caution in the selection of joint owners, this risk can be reduced in other ways. Money market and bank accounts, for example, can be set up in joint ownership so that withdrawals require the signatures of two or more owners rather than one. The sale of stock by one of the joint owners can be prevented by having the stock certificates in your own possession rather than in your brokerage account, since stock certificates cannot be transferred without the guaranteed signature endorsement of all owners. These precautionary measures, however, not only violate the spirit of joint ownership but also reduce the convenience that it offers.

Inflexibility

Once established, joint ownership may be well-nigh impossible to modify or terminate, especially when real estate is involved. It can, of course, be terminated at any time with the consent of all the joint owners, and it is either terminated or modified automatically upon the death of one joint owner, since his share immediately becomes the property of the surviving owner. It also can be dissolved by a court in finalizing a divorce between joint owners or in response to a "partition" lawsuit filed by one of the joint owners asking that the property be divided or sold, with the proceeds divided. But aside from these possibilities, you should regard joint ownership as essentially a "till death us do part" arrangement. This might be satisfactory if you could foretell the future, but most people can't do this very accurately, not only with respect to the stability of their marriage and their relationships with children who are joint owners but also, more important, with respect to death and subsequent inheritance.

Unintended Inheritance

Although automatic inheritability is the most attractive feature of joint ownership, the inflexibility of this form of ownership can result in both unintended inheritance and unintended disinheritance. Often, for example, a parent sets up joint ownership with an adult child for the sole purpose of convenience, so that the child can manage an account with a bank, a broker, or a money market fund in the parent's temporary absence. If the parent should die unexpectedly, however, that child will automatically acquire the joint account balances, and the spouse and other children will receive no share of these accounts. This kind of "inheritance" can be challenged by the survivors who were thus disinherited, but litigation is costly, protracted, and enormously frustrating. Although the problem can be averted by a written agreement, signed by both parent and child, stipulating that no inheritance is intended, a far simpler option would be for the parent to avoid joint ownership and, instead, give the child a durable financial power of attorney to deal with the accounts (see chapter 8) if only convenience and not inheritance is intended.

Joint ownership can also result in disinheritance of children of prior marriages. If, for example, you remarry after the death or divorce of a spouse and you transfer your assets into joint ownership with your new spouse, the children of your first marriage will inherit nothing if you predecease your spouse—an outcome you may not have intended.

But the most significant shortcoming of the automatic inheritability feature of joint ownership stems from the fact that no one can predict which joint owner will die first. Suppose that an elderly widow places her house in joint ownership with her son, intending that he acquire it automatically on her death without the necessity of probate. But if the son should die before she does, ownership of the house reverts to her alone and, upon her death, would become part of her probate estate. On the other hand, if she transfers the house into joint ownership between herself, her son, and her daughter, and the son dies first, then on her own death, ownership of the house would pass automatically to her surviving daughter, and the son's children would receive no share of the property.

All these unintended consequences can be averted if, instead of joint ownership, you establish a revocable living trust. As we shall see in the chapter 4, this form of trust provides automatic inheritability plus control over ultimate disposition if one or more of your primary beneficiaries happen to predecease you. Further, during you lifetime, the trust can be amended with respect to the property involved, the designation of trustees and beneficiaries, and any other circumstances which are subject to change.

As another alternative to joint ownership of bank accounts and securities, most states authorize use of pay-on-death (POD) or transfer-on-death (TOD) beneficiary designations to achieve nonprobate transfers on death. (See chapter 2.) Bank account depositors can designate a POD beneficiary and securities owners can specify a TOD beneficiary. Such a beneficiary, although having no access or control during the owner's lifetime, will automatically acquire the bank account balance or the securities after the owner's death, free of probate administration. These provisions are found in the Uniform Nonprobate Transfers On Death Act (adopted by most states), in some versions of the Uniform Probate Code, and in separate laws enacted by several states.

JOINT OWNERSHIP NOT A WILL SUBSTITUTE

The automatic inheritability feature of joint ownership leads many people to conclude that once they transfer assets into joint ownership, they need not write a will. But there are at least two reasons why joint ownership does not relieve one of this responsibility.

To begin with, you can never be certain that all your assets will be in joint ownership at the specific moment of your death. Almost inevitably your estate will include some property that remains solely owned, because it could not or should not have been placed in joint ownership or because your joint owner predeceased you. Unless you have left a will, this property will be distributed by the probate court to your "heirs at law" specified by state law, and these persons may not be the same individuals you would have chosen as your beneficiaries. (See table 1.1.)

A properly drawn will becomes especially important in the event that you and your joint owner(s) die together in an automobile accident, a plane crash, or some other unforeseeable common disaster. Under the Uniform Simultaneous Death Act, adopted by all states, if your deaths are simultaneous, *each* of you is assumed to have survived the other and, hence, half of all your jointly owned assets (assuming two joint owners) will be regarded as belonging to each of you. This means that each joint owner's estate will be subject to the expense and delay of probate administration and that, in the absence of a will, they will be distributed to each joint owner's heirs as determined by state law.

In case of the simultaneous deaths of joint owners, the separate probate administration of each co-owner's estate can be prevented if both wills contain a "common disaster clause," an example of which follows:

> In the event that my wife and I die simultaneously or under circumstances where it cannot be determined who died first, then it shall be presumed that [I survived my wife],* and all provisions of my will shall be construed based upon such presumption.

Because it specifies the prior death of one spouse (and hence automatic inheritance of jointly held property by the survivor), such a clause avoids double probate and the consequences of the Uniform Simultaneous Death Act, but it points up another limitation of joint ownership, one that is unrelated to simultaneous death. Upon the death of the first of two joint owners, the survivor will be deprived of the probate avoidance advantage unless he or she immediately established joint ownership with a new co-owner—perhaps an adult child or someone else to whom the survivor plans to bequeath the property—or chooses some other strategy that avoids probate. Establishing a new joint ownership is simple enough, but it is often overlooked or neglected, especially by elderly widows or widowers after the death of a mate.

ESTABLISHING JOINT OWNERSHIP

As we have noted, joint ownership can be used for any type of property and can involve any number of joint owners. The co-owners need not share a common residence or even live in the same state,

---

* The wife's will should, of course, specify that "my husband survived me," but the choice of the presumed survivor should depend on individual circumstances.

but in some circumstances they need to record their signatures when the tenancy is established and to be available for a signature endorsement when assets are sold or transferred.

Designating a minor child as a joint owner is not illegal, but it can create problems in some circumstances. Since minors lack legal capacity to sell real estate, stocks, or other types of assets, the sale of a house or stock certificates owned in joint ownership with a minor may require the appointment of a conservator, with the child's share of the proceeds to be maintained in a converatorship account until the child reaches age 18. There is no such restriction with respect to bank accounts, but most parents who consider joint ownership of a bank account with one or more minor children would find a pay-on-death account, a custodial account, or a formal revocable trust a far more advantageous arrangement. All these are discussed in chapter 2.

For many kinds of property, joint ownership is easy to set up. For securities, you need only instruct the broker to register the account in the names of all joint owners and to add the notation JT TEN, which, in securities transactions, establishes rights of survivorship. Bank and money market accounts can be registered in the same way, but on these accounts it is important to make sure that the account specifies rights of survivorship. In fact, you may want to request that the registration of the account read "as joint tenants with rights of survivorship and not as tenants in common."

To transfer real estate into joint ownership, you need only prepare and sign a new deed (see figure 3.1) and record it with the county register of deeds. Motor vehicles can be transferred from individual ownership into joint ownership by the regular transfer procedure provided by the state department of motor vehicles, after which the joint owner will be identified on the vehicle's certificate of title. As we explained in chapter 2, however, it may be advisable to retain a vehicle in sole ownership so as to limit one's exposure to liability from auto accidents.

When other kinds of personal property are acquired, a receipt or a bill of sale is commonly involved; if joint ownership of such property is intended, this document should specify that the co-owners are "joint tenants and not tenants in common." Lacking such documentation, co-owners intending joint ownership should, on acquiring the asset, state their intention in writing and preserve

Figure 3.1

DEED OF REAL ESTATE

KNOW ALL MEN BY THESE PRESENTS: That

whose address is

Quit Claim(s) to

whose address is

the following described premises
situated in the County of   and State of Michigan, to-wit:

for the full consideration of

Dated

Witnesses: Signed and Sealed:

_____   _____(L.S.)

_____   _____(L.S.)

_____   _____(L.S.)

                                         _____(L.S.)

STATE OF MICHIGAN   )

COUNTY OF _____)ss   _____(L.S.)

The foregoing instrument was acknowledged before me on

by

My commission expires   _____

_____   Notary Public _____
                                         County, Michigan
Instrument   Business
Drafted by _____   Address _____

- -

Recording Fee _____   When recorded return to

                                         _____

State Transfer Tax_____   _____

                                         Send subsequent tax bills

                                         to_____

Tax Parcel #_____   _____

Figure 3.2

ASSIGNMENT OF PERSONAL PROPERTY

The undersigned John Doe and Mary Doe (Assignors), whose address is 101 Main Street, Lansing, MI 48823, hereby assign, grant, and transfer to John Doe and Mary Doe, Husband and Wife, as joint tenants with rights of survivorship, all of Assignors' right, title, and interest in and to the following described personal property:

(a) All of the household furnishings, appliances, equipment, tools, books, collectibles, artwork, and all other items of tangible personal property now and hereafter located at or contained in Assignors' dwelling at 101 Main St, Lansing, MI, and any other dwelling occupied by Assignors; and

(b) All of the contents now and hereafter contained in Assignors' safe-deposit box at First of America Bank, and any other safe-deposit box leased to Assignors or either of them.

Date: _____   _____
                                        John Doe, Assignor

                                        _____
                                        Mary Doe, Assignor

WITNESSES:

_____

_____

it with their other important papers. Figure 3.2 illustrates a document sufficient to establish joint ownership of personal property.

TAX CONSEQUENCES

Income Taxes: State and Federal

The assessment of taxes on the income or sale of jointly owned property is arbitrary, to say the least. As a general rule, since each joint owner owns an equal share of an income-producing asset, each is responsible for paying income taxes on the income from his share. But, there are exceptions to this rule, in which income tax liability is based not on the share owned by each tenant but on his or her proportional contribution to the acquisition of the asset. For example, income produced by real estate is taxed on an equal-share basis, that from savings bonds on a proportionate contribution basis. If a father and son own a commercial property as joint owners, each pays tax on half of the income and on half of the capital gain that may result when the property is sold, regardless of their respective contributions to its purchase. On the other hand, if they jointly own U.S. Savings Bonds but the father provided all the money with which they were purchased, it is the father who is responsible for paying the tax on their yield.

Tax liability for interest earned on bank accounts depends on the law of the state in which the bank is located. Some states calculate each joint owner's tax liability on an equal-share basis, others on the basis of each tenant's proportional contribution to the joint account, despite the virtual impossibility of determining each tenant's contributions to a very active account. And the IRS follows state law in assessing tax liability for bank account interest.

When securities are registered in the names of joint owners, each co-owner is taxed on his proportional share of dividends or capital gains or losses regardless of the source of funds used to buy the securities. If, however, the jointly held securities are registered in a broker's "street" account, the tax liability of each joint owner is governed by state law, which should be consulted.

Obviously, then, whether or not joint ownership offers an advantage with respect to income taxes depends both on the nature of the asset and on your relationship with the joint owner. In general, no matter whether tax is assessed on a contribution basis or a share basis, husband and wife will derive no tax advantage from joint ownership as long as they file joint tax returns, although there may be some advantage if they file separately. Joint ownership between a parent and an adult child who is in a lower tax bracket can yield a tax advantage in connection with real estate or registered securities, since the child will pay less tax on his half share, whether or not he contributed to the purchase.

Many parents assume that they can reduce or avoid income tax by setting up a joint bank or money market account with a lower-tax-bracket child who contributes nothing to the account but his name. By furnishing the financial institution with the child's taxpayer identification number (usually his Social Security number), they assume that the institution will identify all earnings from the account as belonging to the child. In fact, this tactic does not relieve the parent of any obligation for paying tax on half the yield in states that use the share basis, or on all the yield in states that assess on the basis of proportional contribution. If, however, the parent makes a gift of all or part of the account funds to the child and the child then deposits this gift in a joint account with the parent, it would seem that the child has become a contributor to the account and hence can assume responsibility for some or all of the tax.

When a surviving joint owner sells assets of which he or she has become sole owner, complex rules apply in determining capital gain or loss for income tax purposes. As with any gain or loss, the seller's "cost basis" must be determined; usually it is the actual cost of, or price paid for, the property. The "cost" of any property included in a decedent's taxable estate, however, is given a "stepped-up" basis—to its market value on the date of death, or, optionally, six months after death.

However, transferring property at death by joint ownership may make it impossible to take full advantage of this tax-saving device. Joint ownership between husband and wife may well produce an unfavorable cost basis for the surviving spouse; that's because for federal estate tax purposes, only one-half of the property involved would be included in the estate of the first spouse to die. Thus, only one-half of the property would receive a stepped-up cost basis, giving rise to potential capital gains tax on behalf of the surviving spouse in the event that the property should subsequently be sold.

If, therefore, you own assets that have appreciated substantially, you should consider the advantages of retaining the assets in your own name, and transferring them at death by use of a will, a revocable trust, or a transfer-on-death securities account, thus giving your survivors the benefit of a full stepped-up tax basis and a resultant saving of capital gains tax.

Federal Gift Tax

Any gift of more than $12,000 (or $24,000 with a spouse's consent) may subject the donor to federal gift tax. See chapter 6. Whether the creation of joint ownership gives rise to any gift tax liability, however, depends on the respective contributions of each tenant, the relationship between the tenants, and the nature of the asset.

If two persons set up joint ownership to which each contributes an equal amount, no gift has been made and no gift tax liability is incurred. If two spouses set up ownership and only one of them has contributed to it, a gift amounting to half of the value of the joint property has occurred, but no gift tax is payable because the law provides an unlimited marital deduction for gifts between spouses. Thus, the husband who, upon marriage, transfers his house or his securities portfolio into joint ownership with his wife has made her a gift, but the gift is not subject to any gift tax.

When the respective contributions of two joint owners are unequal and the co-owners are not spouses, the question of whether a gift has been made and whether it is subject to federal gift tax depends on the nature of the jointly owned asset. If, for example, a parent is the sole contributor to a joint bank account with a child, no gift has been made until the child actually withdraws funds from the account. A gift occurs once the child withdraws the money, but if he withdraws at a rate of less than $12,000 a year (or $24,000 with consent of the parent's spouse), the gift will not be taxable. There is no reason why the child cannot withdraw money from time to time and immediately redeposit it in order to avoid gift tax and to assume some of the income tax liability for interest earned by the account, presumably at a lower tax rate.

The rule governing bank accounts applies also to U.S. Savings Bonds. When bonds are registered in joint ownership, no gift is deemed to have occurred until the noncontributing joint owner re-registers the bonds in his or her own name.

Securities are a different matter. If the securities are simply held in joint ownership in a broker's street account, no gift has occurred. But if a donor *registers* the securities in joint ownership with a child, a gift of half of the securities has occurred, because in theory, the child has a right to liquidate his or her share of the securities immediately. In such a situation a gift tax can be avoided by transferring once a year into joint ownership securities worth less than $12,000.

Jointly owned real estate is governed by the same rule as registered securities: a gift occurs at the moment that the joint ownership is established. As in the case of registered securities, this is because the noncontributing joint owner has the right to sell his or her share of the jointly held asset.

For most people the tax consequences of making a gift are probably less significant than they may appear because the mere fact that a gift has been made does not mean that gift tax is immediately payable. Gifts of any amount between spouses and gifts of less than $12,000 per year to nonspouses are tax exempt. In addition, each person has a lifetime gift tax exemption of $1 million.

Federal Estate Tax

The IRS's treatment of jointly owned property for federal estate-tax purposes is somewhat complex. Property held in joint ownership passes automatically to the surviving joint owner(s) on the death of the first co-owner and should, logically, not be considered part of the deceased's estate. But this is not true for estate tax purposes. The IRS regards the *full value* of all jointly held property as part of the deceased's taxable estate. There are, however, three important exceptions to this general rule.

First, if a surviving joint owner is a spouse of the deceased, only one-half of the jointly held assets will be counted as part of the deceased's taxable estate and, because of the unlimited marital deduction, even that half will not be taxed.

Second, if a surviving joint owner who is not a spouse of the deceased can prove that he or she bought the jointly held asset, or contributed to its acquisition or improvement, the proportion contributed will be excluded from the deceased's taxable estate.

Third, if the jointly held property was originally given or bequeathed to the joint owners, only the deceased owner's share will be included in his estate for tax purposes.

Many people believe that because joint ownership usually avoids probate, it also avoids the federal estate tax. This is not true. Unless one of the foregoing three exceptions to the general rule is applicable, the *full value* of the decedent's jointly held property is included in his taxable estate for purposes of computing federal estate-tax liability. The federal estate tax is based on the fair market value of all property included in the estate, either as of the date of death or, at the executor's option, six months after death.

The minimum value of an estate subject to estate tax is $2 million during years 2006 through 2008. (See chapter 6.) Given this threshold, the federal estate tax is likely to affect only a small, affluent percentage of the population. But since neither your future affluence nor the rate of inflation nor the actions of future Congresses can be predicted accurately, the tax consequences of joint ownership should always be considered. Joint ownership can, for example, result in double taxation if jointly owned property is taxed on the death of the first joint owner and then again on the later death of the surviving owner.

TERMINATING JOINT OWNERSHIP

Joint ownership can be terminated or altered in any of four ways: (1) by death of one of the co-owners, (2) by an act of one of the co-owners, (3) by mutual consent of all of them, and (4) by order of a court of law.

When, as is most commonly the case, joint ownership is terminated by the death of one joint owner, the surviving owner(s) need do nothing immediately, since they can enjoy the property and its earnings just as they did prior to the death. If, however, only two joint owners were involved, the property reverts to sole ownership and the surviving joint owner should promptly consider setting up joint ownership with a new co-owner (if joint ownership still seems advantageous) or using an alternative form of ownership such as a revocable living trust. See chapters 2 and 4.

In any event, a transfer to reflect the change in ownership should be made before the property is sold. In most cases, this involves essentially the same procedures described in connection with establishing the joint ownership: reregistration of stock certificates and similar records and recording of death certificates and possibly new deeds or other documents affecting the title to real estate. In some states, in order to effect a transfer at death, the surviving joint owner may be required to produce a document from the state tax authority indicating that the deceased joint owner's death taxes have been paid in full or that none are owed.

Joint ownership can be terminated at any time by mutual agreement between or among the co-owners. In some circumstances, however, one co-owner may sell or give away his share independently. When this occurs, the new owner does not become a joint owner. Instead, he becomes a tenant in common (see p. 73). For example, if three brothers jointly own a piece of real estate and one of them sells his share to a stranger, the two remaining brothers retain their two-thirds interest in joint ownership with rights of survivorship but the stranger, as a tenant in common, has no such survivorship rights.

Joint ownership may be terminated and the asset divided between or among the co-owners by a court in the course of a divorce proceeding or in response to a "partition" lawsuit initiated by one of the joint owners who is no longer interested in joint ownership. In such cases, if the property is not readily divisible, the court may order that it be sold and the proceeds divided among the joint owners.

TENANCY BY THE ENTIRETY

A hybrid form of joint ownership, *tenancy by the entirety*, offers two significant advantages over standard joint ownership, but also has two limitations. First, it is recognized by only 24 states, and some of these restrict its use to real property only. Second, in all the states that do recognize this form of co-ownership, it can be used only by married couples. If these limitations do not disqualify you, you may consider it in lieu of joint ownership for at least some of your property.

Tenancy by the entirety has its roots in English common law, which held that upon marriage the two partners became an "entirety," which could hold property in its name rather than in the name of the individual partners. Tenancy by the entirety was the earliest form of co-ownership and, although it has been modified in some respects, it still retains some unique characteristics.

Like joint ownership, tenancy by the entirety provides for automatic inheritance by the surviving spouse, but with greater certainty and finality. As we have noted, automatic inheritance by a surviving joint owner may be challenged in the courts on grounds that it was unintended. Experience indicates, however, that inheritance by the survivor of a tenancy by the entirety is much less likely to be challenged successfully, apparently because courts feel that the co-owners really intended inheritance by survivor.

More important, perhaps, tenancy by the entirety provides greater protection against the creditors of one of the co-owners. Not only does it immunize the joint property against such claims after the death of the debtor but also, unlike joint ownership, in many states it provides the same protection during the co-owners' lifetimes.

There are some situations in which this protection is not as useful as it may appear to be. If, for example, you apply for a personal loan, a credit card, or any other kind of credit that requires submission of a statement of net worth, and if all your assets turn out to be held in tenancy by the entirety, no sensible lender is likely to approve the loan unless it is co-signed by your spouse, in which case your co-owned property gets no protection because the co-signed loan is a debt for which the entirety is responsible. On the other hand, if you are sued as an individual for negligence and the damages exceed your liability insurance coverage, none of your property held in tenancy by the entirety can be attached to satisfy the damage claim.

The thought may occur to you at this point that, immediately after incurring a debt or losing a lawsuit, you could protect the bulk of your assets by quickly transferring them into a tenancy by the entirety. But this tactic, known as a *fraudulent conveyance*, will be of no avail if your creditors can persuade a court that you made the transfer with the intention of defrauding them.

TAX CONSEQUENCES OF TENANCY BY THE ENTIRETY

With respect to income, gift, or estate taxes, tenancy by the entirety offers no advantages or disadvantages that distinguish it from standard joint ownership. The earlier discussion of the tax aspects of joint ownership applies to tenancy by the entirety in all respects.

ESTABLISHING A TENANCY BY THE ENTIRETY

In its original form, which has been retained by a number of states, tenancy by the entirety is applicable only to newly acquired property, not to property owned previously by either of the spouses or by both of them under some other form of co-ownership. That is, spouses may buy a new house or 100 shares of Xerox stock in tenancy by the entirety, but they are not permitted to transfer their present home, securities, or other assets into this form of ownership.

A number of states have removed this restriction, but in states that have retained it you can circumvent it by transferring any currently owned property to a third party, sometimes called a "straw man," who will in turn transfer it back to you and your spouse as a tenancy by the entirety. You can, for example, deed your current home to an adult daughter, who can then deed it back to you and your spouse as tenants by the entirety. If, however, this back-and-forth non-spousal transfer exceeds $12,000/$24,000 in value, it may be a taxable gift, thus requiring the filing of a gift tax return.

TERMINATING A TENANCY BY THE ENTIRETY

Like joint ownership, tenancy by the entirety is most commonly terminated by the death of one of the spouses, at which time ownership of the entireties property passes to a surviving spouse. It can also be terminated by mutual consent of the spouses. By law, a divorce automatically terminates a tenancy by the entirety, transforming it into a tenancy in common unless other provisions are made in the divorce decree.

TENANCY IN COMMON

The third form of co-ownership, *tenancy in common*, is similar to joint ownership in that it can involve two or more people, who need not be related, and it can be used for the ownership of any kind of property, real or personal, tangible or intangible. But the differences are far more important than the similarities.

The most important difference is that a tenancy in common provides no rights of survivorship. Instead, each co-owner's share belongs exclusively to him. During his lifetime he has the right to sell it or give it away, and on his death his share becomes part of his probate estate, instead of passing to the surviving co-owner.

A second difference relates to the share of the property owned by each tenant in common. In joint ownership and in tenancy by the entirety, each co-owner is assumed to own an equal share—that is, one-half in a tenancy by the entirety or a joint ownership involving two co-owners, or one-third in joint ownership involving three. In a tenancy in common, by contrast, the share owned by each tenant is clearly specified and it need bear no relationship to the number of co-owners involved.

In many respects, owning something as a tenant in common is rather similar to owning 100 shares of corporate common stock. As a corporate stockholder, you own a specified share of the company, you are entitled to a specified share of the distributed profits, you have the right to sell, give away, or bequeath your shares, and you are obligated to pay tax on the income that your shares produce. Your stock is subject to claims by your creditors, both before and after your death, and on your death it becomes part of your probate estate and passes not to the surviving stockholders but to the beneficiaries designated in your will, or to your heirs at law if you die without a will.

Since tenancy in common lacks the advantage of automatic inheritability and offers neither tax advantages nor protection against creditors' claims, you may wonder why we have devoted space to it. Actually, in some circumstances tenancy in common can be a very useful form of ownership, and there are various reasons why you should have some understanding of it.

For one thing, there are situations in which automatic inheritability is undesirable. Suppose, for example, that you would like your two adult children and their families to share ownership of your vacation home after your death. If you will it to them as joint owners or if you transfer it into joint ownership during your lifetime and if one of them should die shortly after you do, the deceased child's share will pass automatically to his or her surviving sibling and the deceased child's family will have no rights in it. If, on the other hand, you will it to them as tenants in common, each can bequeath his share to his family and, in case of disagreement, the vacation home can be sold and the proceeds divided.

In other situations, a tenancy in common can serve as a convenient form of temporary partnership among friends, neighbors, or business associates. If, for example, a bank offers a certificate of deposit that carries a highly attractive interest rate but requires a minimum of $100,000, there is no reason why you and four friends could not each invest $20,000 and buy it as tenants in common. This kind of arrangement is useful for many kinds of investment, such as real estate, mortgages, or large blocks of stock, that are too expensive for an individual. Tenancy in common is useful, too, for a part-time enterprise: collaboration on a book, for example, or the establishment of a small home business. To cite a more modest example, if you and a neighbor would both like to own a riding lawnmower or a snowblower but hesitate to spend a considerable amount of money for something that each of you will use only a few hours each season, there is no reason why you could not buy one machine as tenants in common, sharing its cost, maintenance, and use.

TAX ASPECTS

Because a tenant in common owns his share outright, the tax consequences of tenancy in common are identical with those of sole ownership. The tenant is solely responsible for paying income tax on its yield or sale, and the property becomes part of his estate for both federal and state death tax purposes.

ESTABLISHING A TENANCY IN COMMON

By Agreement

When a tenancy in common is set up by agreement among two or more people, the arrangement, no matter how informal, should nevertheless be reduced to writing in a document that specifies not only the contribution to and the share owned by each co-owner but also his responsibilities and his vote in any decisions that will be made about the use, maintenance, or disposition of the property involved.

If the property consists of real estate, the wording of the deed or land contract should clearly indicate a tenancy in common. The same holds true for other kinds of property. Both banks and brokerage firms are familiar with tenancy in common, and either the bank signature card or the brokerage account should be marked TEN COM, although even in these cases a written document specifying tenancy in common and the share owned by each co-owner will provide the co-owners with additional protection. When other kinds of personal property are involved, a bill of sale or a separate document can indicate that a tenancy in common and not a joint ownership is intended by the co-owners.

By Court Action

A tenancy in common may also be established by a court of law. In many divorce settlements, especially in community property states, the court may order that all property held by the couple in joint ownership or tenancy by the entirety be converted into a tenancy in common so as to abolish inheritability and to ensure that each co-owner has the exclusive right to control and dispose of his or her share.

Court action may also create a tenancy in common when a creditor makes a successful claim against property held in joint ownership. To satisfy the creditor's claims, a court may order that the debtor's share of jointly owned property be turned over to the creditor, who then becomes a tenant in common with the remaining co-owners.

By Transfer

In some circumstances a tenancy in common may be established by transfer of property owned solely or in joint ownership. If, for example, one joint owner sells his share to a third party, the third party becomes a tenant in common with the remaining joint owner(s). Similarly, the sole owner of a piece of property—income producing real estate, for example—may sell whatever portion of it he chooses to someone else, who then becomes a tenant in common with the original owner.

By Default

Occasionally a tenancy in common is established by error—through ignorance or as the result of a carelessly drawn deed, land contract, or will. Although, as we have noted, there are situations in which you would like to bequeath something to your survivors as tenants in common, there are many other situations in which you may intend joint ownership. You may, for example, want to leave your vacation home to your wife and your son in joint ownership in order to ensure rights of survivorship. If so, your will should identify the beneficiaries as "Mary Smith and Robert Smith as joint tenants and not as tenants in common." If, instead, your will simply says, "I leave my vacation home to my wife, Mary Smith, and my son Robert Smith," the probate courts of most states will resolve any ambiguity in favor of tenancy in common.

Similar problems can arise when a bank or brokerage account is established. Particularly in small banks and local branches, bank officers may not be aware of the distinctions among the three forms of co-ownership, and an account intended to be in joint ownership may be registered erroneously as a tenancy in common if you do not clearly specify which form you prefer.

In general, when most types of property are transferred to two or more persons, the law presumes that a tenancy in common was intended unless the transfer document clearly specifies joint ownership or some other form of ownership. The one exception to this presumption involves real estate. In some states, when a deed transferring real estate to husband and wife fails to specify the form of ownership, the presumption is that the spouses intended to own it as tenants by the entirety.

TERMINATING A TENANCY IN COMMON

If a tenant in common sells his share, the tenancy continues, because the purchaser becomes the new co-owner. If, however, all tenants in common agree to divide the property among themselves (if, for example, it consists of 1,000 bushels of grain), the tenancy in common ends. Moreover, the tenancy terminates if the property is sold by common consent, although the proceeds are regarded as held as a tenancy in common until the money is distributed pro rata among the owners.

4

TRUSTS AND
THEIR VERSATILITY

If you have relatively few assets and their value is only moderate, and if your family situation seems unlikely to change, one of the forms of co-ownership described in chapter 3 may suit your needs. Joint ownership provides automatic inheritability and can, at least to some extent, protect your assets against creditors' claims and may reduce your tax burden. Above all, it usually costs little to set up. These advantages may well outweigh its inherent disadvantages.

But if your assets are numerous, diverse, and increasing in value, it can be something of a chore to place each bank account, each stock and bond, each piece of real estate, and each of your other valuable possessions into one or another form of co-ownership. More important, if your future financial needs are unpredictable or if your relationships with family and others are unstable or complex, the inflexibility of joint ownership can sometimes present serious problems. In such circumstances, you may be able to enjoy all the advantages of joint ownership and considerably greater convenience, flexibility, and security if you transfer part or all of your assets into some type of trust.

Because we have all encountered, in novels and movies, characters who live in luxurious idleness, supported by "a trust my grandfather set up for me," many of us think of a trust as an instrument that only the very rich use to avoid taxes or to exercise fiscal control over their playboy, spendthrift, or black-sheep children. Trusts, some middle-income people assume, are for the Rockefellers and Vanderbilts, not for themselves.

In reality, trusts of one kind or another are becoming increasingly common among people whose net worth is far below the millionaire level. As tax burdens rise, as people accumulate more assets and hence become more concerned with estate planning and probate avoidance, as family stability diminishes and remarriage and cohabitation become more common, and as more lawyers become familiar with trusts, the old stereotypes are disappearing. Instead, there is increasing recognition of a trust's many advantages and a growing realization that a trust is neither difficult nor unduly expensive to set up. In fact, as we shall see shortly, you may already have some property that is now in some type of a trust, even though you may not be aware of it.

TRUSTS—THE BASIC CONCEPT

When you establish a trust, you turn over the ownership and management of your property to a trustee. This may strike you as a disconcerting and risky idea but, although the trustee "owns" the property, you need not relinquish ultimate control over your property or over the actions of the trustee. (In fact, you may, if you wish, serve as the trustee or co-trustee of your own trust.) The basic reason for the transfer of ownership to the trustee is that it changes your legal relationship to the property, and this change offers you some important advantages that are not available under either sole ownership or joint ownership.

There are several types of trust, each with distinctive features that serve specific purposes. But despite the variations, a general definition is possible: A trust is a legal entity (similar in some respects to a corporation) that is permitted to own, manage, reinvest, and ultimately distribute any kind of property. The property it manages is transferred into the trust by one or more *grantors* (sometimes called settlors or trustors), and the trust is administered by one or more *trustees* for the current or future benefit of one or more *beneficiaries*.

The most widely used form of trust—the revocable living trust—has four very significant characteristics. First, and most important, in this form of trust *any or all of the three roles—grantor, trustee, or beneficiary—may be filled by the same person or persons.* Moreover, the grantor may at any time replace the current trustees or beneficiaries with new ones. Thus, if you establish a revocable living trust, as grantor you can, if you wish, serve as your own trustee or you can designate, either as trustee or as co-trustee, a relative, a friend, a bank, or a trust company. If you prefer, you can serve as trustee during your lifetime and designate one or more successor trustees to take over management of the trust when you no longer want to serve, if you become incapacitated, or when you die. The same flexibility applies to your designation of beneficiaries. You may, for example, designate yourself and/or your spouse as trust beneficiaries during your lifetime, and your children or any other person or institution as beneficiaries after your death. And you can change beneficiaries whenever you like, prior to your incapacity or death.

In a revocable living trust, whether or not you serve as a trustee, you are, as a grantor, fully entitled to move property into and out of the trust or to sell or gift off trust property at any time and to use whatever income the trust-held property earns. In short, you can retain full control over trust assets, as well as the actions of the trustee, even though in a strictly legal sense the assets are titled in the trustee's representative name, not in your individual name.

The second significant characteristic of a revocable living trust is that *the assets held in trust are not part of your probate estate.* Upon your death, they can pass to the beneficiaries you designate in the trust document just as swiftly as they would if held in joint ownership.

Third, *a trust can serve as your beneficiary.* That is, upon your death, your will can bequeath everything you possess to the trust. This tactic does not avoid probate but, as we shall see, it assures you far more control over your property after your death than you can enjoy through joint ownership or through a will that bequeaths your assets directly and unconditionally to your beneficiaries.

Lastly, *a trust can outlive the grantor by many decades,* since any trustee can be succeeded by another. This longevity extends your control over your property long after your death, since whatever assets you place in a trust can be passed on not only to your immediate beneficiaries but also to future generations under conditions that you can now specify in the trust document.

ADVANTAGES OF TRUSTS

Trusts are proliferating because they provide all the advantages of joint ownership—and more. Since not all types of trust offer the same advantages, the discussion that follows does not apply to all of them. But because some advantages will appeal to you more than others, a thoughtful reading may help you identify the type of trust that best suits your purposes, your assets, and the needs of your survivors.

CONVENIENCE PLUS MANAGEMENT

A trust can offer you even more convenience than joint ownership. If you are hospitalized or traveling, or otherwise unavailable or incapacitated, the trustee (or your co-trustee or successor trustee if you are serving as your own trustee) can manage your assets for you. After your death, the trustee or successor trustee can continue managing the trust assets for as long as you specify in the trust document, making partial distributions to your beneficiaries according to your instructions, investing and reinvesting, and ultimately making final distribution to beneficiaries.

In addition to convenience, a trust offers the grantors an opportunity for continuous professional management of their assets. If, for example, your assets include a securities portfolio, and if you are unsophisticated about the stock market or simply unwilling to devote time and attention to monitoring your securities, designating a bank or trust company as the trustee may give you a higher yield than you could achieve by yourself. Professional trustees may be of value, also, if your property includes income-producing real estate, which you can't or don't want to manage personally. The fees charged by some professional trustees, however, are not inconsiderable and may well cancel out any gains achieved through professional management.

FLEXIBILITY DURING LIFE

If either your future financial needs or the stability of your marriage is unpredictable, a trust can give you far more flexibility and control than joint ownership. As we have seen, joint ownership can be difficult to unwind or revoke, and any assets you place in joint ownership will pass, at least to some extent, out of your exclusive control. If, for example, you transfer most of your assets into joint ownership with your spouse, you may not be able to use them for a new business venture without your spouse's consent. Should you divorce, your spouse will receive at least half of the jointly held assets whether or not he or she helped you acquire them. Moreover, if you remarry, any assets you place in joint ownership with your second spouse cannot be given or bequeathed to the children of your first marriage without your new spouse's consent.

If, on the other hand, you transfer your assets into a revocable trust, you retain full control over them and can use them for any purpose at any time prior to your incapacity or death. You can provide for automatic inheritance by your spouse by naming him/her as the trust's beneficiary, but you can easily change beneficiaries at any time if your marital situation should change, and you can make provisions for children from a prior marriage or for anyone else you choose. In some states, in fact, a trust can be used to disinherit a spouse, a result that cannot be accomplished through use of a will.

A trust, then, can remain revocable during your lifetime and still achieve prompt transfer at death without probate administration. In addition to avoiding probate, a trust can serve most of the purposes of a will. Like joint ownership, however, it does not relieve you of the need to make a will.

CONTROL AFTER DEATH

If you bequeath your property outright to beneficiaries by means of a will, you will have no control over it after your death. Under state law, the probate court will require your executor to liquidate your estate as expeditiously as possible and to distribute the proceeds to your beneficiaries, regardless of whether prompt liquidation is advisable or whether your beneficiaries are able and willing to use the proceeds judiciously.

Thus, for example, if you own a promising business, it will almost certainly have to be sold promptly on your death, even though it might triple in value if it were permitted to operate for another two or three years. But if, instead, you transfer your business to a trust and designate a competent trustee, there is no reason why your business could not continue to operate indefinitely after you die or at least until it reached its full potential value.

In addition to protecting your assets from premature liquidation, a trust can be far more effective than joint ownership in protecting them from dissipation by your surviving beneficiaries. When one joint owner dies, the fate of jointly held property depends on the financial acuity of the surviving co-owner. If, for example, the surviving joint owner is an elderly widow, she may be susceptible to investment schemes or confidence games. Or if the survivor is an immature or unstable child, his or her inheritance may be dissipated in other ways. If, on the other hand, the property is held in a trust managed by a competent trustee, you, as grantor, can set the conditions and the timetable under which the inheritance will be passed on to your beneficiaries, and you can enjoy greater confidence that its value is likely to be preserved or increased.

This assurance of stability and continuity becomes even more important if you have a disabled child or some other dependent who is likely to require lifetime care. In such circumstances a trust can protect the beneficiary's financial interests even though a guardian may have to be appointed to make custodial decisions and take care of the ward's other personal needs. For example, if you have nominated your sister as the guardian of your minor son, your sister will, on your death, assume custody of the child and responsibility for meeting his day-to-day needs. But if your sister has no ability or desire to manage money or other assets, the child's inheritance could be placed in a trust with a local bank named as trustee to manage the assets and make periodic distributions to the child's guardian. And if your child is disabled, you may want to set up a "special needs trust" to provide for the child without rendering him ineligible for governmental benefits. For more on this type of trust, see chapter 7.

In order to ensure that the trustee bank manages the inheritance competently, remains responsive to the child's needs, and does not charge unreasonable annual fees, your trust document can specifically grant to the guardian the power to discharge the trustee bank and to appoint as successor trustee "any bank or trust company in the U.S.A. which is authorized by law to administer trusts."

PROTECTION AGAINST CREDITORS' CLAIMS

All types of trusts provide protection against creditors' claims after the death of the grantors. Some types offer such protection during the grantor's lifetime as well, but, as we shall see, this protection may come at a very high price.

TAX ASPECTS

Some types of trust offer the possibility of reducing or totally avoiding income tax, federal estate tax, or both. An irrevocable trust, for example, allows you to shift income tax liability for the yield on its assets from yourself to beneficiaries who may be in a lower tax bracket. But most such trusts require you to relinquish—at least temporarily and more often permanently—any control over the assets and any benefit from their yield. Except on a small scale, they offer advantages only to those who are rich enough to dispense completely and irrevocably with a part of their assets.

A generation-skipping trust, which may be established during your lifetime or by your will after your death, can avoid double liability for federal estate tax. If, for example, you willed some assets to a child of yours and he, in turn, willed all or part of them to his child, the assets could be subject to federal estate tax twice, first as part of your estate and later as part of your child's estate. If, however, you set up a generation-skipping trust with a grandchild as beneficiary, your child may receive the trust income and your grandchild may eventually inherit the assets, but federal estate tax will be payable, if at all, only once—by your estate upon your death.

THE REVOCABLE LIVING TRUST

Trusts can be classified in many ways, but for our purposes the most useful approach is to distinguish between *revocable* and *irrevocable* living trusts. Although the revocable trust lacks some of the advantages offered by the irrevocable trust, it is far more widely used—and for good reasons. We shall deal first, therefore, with the revocable living trust and then, more briefly, with the irrevocable version.

The most important feature of a revocable living trust is implied by its name: You, as grantor, can freely transfer property into and out of the trust, change your designation of the trustees and beneficiaries, alter or modify the conditions under which the beneficiaries are entitled to receive their benefits, or even terminate the trust altogether at any time before you become mentally incapacitated or die. This revocability feature offers you complete freedom and control; it permits you to appoint a trustee, monitor his performance, and replace him as often as necessary until you find someone thoroughly competent to manage the trust after your incapacity or death.

The principal reason for establishing a revocable living trust is the avoidance of probate. If you become incapacitated, the trustee manages your assets without the expense, frustrations, and indignity of probate court guardianship proceedings. On your death, none of the property held in the trust is probatable, because it is titled in the trustee's name, not in yours. Thus, by transferring all your property into such a trust, you avoid not only the inevitable costs, delays, and frustrations of probate but also the attendant publicity. Probate is a public procedure; through probate records, anyone interested can find out the nature and value of your probate estate and identify the beneficiaries of your will, but the after-death transfer of assets from a trust to its beneficiaries can be completely private.

Many people believe that by setting up a revocable living trust they can reduce or avoid income, estate, or gift taxes. This is not true. Because the trust is revocable and the grantor has full use of trust-owned property, the grantor remains fully responsible for income tax on the property's earnings, and the full value of the trust's assets is included as part of his taxable estate for estate-tax purposes. When a grantor transfers property into a revocable living trust, no gift tax is involved because no gift is considered completed until after his death, when the property is managed for and distributed to the trust-designated beneficiaries.

THE TOTTEN TRUST

An easy way to familiarize yourself with the basic principles of a revocable living trust is to try out, on a small scale and at no cost, a somewhat limited version known as a *Totten trust* or *discretionary revocable trust account*. This type of trust is recognized by most states and is quite likely to be available at your local bank. Setting it up involves nothing more than filling out a special signature card designating yourself as trustee and your spouse, child, or anyone else you choose as the account's beneficiary (see figure 4.1).

Like any other bank account, a Totten trust account is used for cash deposits, but it differs from a conventional bank account in three respects: (1) it provides for the designation of one or more trustees and one or more beneficiaries; (2) upon your death, the balance of the account passes automatically to the account-designated beneficiary without probate administration; and (3) funds in the account are usable by you at any time but they cannot be withdrawn by your beneficiary or attached by his creditors during your lifetime or reached by your creditors after your death.

If you have read chapter 3, you may wonder why a Totten trust is preferable to joint ownership, since both types of ownership avoid probate by providing for automatic inheritance. There are two reasons. First, once joint ownership is established it may well be irrevocable, whereas the Totten trust permits you not only to use the money at any time and for any purpose during your lifetime but also to change beneficiaries whenever you choose. Second, some forms of joint ownership permit either co-owner (even the non-contributor) to withdraw and use all the jointly held funds, whereas the beneficiary you designate in a Totten trust cannot withdraw any of the funds until your death. Both of these differences give you a degree of control that simply may not be available with joint ownership.

Although the Totten trust is restricted to savings accounts offered by banks, it illustrates the considerable flexibility provided by the typical revocable living trust. You have full use of the money during your lifetime. Moreover, when death seems imminent you can liquidate most of your property, deposit the proceeds in a Totten trust, and thus avoid probate of the entire balance.

The Totten trust has, however, a number of limitations. Because it is restricted to bank deposits, it provides no opportunity for increasing the yield at a higher rate than the usually conservative rates offered by banks. And, although you can designate an account beneficiary, you cannot specify either the age that the beneficiary must reach or the conditions he or she must meet in order to claim the inheritance. Unlike a formal revocable living trust, which can outlive you, the Totten trust terminates automatically on your death, at which time the account balance passes immediately to the designated beneficiary or to the beneficiary's conservator if the beneficiary is a minor. And, like all revocable living trusts, the Totten trust offers you no tax advantages whatever.

Despite its limitations, the Totten trust can offer you some experience with a revocable living trust. If you don't like it, you can always close it out with no loss or you can maintain it with a minimum balance so that it stands ready for use if your financial situation or your life expectancy changes. If it does seem clearly useful, you can either continue to use it actively or you can realize the same advantages with far more flexibility by creating a more formal revocable living trust.

THE FORMAL REVOCABLE LIVING TRUST

Setting up a revocable living trust is a serious and not inexpensive undertaking. It requires that you think carefully about your choice

Figure 4.1

TOTTEN TRUST ACCOUNT CARD

DISCRETIONARY REVOCABLE TRUST ACCOUNT

Date _____   Account No. _____

     (1) _____ As Trustee}   Or the
          Social Security Number   Survivor
and (2) _____ As Trustee}   Thereof
      Social Security Number
For _____ Beneficiary}   Or the
                            Survivor
and _____ Beneficiary}   Thereof
Type (Last Name)   (First Name)   (Middle Name)
As trustees with right of survivorship, the undersigned hereby apply for membership in the

CAPITOL SAVINGS & LOAN ASSOCIATION
112 E. Allegan St.   Lansing. Michigan

and for issuance _____ of Account thereof in their names as trustees described as aforesaid, subject to the Laws of the State of Michigan, the rules and regulations of the Savings and Loan supervisory authority of the State of Michigan and the Articles of Incorporation and By-Laws of the Association, as they now are or as they may hereafter be amended. You are directed to act pursuant to writing bearing the signature of anyone of said trustees, shown below, in all matters related to this account. It is agreed by the signatory parties with each other and by the parties with you that any funds placed in or added to the account by anyone of the parties whether in his trustee or individual capacity is and shall be conclusively intended to be a gift and delivery at that time of such funds to the trust estate. If there is only one trustee, beneficiary or grantor then the plural form of designation shall be considered singular in the application and trust agreement.

Signature _____ As Trustee
                           Address

Signature _____ As Trustee
                           Address
As Trustees for _____
Address _____ Beneficiaries of the Survivors
or survivor thereof as specified in trust agreement on reverse side hereof.
Revocable Joint or Individual Trust Account for 1 or more Beneficiaries.
(front side)

Figure 4.1

TOTTEN TRUST ACCOUNT CARD *(continued)*

DISCRETIONARY REVOCABLE TRUST AGREEMENT

Trust Agreement Regarding Account No. _____

The funds in the account indicated on the reverse side of this instrument, together with earnings thereon, and any future additions thereto are conveyed to the trustees (who are also grantors herein) for the beneficiaries or the survivor as indicated. The conditions of said trust are: (1) The trustees are authorized to hold, manage, invest and reinvest said funds in their sole discretion: (2) The undersigned grantors of the survivor thereof reserve the right to revoke said trust in part or in full at any time and any partial or complete withdrawal by the trustees, or survivor thereof, if they are the grantors shall be a revocation to the extent of such withdrawal, but no other revocation shall be valid unless written notice by said trustees, grantors or survivor thereof is given to the Institution named on the reverse side of this card: (3) This trust, subject to the right of revocation shall terminate upon the death of all the grantors or upon the death of all said beneficiaries prior thereto. If at the death of all grantors any of said beneficiaries are surviving the proceeds shall be delivered to said surviving beneficiaries; if all the beneficiaries die prior to all the grantors then said trust forthwith terminates and becomes the property of the grantors or the survivor thereof; (4) The Institution in which such funds are invested is authorized to pay the same or to act in any respect affecting said account before or after the termination of this trust upon the signature of anyone of the trustees or the survivor thereof and has no responsibility to follow the application of the funds.

Date _____

_____ Grantor _____ Grantor
(back side)

---

of a trustee because an unsuitable trustee, even though you can replace him before you die, can do considerable damage before you discover it. A revocable living trust also requires a comprehensive and carefully worded trust document, which should be prepared by a lawyer skilled in estate planning. But before spending your own time thinking about the choice of a trustee and your lawyer's time formulating the trust document, you need to make some clear decisions about what you expect a trust to accomplish for you.

What probably motivates most people to set up a revocable living trust is the desire to avoid probate of their estates. Although joint ownership also avoids probate, a trust offers greater protection in some respects. Like joint ownership, it may in some states protect your property against creditors' claims after your death; in addition, it is less vulnerable to lawsuits brought by disinherited heirs in an attempt to contest your will or to challenge the automatic inheritance of your jointly owned property. Indeed, a trust can be used to disinherit most of your lawful heirs.

The probate avoidance feature of a trust is especially valuable if your assets include a business of some sort. If you bequeath your business through a will, it may have to come to a halt while your estate is being probated; the probate court may even require its immediate liquidation. If your business is transferred through use of a trust, however, it can continue without interruption, except for any administrative or operational problems created by your own death.

If, on the other hand, no ongoing business is involved and you simply want to avoid probate administration of your assets at death, you may serve as your own trustee (or as co-trustee with your spouse or an adult child) and designate as successor trustee the same kind of person you would choose as a executor if you merely used a will: your spouse, a trusted younger relative or friend, or perhaps a bank or trust company if your estate is large or complex. On your death, the successor trustee will see that all trust assets are properly managed until they are distributed to the beneficiaries according to the terms of the trust, after which the trust will then terminate.

But a trust can do much more than eliminate probate administration. Its ability to survive your death can give you control over your assets long after death. If you pass property on to your beneficiaries outright by will or through joint ownership, and if you die prematurely, your property will pass immediately to your beneficiaries even though your spouse may be unable to manage it or your children, though legally adults, may not be mature enough to protect it and use it productively. If, instead, you pass your property on by use of a trust, you can not only protect your assets against misuse or dissipation but you can also extend for many years the protection of a spouse, a child, or anyone else who may not be competent to manage them. If this is your purpose, the trustee or successor trustee you choose should have not only the skills needed to manage your assets but also the ability to deal humanely and sensitively with the needs of your beneficiaries or their guardians.

In addition to protecting your assets after your death, a trust can, during your lifetime, relieve you of the responsibility of managing your property, whether it consists of real estate, personal property, or both. If you choose a bank or trust company as trustee, you can empower the trustee to manage all your assets, to sell or trade them on a discretionary basis, and to send you an income check each month or at other regular intervals.

This, of course, entails some risk, because some institutional trustees, including those who serve as trustees for huge pension funds, have in recent years shown poor investment judgment. But if you set up a revocable living trust of this kind and monitor it carefully, you have the opportunity to evaluate the trustee's performance and to make a change if you are not satisfied. We shall deal in detail with the choice of trustee later in this chapter, because your choice will depend in large part on the type of revocable living trust you choose.

CHOOSING A TYPE OF TRUST

Having noted the various functions that a revocable living trust can perform, you can now choose the type of trust that best suits your purposes. To begin with, you need to decide whether your trust should be *funded* or *unfunded*.

A funded trust, as the name implies, is one that owns and manages the grantor's property immediately on its establishment. No revocable trust can be used to avoid probate unless or until it is funded with your assets prior to your death, because only property that belongs to the trust is removed from the grantor's probate estate.

Unfunded trusts are empty or "dry" at the time of their creation; they are set up in anticipation of future transfers. Although some states prohibit the establishment of unfunded trusts, this restriction can be easily circumvented by creating the trust with a token amount. Unfunded trusts do nothing to avoid probate if they are not funded before death, but they offer certain other advantages. Each of the types discussed below is intended to serve a specific purpose.

A *standby trust* is one that can go into action when the grantor is unavailable (if he is traveling abroad, for example) or becomes incapacitated. The trustee, who of course should not be the grantor, simply manages property that the grantor transfers into the trust when circumstances require it.

A *revocable life insurance trust* serves as the beneficiary of the grantor's life insurance proceeds. It is unfunded until, on the grantor's death, it receives the proceeds of his policies, which it then manages and distributes to the beneficiaries he has named in the trust document according to the conditions specified in the trust.

There are several reasons why it may be more sensible to name such a trust rather than your individual survivors as the beneficiary of your life insurance proceeds. If, for example, your spouse is unsophisticated in handling money, trust management can prevent your life insurance proceeds from being squandered, thus depriving your children of benefits intended for them. Or if your children, who may be either primary or contingent beneficiaries, seem unlikely to spend the proceeds in ways of which you approve, the trustee can exercise total control. Perhaps more important, a trustee who is chosen judiciously and given sufficient discretion by the trust document can deal fairly and sensibly with situations that arise after your death: the incapacity or premature death of one or more of your beneficiaries, the birth of a disabled grandchild, or some other unforeseeable events.

Unlike an irrevocable life insurance trust, discussed in the last section of this chapter, the revocable living life insurance trust offers no advantages with respect to income tax or federal estate tax. It may, however, depending on your state's laws, protect your life insurance proceeds from claims of creditors and it will protect the proceeds from the delays and costs of probate administration—problems that are unavoidable if you name your estate or your executor as the beneficiary of your life insurance proceeds.

An *unfunded trust*, accompanied by a "pour-over" will, serves essentially the same purpose as a life insurance trust except that its function is broader: It can become the beneficiary not only of your life insurance proceeds but also of part or all of your estate, which is "poured over" by your will to the trustee of a trust. Like the life insurance trust, it helps to protect and enhance your assets, but it also provides privacy during the probate process. When a will is probated, your estate becomes a public record for all to see. Hence, if your will specifies individual bequests, anyone interested can find out whom you disinherited as well as who your beneficiaries are, what share of your assets each received, and their respective values. But if the sole beneficiary of your will is the trustee of a pre-existing trust, and if only the trust document spells out what you are leaving to each beneficiary, curious outsiders can learn only the total amount of your estate and not its ultimate distribution to the individual beneficiaries.

Although each of the unfunded trusts we have described may be useful, you should bear in mind that none of them except the life insurance trust can be used to avoid probate, because they become funded only through your will. Moreover, such trusts, because they become operative only after your death, offer you no opportunity to monitor the performance of the trustee. On the other hand, there is no reason why a funded trust, which does avoid probate, cannot be used for each of the purposes served by unfunded trusts.

One reason for establishing an unfunded rather than a funded trust is that you will pay no trustee fees as long as the trust remains empty. Some people set up an unfunded trust in anticipation of assets they do not yet have or as a future recipient of assets they prefer to retain in other forms of ownership for the time being. Furthermore, as we have noted, an unfunded living trust accompanied by a "pour-over" will established before death provides survivors with more privacy than a testamentary (will-created) trust.

CHOOSING A TRUSTEE

As should be apparent by now, the choice of a trustee depends largely on the purposes for which you are creating the trust. If you have hitherto managed your assets competently, and if your purpose is simply to avoid probate and to pass your property on to your beneficiaries immediately after your death, you may appoint yourself as trustee and designate as successor trustee your spouse, an adult child, a sibling or other relative, or a close (and preferably younger) friend. In such circumstances the trust is likely to be short-lived and the assets are unlikely to require long-term professional management. Bear in mind, however, that the successor trustee may take over long before you die—for example, should you become incapacitated.

If, on the other hand, you want the trust to continue for some time after your death in order to protect and gradually distribute the assets to one or more of your beneficiaries, your choice of trustee becomes somewhat more difficult. On the one hand, a bank or a trust company offers you the advantages of continuity, management experience, and careful attention to your investments. But such institutional trustees, aside from costing the trust more in the way of fees, may very well fail to deal with your beneficiaries' needs or changing circumstances with the sensitivity and understanding that a relative or a close friend of yours could be expected to show. On the other hand, a relative or a friend who is highly empathetic may have disastrously poor financial judgment.

Some grantors resolve this dilemma by appointing as co-trustees a bank for financial management and a friend or relative to recognize and satisfy the beneficiaries' personal needs. Even if the trust document is carefully drawn, however, this arrangement may produce conflict and possible impasse between the co-trustees. In fact, banks and other institutional trustees, in anticipation of such time-consuming conflicts, may charge higher fees when a co-trustee is involved.

Institutional trustees may not be ideally suitable for a trust with assets of less than $100,000. Because some state laws generally limit trustees' annual fees to a percentage of the value of the trust assets or of the income produced by these assets, many institutional trustees consider trusts of moderate value to be more trouble than they're worth and hence do not devote much time or care to their management. Large urban banks rarely accept trusts whose asset value is less than $300,000. And even when motivated by the high fees to be earned from very large trusts, some professional managers perform poorly in terms of investing trust assets.

Generally speaking, your primary concern in choosing an individual as a trustee should center on his or her integrity, experience, judgment in managing the assets, and understanding and flexibility in dealing with the beneficiaries. You should also be concerned with trustee life expectancy and reject a person whom the trust seems likely to outlive. Since no trustee is likely to meet every one of these criteria, some compromise is almost inevitable. In addition, it is essential to name one or more successor trustees because of the possibility that the trustee you have named may die, or become unable to accept the trusteeship, or resign after accepting it.

In choosing an institutional trustee, the length, breadth, and quality of its trust experience are important considerations. How long has its trust department been in existence? Does the trust department consist of a single young trust officer or does it have several officers backed by a team of managers skilled in investments? Most important, what rate of income and growth has it achieved recently in managing its trust portfolio?

ESTABLISHING A TRUST

The basis of every trust is a document that defines the terms of the trust in much the same way as a charter and bylaws govern the activities of a corporation. The trust document spells out quite explicitly what the trustee(s) may and may not do, how long the trust is to exist, whether it is revocable or irrevocable, who the beneficiaries are, when and how they are to receive the trust income and assets, and what conditions they must meet in order to receive them. If you bear in mind that any beneficiary can at any time file a lawsuit charging the trustee with violating the terms of the trust, or breaching his fiduciary responsibilities, you can readily see that the trust document must be drafted with great care if it is to carry out your wishes precisely and effectively.

Figure 4.2, an example of a basic revocable living trust, illustrates the general style and content of a trust document. You should not use it as a model for a trust of your own, because every trust document must reflect not only the basic purposes of the trust but also the specific intentions of the individual grantor and, in some instances, the special circumstances of each beneficiary as well as the special nature of any of the assets. It is almost impossible for a pre-printed form to do this accurately and precisely. Moreover, a trust document must be carefully coordinated with your will, with any property held in joint ownership, and with all your other estate planning strategies, in order to avoid contradictions and inconsistencies.

In recent years, a number of books have been published that offer do-it-yourself instructions for preparing a trust document. In addition, a number of telemarketing firms have exploited the public (mainly the elderly) by offering living trust preparation to people who have no need for it. At best, such firms overcharge their clients; at worst, they persuade the clients to move their assets into dubious investments on which the firms earn commissions. Both the books and the telemarketers offer a one-size-fits-all trust document that consists almost entirely of "boilerplate." For these reasons,

Figure 4.2

REVOCABLE LIVING TRUST

DECLARATION OF TRUST made May 8, 2007, by JOHN DOE, MARY DOE, WILLIAM DOE, and JANE HARRIS, hereinafter called "Trustees," with reference to the following facts:

(a) John and Mary are husband and wife and hold title to all of their property as joint tenants or tenants by the entireties;

(b) William Doe and Jane Harris are their only children; each of them has children;

(c) John and Mary would like to avoid probate, not only in the event of the death or disability of one of them, but also on the death of the survivor of them, but want assurance that, in the event of the disability of one or both of them, property will be applied toward his, her or their care and, upon the death of the survivor of them, will be distributed to their issue who survive such survivor, per stirpes;

(d) The parties have decided upon holding such property in joint tenancy, with full rights of survivorship, and without any mention of a trust on the record, but with a declaration and acknowledgment that those who succeed, or the one who succeeds, to the title on the death or disability of another or others are, or is, actually holding as trustees, or trustee, for the purposes and on the conditions hereinafter set forth.

THE PARTIES AGREE:

1. *Establishment Of Trust.* Any property assigned, heretofore or hereafter, by John and/or Mary to the Trustees, as joint tenants or otherwise, shall be deemed trust property and Trustees agree to hold the same in trust for the purposes and on the conditions hereinafter set forth.

2. *Reservations.* John and Mary (or the survivor of them) reserve(s) the right to amend or revoke this trust and Trustees agree to reassign or reconvey to them or the survivor of them any property affected by the exercise of such right.

3. *Trustee.* If one acting as a trustee shall become disabled as defined in the paragraph entitled "DISABILITY" in Article V, he shall be deemed to have resigned.

If none of the parties is acting as a trustee, the executor of the last to act or, if he has none appointed within thirty (30) days after he ceases to act, EAST LANSING STATE BANK shall become trustee by filing with a beneficiary hereunder a written acceptance of trust.

Individual trustees shall be reimbursed for their reasonable out-of-pocket expenses, but shall receive no additional compensation for their services. A corporate trustee shall be entitled to reimbursement for expenses and fees in

Figure 4.2

REVOCABLE LIVING TRUST *(continued)*

accordance with its published fee schedule in effect at the time the services for which the fee is charged are performed, and if there is no such fee schedule then in effect, such fees as, from time to time, are recognized in the area as ordinary and reasonable for the services it performs.

4. Distribution.

During the Lives of John And Mary

Income: While both John and Mary are living and not disabled, all of the net income shall be paid to them or at their direction. If both of them become disabled, Trustees shall, in their discretion, apply income for their benefit or accumulate income and thereafter treat it as corpus. After the death of John or Mary, Trustees shall likewise pay or apply net income to or for the benefit of the survivor of them.

Corpus: Trustees may pay to either John or Mary from the corpus of the trust from time to time, such further accounts (even to the exhaustion of the trust) as in their discretion they deem necessary or advisable to properly maintain him or her in the style to which he or she is presently accustomed, and shall do so if he or she becomes disabled; such payments may include amounts to or for the benefit of persons dependent upon them for support and premiums on life insurance on either of them or such persons whether or not such policies are payable to this trust.

On Death: Upon the death of John or Mary, Trustees shall pay the expenses of his or her last illness and burial and all debts and taxes and other charges against him or her or arising because of his or her death which shall seem proper; upon the death of the survivor of them, Trustees shall pay such expenses, debts, taxes and charges arising because of the survivor's death and shall pay over all remaining property, both corpus and accumulated income, to the issue of John and Mary surviving such survivor, per stirpes, their children to be the stock.

Notwithstanding the foregoing, if any distributee has not attained his majority, his share shall be continued in trust, with Trustees accumulating income and distributing to him so much thereof and of corpus from time to time as they deem for his best interests and welfare and upon his reaching his majority, paying over to him property, if any, remaining; and, in the event of his death, paying property on hand to his executor.

5. Miscellaneous.

Survival Defined. No person shall be considered to have survived another if he shall die within thirty (30) days after the death of the other.

Disability. If two medical doctors determine that a beneficiary or a trustee is suffering from physical or mental disability to the extent he is incapable

Figure 4.2

REVOCABLE LIVING TRUST *(continued)*

of exercising judgment about or attending to financial and property transactions, such determination reduced to writing and delivered to any beneficiary or contingent beneficiary under this agreement, or to another trustee, shall be conclusive for the purposes of this agreement.

6. *Administrative Powers.* Trustees shall have the power to retain, sell, invest and reinvest, loan, improve, lease and borrow.

7. *Accounting.* So long as Mary lives and is not disabled, Trustees need keep no accounts because of the control which she has retained. However, in the event of the disability or death of Mary, Trustees shall keep an account of receipts and disbursements and of property on hand at the end of the accounting period and shall deliver copies to the beneficiaries or, if one is a minor, to one with whom he makes his home. .

8. *Exculpatory.* No purchaser from or other person dealing with Trustees shall be responsible for the application of any purchase money or other thing of value paid or delivered to them, but the receipt of Trustees shall be a full discharge; and no purchaser or other person dealing with Trustees and no issuer, or transfer agent or other agent of any issuer of any securities to which any dealing with Trustees should relate, shall be under any obligation to ascertain or inquire into the power of Trustees to purchase, sell, exchange, transfer, mortgage, pledge, lease, distribute or otherwise in any manner dispose of or deal with any security or any other property held by Trustees or comprised in this estate.

The certificate of the Trustees that they are acting according to the terms of this instrument shall fully protect all persons dealing with the Trustees.

9. *Conflict Of Laws.* All questions concerning the validity, construction and administration of the trust shall be determined under the laws of the State of Michigan.

IN WITNESS WHEREOF, the parties have executed this instrument.

Witness:

_____	_____
Lawrence L. Black	John Doe
_____	_____
Belinda B. Blue	Mary Doe
	_____
	William Doe
_____	_____
	Jane Harris

Figure 4.2
REVOCABLE LIVING TRUST *(continued)*

STATE OF MICHIGAN)
COUNTY OF INGHAM)ss

On this 8th day of May, 2007, before me, a Notary Public, in and for said County, personally appeared John Doe, Mary Doe, William Doe, and Jane Harris, to me known to be the same persons described in and who executed the within instrument, who acknowledged the same to be their free act and deed.

INSTRUMENT PREPARED BY: _____

Lawrence L. Black   Belinda B. Blue, Notary Public
Attorney at Law   Ingham County, Michigan
101 Main Street   My Commission Expires: 1/1/09
Lansing, Michigan 48933   Lansing, Michigan 48933

---

you should not rely on these sources for preparation of your own trust document.

Your choice of a lawyer may be almost as crucial to the success of your trust as your choice of trustee. Above all, the lawyer you choose should be skilled in estate planning. If your regular lawyer has no such experience but you think that asking him for a referral may hurt his feelings, you can probably find one through the referral service of your local bar association, through the clerk of your county probate court, or by a call to your bank's trust department.

Some estate lawyers charge their clients on an hourly basis the fees ranging from perhaps $150 per hour for young lawyers in rural areas to well over $300 for high-prestige urban law firms. Others charge a set fee for preparing and funding a trust, the amount ranging from $1,000 to $2,000. Drafting a trust should not involve more than five or six hours of a lawyer's time, and this money is likely to be well spent if it protects you against the deficiencies of do-it-yourself books and ready-made forms.

Although any lawyer skilled in estate planning is likely to draft a satisfactory trust document, the checklist shown in table 4.1 should guide you in your preliminary discussions with your lawyer and should help you to make sure that the document he or she produces reflects your intentions and meets all your needs.

TABLE 4.1
Elements of a Trust Agreement

What a trust MUST include	*What a trust MAY include*
Name of grantor	
Name of trustee and successor trustee	Selection of individual or corporate trustee; standby provision for trustee to take over when grantor is ill, absent, or dead
Name of beneficiaries and alternate beneficiaries	Selection of individual or charitable beneficiaries; authority of beneficiary to replace trustee
Purposes of trust	
Duration of trust	
Whether trust is revocable or irrevocable	
Powers granted to trustee	Scope of trustee's discretion; trustee's power to distribute principal and income
Manner and timetable of income and principal distribution to beneficiaries	Conditions and limitations on the distribution of spendthrift provisions; sprinkling provisions;
Description of assets transferred to trustee (unless trust is unfunded)	

IRREVOCABLE LIVING TRUSTS

Revocable living trusts, despite their many advantages, do not relieve the grantor of liability for income tax or his estate from liability for federal estate tax on trust assets. If you are concerned about reducing your tax burden, you may want to consider an irrevocable living trust. An irrevocable trust can serve all the purposes of a revocable living trust, but the trust itself—or its beneficiaries if trust funds are distributed—pays the taxes on its income, usually at a lower rate than you would. The trust also offers possible relief from federal estate tax.

This tax relief, however, has a number of rather stringent conditions attached to it. Once you have set up an irrevocable trust, you cannot ever change it, and any assets you transfer into such a trust pass out of your ownership permanently. You may never use either the principal or the income of such a trust for your own benefit, or to pay your debts, or to support a dependent whom you are legally obligated to support. Although you may serve as a trustee, your powers are limited to management of the assets; you are not permitted to make any changes that might affect the interests of the beneficiaries. In short, far more assuredly than diamonds, an irrevocable trust is "forever."

Despite the attractiveness of income tax relief, most people cannot afford to part forever with a substantial part of their assets. Indeed, irrevocable trusts of any significant size are used almost exclusively by the very rich, who make up probably less than one percent of American families. There are, however, some "mini" forms of irrevocable trust—the *custodial account for minors* and the *trust for minors*—that are used commonly by middle- to upper-middle-income persons to avoid taxes and to provide for the future needs of their children or grandchildren.

CUSTODIAL ACCOUNT FOR MINORS

Authorized by the Uniform Gifts to Minors Act or the Uniform Transfer to Minors Act, one or the other of which has been adopted by all states, a custodial account for minors is a simple, informal, and cost-free device for making gifts to minors, usually one's children, grandchildren, or other relatives. These gifts can take the form of bank accounts, money market accounts, securities, mutual funds, and, in states that have adopted the Uniform Transfers to Minors Act, life insurance policies, other kinds of personal property, and real estate. The gifts may be of any value, and they may be made cumulatively. That is, the donor can open a custodial account for a child in a very modest amount and add to it in any amount as frequently as he or she chooses.

Funds in a custodial account can be shifted from one form of investment to another as long as they are not removed from the custodianship or used for the benefit of anyone except the minor. There is no limit, moreover, to the number of accounts that a donor can establish for one minor, to the number of minors for which one donor can open accounts, or to the number of donors who can open an account for the same minor.

Simple though it is, the custodial account has two of the characteristics of an irrevocable living trust. First, the custodian, who functions much as does the trustee of a formal irrevocable trust, may not use the funds for his own benefit and is legally responsible for safeguarding them and investing them prudently for the exclusive benefit of the minor. Second, the gift or gifts made to the account are irrevocable; for this reason any income tax on its yield is payable by the minor, not the donor.

Establishing a custodial account involves nothing more than obtaining a Social Security number for the minor and filling out a signature card at a bank (see figure 4.3) or opening an account with a mutual fund or a brokerage firm. Like many parents and grandparents, you may decide to use such an account to accumulate funds for the minor's college education or some similar long-term goal.

There are, however, some important differences between the custodial account for minors and a formal irrevocable trust. Whereas a formal irrevocable trust can specify the age at which a beneficiary may get control of the funds and the conditions he must meet in

Figure 4.3

CUSTODIAL ACCOUNT FOR MINOR

GIFT TRANSFER

I hereby deliver $_____ to Capitol Savings and Loan Association, a Michigan corporation for credit to an Optional Savings Account in the said institution in the

name of _____
                             Name of Custodian

as Custodian for _____
                             Name of Minor

under the Michigan Uniform Gifts to Minors Act.

This gift of money to the minor named, which gift shall be deemed to include all earnings thereon and any future additions thereto, is irrevocable and is made in accordance with and to include all the provisions of the said Statute of this State as it is now or hereafter may be amended.

_____   _____
           Date   Signature of Donor

NOTE: The use of this Gift Transfer Form is optional; however, it is recommended that it be used.

The Donor and the Custodian may be the same person.

(front side)

Figure 4.3

CUSTODIAL ACCOUNT FOR MINOR *(continued)*

Date _____   Account No. _____

Last Name of Custodian   First Name   Middle Name

as Custodian for _____
                     Last Name of Minor   First Name   Middle Name

under the Michigan Uniform Gifts to Minors Act, hereby makes application for membership in the

CAPITOL SAVINGS AND LOAN ASSOCIATION

and for the issuance of an Optional Savings Account subject to the Laws of the State of Michigan, the rules and regulations of the Savings and Loan supervisory authority of the State of Michigan and the Articles of Incorporation and By-Laws of the Association, as they now are or as they may hereafter be amended.

_____ as Custodian for
                     Signature

_____under the
                     Name of Minor

Michigan Uniform Gifts to Minors Act.
Custodian Savings Account for Minor under "Michigan Uniform Gifts to Minors Act".
There can only be 1 custodian and 1 minor.
Form 149 2M 10-67

(back side)

order to get them, a custodial account permits no such restrictions; the minor automatically gains control of the account when he or she reaches majority—in most states, at the age of eighteen. Thus, on his eighteenth birthday, your child may, if he chooses, use the money to buy a $50,000 sports car rather than a freshman year at an Ivy League college and there is no way in which you can prevent his using the money in this way.

Moreover, neither the principal nor the income from a custodial account may be used for goods and services that the child's parents are obligated to provide. Money in a custodial account may, for example, be used for music lessons, summer camp, a new bicycle, or other "special" items but not for the child's food, clothing, medical care, or similar day-to-day expenses typically viewed as parental obligations.

The deposits to a custodian account may be subject to federal gift tax, since each deposit constitutes a completed gift. Normally, this is not a problem because annual gifts of $12,000 (or $24,000 with the consent of the donor's spouse) are not subject to this tax. But if the donor is also the custodian, the account balance as of the donor's death will be included in the donor's estate for federal estate tax purposes should he die before the minor reaches the age of majority. For this reason, it may be advisable for the donor not to serve as the custodian. The donor might, for example, name his wife as custodian; a donor grandparent might name either the child's father or mother.

When your children reach age 13, the federal government taxes income in custodial counts at the child's tax rate, which presumably will be lower than yours. For younger children, because of the "kiddie tax" the federal government taxes income from the child's custodial account at *your* tax rate.

The simplest form of custodial account is a bank account opened in the name of "Mary Smith, Custodian for William Smith, Jr., under the Uniform Gifts to Minors Act (or Uniform Transfers to Minors Act) [your state]." A minimal deposit will open a passbook account to which you can add at any time, or a larger amount can be used to buy a certificate of deposit. As the account increases in value through additional deposits or earned interest, you may decide to transfer the money into a brokerage or mutual fund account bearing the same title as the bank account. Either of these accounts carries the minor's Social Security number, and the minor is responsible for all taxes on its yield. Bear in mind, however, that once you deposit money into such an account it is an irrevocable gift and you can never again use it for your own purposes.

THE TRUST FOR MINORS

If you like the concept of a custodial account but feel uncomfortable about the prospect of the minor getting control of the account's assets at age 18 or 21, you may want to consider a formal trust for minors, known also as a Section 2503(c) trust (a reference to the section of the Internal Revenue Code that authorizes it). There are four differences between a custodial account and a trust for minors. First, under a trust for minors, the minor does not get control of the trust assets until at least age 21. Second, at age 21 the beneficiary may, if he chooses, extend the life of the trust indefinitely in order to take advantage of the trustee's responsible (and perhaps highly productive) management. Third, a trust for minors can be drafted to include several minors instead of only one. And, lastly, assets in a trust for minors may include real estate as well as any type of personal property.

As in the case of a custodial account, any tax on income generated by the assets in a trust for minors, if distributed to the minor, is payable at the minor's rate as long as the child is at least age 14 and the distributions are not used to discharge your legal obligations (as a parent) to support the child. However, your contributions, if they exceed the annual, $12,000/$24,000 annual gift tax exclusion, may be subject to federal gift tax.

Your choice of trustee for a trust for minors should be based on the nature and the value of the trust assets. There is nothing to prevent you from serving as trustee (perhaps with your spouse as co-trustee), but if the trust assets are complex or of substantial value, you may decide that a professional trustee is a better choice.

THE FORMAL IRREVOCABLE LIVING TRUST

An irrevocable living trust can be just as versatile as the revocable living trust and can be established to serve the same purposes. The most important difference, aside from irrevocability, is that income tax on the yield from irrevocable trust assets is payable not by the grantor but by the trust itself or by the beneficiaries if they receive periodic distributions, in either case presumably at a lower bracket rate than what the grantor would pay. In addition, funds transferred to an irrevocable trust are completely unreachable by the grantor's creditors because they in fact no longer belong to the grantor. However, because the grantor can make no changes once the trust has been established, the trust document must be drafted with the greatest care and the choice of trustees must be made as judiciously as possible.

TRUSTS AND THE PROTECTION
OF BENEFICIARIES

We have emphasized the use of trusts to avoid probate and to reduce income taxes and, in some circumstances, to reduce federal estate tax. These advantages, however, are incidental to the fundamental purpose of a trust: to carry on, after the grantor's death, his or her efforts to ensure the welfare of his designated beneficiaries.

As we have noted, transferring assets through a will or through joint ownership gives immediate and unconditional control of them to a surviving beneficiary who, for one reason or another, may not be able to conserve them, increase them, or use them wisely. Transferring them by means of a trust, on the other hand, can do much to protect the assets against loss or dissipation, to ensure that they are used in ways of which you would approve, and thus to promote your designated beneficiary's long-term welfare.

If, for example, your wife is inexperienced or simply uninterested in managing assets of substantial value or complex makeup, a professional trustee is more likely to protect or increase them than she is. But even if she is both capable and motivated, she may be unable to resist the importunate demands from relatives, friends, and suitors that many widows face when they inherit large sums of money. In such a situation, a professional trustee can serve as a buffer.

A trust can also protect the interests of your children, both minor and adult. Most parents ensure the welfare of minor children by designating in their wills a guardian or, if a substantial inheritance is involved, two protectors: *a guardian of the person* and *a conservator of the property*. A serious limitation of this arrangement is that the guardian or the conservator must manage the child's inheritance under the strict supervision of the probate court, and courts are often both conservative and inflexible in their supervision. Moreover, these arrangements terminate automatically when the child reaches the age of majority (18 in most states), regardless of the child's ability or inclination to manage what he or she may consider a windfall. If, however, you establish a trust for the children, the trustee serves the function of the conservator, free from supervision by the probate court and able to exercise as much discretion as you provide in the trust document and for as long as you wish to postpone the ultimate distribution of your estate.

A probate court conservatorship automatically terminates when the child reaches the age of majority, but even "adult" children may require protection against their own immaturity or irresponsibility, especially if large sums of money are involved. For example, if an adult child of yours seems to believe that money is something that should be spent immediately on whatever catches his eye, you might consider incorporating in your trust a *spendthrift* provision, which instructs the trustee to dole out the assets in limited amounts—for necessities only, perhaps—and which prohibits the beneficiary from selling his future income from the trust (usually at a deep discount) to various financial institutions that buy such interests. Alternatively, you might incorporate an *incentive* provision, under which the amount of each payment to the beneficiary is linked to income that the beneficiary earns through his own efforts.

Occasionally, money left to adult children may be dissipated not by the children themselves but by their spouses, especially if a divorce occurs shortly after receipt of the inheritance. This can be averted and the money kept in the family by drafting the trust document so that the inheritance, or a part of it, goes directly to the children of the marriage. If an adult child's marriage seems currently unstable, the trust can be drafted so that no payments are made until the instability has been resolved.

Given sufficient discretion, a trustee can cope with problems that you cannot foresee at the time you set up the trust, such as sharp differences in the affluence of your children, or severe financial stress suffered by one of them years after your death. If you establish a *sprinkling* trust, the trustee, instead of distributing predetermined shares of assets or income to each child, can alter the shares to meet each child's current needs and can shift distribution from one beneficiary to another as these needs change.

A sprinkling trust provision can be useful even when no financial crisis is involved. Suppose, for example, that a grandchild needs $20,000 for a year of college tuition. If the trust were to pay the trust income of $20,000 to the child's father, who is in the 31% tax bracket, the child would receive only $13,800 after the father had paid income tax on this amount. If, instead, the trustee had the discretion to pay the $20,000 of trust income directly to the child, the loss through taxation would be significantly less.

Each of the strategies we have discussed enables you to have your wishes carried out for many years and possibly decades after your death. All of them, however, embody an obvious risk: that "the dead hand of the past"—your own—will constrict or even damage the lives of your surviving beneficiaries. It is therefore important to recognize that some of your beneficiaries, because they are more than a quarter of a century younger than you, live in a different world from yours, face different problems, and have different standards and aspirations. Too rigid a trust document may protect your assets but may cripple the very people whom the assets are intended to benefit.

⇝ 5 ⇜

INSURING YOUR LIFE

No matter what your income level, you are likely to function financially unless your income is interrupted by your unemployment or death or your savings are wiped out by a major illness in the family. No private insurance company is reckless enough to offer a policy that protects you against unemployment (and the unemployment insurance provided by the government is both inadequate and temporary), but policies are, of course, available to protect your survivors should you die and to help you with the sometimes catastrophic costs of illness.

Whether or not you can afford adequate coverage depends on the fringe benefits your employer provides, the availability of group insurance through a credit union or other association, your personal health status, and, to some extent, the laws of your state that regulate insurance. But since most life insurance is marketed to individuals by private profit-making companies, you are likely to encounter as much hype and flimflam from insurance salesmen as you are from their counterparts who sell encyclopedias door-to-door. Your best protection against them is a clear understanding of what you want to buy—which may be quite different from what the insurance company would prefer to sell you.

LIFE INSURANCE

A life insurance policy is nothing more than a form of legalized gambling. The insurance company bets that you're not going to die within the next year. You bet, using your premium as the stake, that you will. If you die, you "win" the bet and the insurance company pays off to your designated beneficiaries. If you don't, the insurance company keeps your premium and you renew the bet by putting up next year's premium.

What are the odds the insurance company uses to set your premiums? Actuarial tables predicting death rates and life expectancies are so accurate that these odds—like the odds in a game of craps or Blackjack—are very precisely known. But if the insurance company were to base its bet with you on these odds, it would actually lose money, since it would pay out as benefits precisely what it took in as premiums and get nothing for its administrative costs or its stockholders. Hence the insurance company, like the gambling casinos, must offer you odds that are somewhat more favorable to itself than the true odds.

This margin in favor of "the house" will vary from one company to another because some may be more administratively efficient than others. But no insurance company is satisfied with the profit that this margin provides. Instead, since they accumulate your premiums until you die, they invest this vast amount of cash in all sorts of financial ventures—mortgages, real estate, money markets, and other investments. And, since it is these ventures that provide the bulk of their profits, they are eager to collect from you just as high a premium as possible by offering you all sorts of expensive "bells and whistles" policies that go beyond the basic function of protecting your survivors.

The question you need to answer, then, is whether these extras really work to your advantage or whether the higher premiums do nothing more than provide the company with investment capital at your expense. The answer is not the same for everyone, but you may be able to make a sound decision by reviewing the alternatives described below.

How Much Insurance Is Enough?

Because the basic purpose of life insurance is to protect your survivors against the loss of your income, the amount of coverage you need depends entirely on your personal situation and will change at various stages of your life. At any given time, the proceeds of your insurance policies should, when added to your other assets, allow your spouse and children to maintain the standard of living they now have, but translating this into dollars requires careful thought and calculation.

One commonly used rule of thumb suggests that your insurance coverage should equal three to six times your annual income, but this formula is so broad as to be almost useless. The coverage you need depends on the current and future earnings of your spouse, the ages and educational needs of your children, income you may be receiving from other investments, the maturity of your home mortgage, your other assets, and your estimate of what your survivors' costs of living are likely to be until your children begin supporting themselves.

A careful calculation along these lines will lead you to two conclusions. The first is that the amount of insurance coverage you need won't remain constant for the next 30 or 40 years. If, at the moment, your youngest child will be dependent on you for the next 18 years or so, if your mortgage payments will go on for perhaps 20 years, and if your spouse's income earning potential is low, you will probably need enough coverage to provide your survivors with 60 to 75% of your current after-tax income. But 20 years from now, with your children self-sufficient, your mortgage paid off, and your accumulated assets worth more than the face value of your policy, you may need only 40%. From this point of view, the best policy is one that permits you to lower your coverage as time goes on.

On the other hand, there is the problem of inflation. During World War II, the government offered members of the armed forces a life insurance policy with a maximum face value of $10,000 at very low cost. There were few takers for the maximum because it represented, at the time, about five times the average annual income.

Today, of course, this face value provides survivors with less than one year of income, at substantially below the poverty level. The question is, then, whether you can calculate a fixed-dollar coverage that will be eroded by inflation at more or less the same rate as your need for coverage diminishes. Since the inflation rate is entirely unpredictable, and since your personal situation is not entirely predictable, the best plan may be to choose a policy or policies that allow you maximum flexibility—a subject to which we'll return shortly.

WHERE TO BUY

Life insurance salesmen, no matter how well qualified, work on a commission basis and continue to receive commissions on your policy as long as you continue to pay premiums. Obviously, then, they are interested in selling you as expensive a policy as they can persuade you to buy. Representatives of a single insurance company will, of course, favor their company's product even though a competing company's policy may be more suitable, but even independent agents, who sell policies for a number of companies, are motivated by the size of their commissions. Ultimately, you will probably buy at least some insurance through an agent, but you will be far better off if you do your own research and ask the agent for a premium quotation on the precise type and amount of coverage you've chosen rather than soliciting and following his advice. Even if the agent insists on advising you, the more you've learned about insurance and the more pointed your questions, the less likely you are to be misled. In recent years the insurance commissioners of several states have charged some agents of highly reputable companies with deliberately misleading prospective clients.

Eliminating the services of an agent can reduce your premium costs substantially, and this is possible in two ways. In some states—notably New York—savings banks sell life insurance direct to the buyer, at rates so low that private insurance companies have lobbied strenuously to limit the amount of coverage the banks are allowed to sell. A bank policy is not likely to offer you enough coverage, but making such a policy a part of your coverage can save you money.

A second possibility, more widely available, is the group policy available through employers, credit unions, professional associations, and fraternal organizations. The group premiums are lower because the policies are negotiated directly with the insurer and because administrative costs are low. Moreover, the policies are generally sound because they have been reviewed by experts, and many of them do not require a medical examination. But they have a couple of disadvantages. Your coverage under an employer-sponsored life insurance policy may terminate if you leave your job—or the insurer may cancel the group policy and leave you without coverage. Nevertheless, although you may want to consider a group policy only as a supplement to other policies, it is likely to offer the highest level of coverage for the lowest premium—an advantage especially important for young parents.

TYPES OF POLICY
What makes buying a life insurance policy extremely confusing is the enormous variety of types available, as well as the wide variation in premium costs for each type. Our descriptions of the basic types will be followed by suggestions for comparing costs within each type.

Term Insurance
Although it is by far the best buy for many young parents, an agent is likely to tell you little or nothing about term insurance—or, indeed, may argue strongly against it—because its low premiums earn him only a scanty commission. Term insurance is a no-frills policy that provides you with protection and nothing but protection. Your premiums buy nothing more than the promise that the policy will pay its face value should you die during its term. Unlike other policies, it is not an investment; it pays no dividends; it accumulates no cash value; you cannot borrow money against it; and it becomes worthless either when you stop paying premiums or at the end of its term. All this may strike you as unattractive, but if you are interested in getting the highest coverage for the lowest premiums, the term policy is unmatchable.

The term of such a policy ranges from five to 20 years, and the premium remains fixed for the duration of the term. The more desirable term policies are renewable term after term without medical examination, although the premium will escalate at each renewal. Thus, if you buy a 20-year term policy, your premiums remain fixed; if you buy a five-year term your premiums will rise each time you renew it, but you have the option of decreasing your coverage in the later years. In addition, some term policies carry the privilege of conversion to whole-life policies at the expiration of each term.

Another type of term policy—especially desirable if your mortgage is currently high—is known as "decreasing term." Such a policy offers, for a constant but attractively low premium, a high initial face value which decreases steadily over 20 or 30 years as your mortgage decreases or as your other assets accumulate sufficiently to make insurance coverage less essential. Yet another type, the "increasing term" policy, on the other hand, provides for rising amounts of coverage to protect your survivors against inflation.

For most persons, term policies are probably the best buy for all, or at least most, of their life insurance coverage—not only because they provide the highest coverage at the lowest cost but also because they are flexible with respect to coverage.

Whole Life Policies

Unlike the term policy, whole-life policies—also called ordinary life, straight life, or cash value policies—require premium payments which remain fixed for your entire lifetime and are based on the age at which you buy the policy. If you buy such a policy at an early age, your premiums will be somewhat higher than for a term policy for the first few years but lower than the premiums you will pay when you renew the term policy later on.

Whole-life policies combine protection with investment. That is, part of your premium buys protection but part of it buys a continuously increasing "cash value." This cash value may, in some cases, pay periodic dividends—or it can be used to pay future premiums if you develop cash flow problems, or it can be borrowed against, usually at a favorable interest rate, or it can be transferred to you if you decide to terminate the policy by "cashing it in." If you borrow against your policy's cash value, you need not repay the loan as long as you continue making interest payments, because the insurance company can always deduct the principal from the face value of the policy at the time of your death.

The whole-life policy has a close relative with similar features. The "limited payment," or "20-year payment" policy requires premium payments for a fixed number of years (typically 20 or 30) or until a certain age (typically 65), after which it remains in force without further payments. Obviously the premiums for such a policy will be higher than for the straight-life policy, and you will be paying them early in life when your income is likely to be lower than it will be when you no longer need to pay them.

Whether a whole-life policy strikes you as preferable to term insurance depends to a large extent on your self discipline in saving money and on your skill in investing it. Because whole-life policies earn them higher commissions, insurance salesmen are likely to stress the advantages of dividends or the steady, tax-free growth in cash value as a result of the company's investments. But independent analysts argue that insurance companies are extremely frugal with dividends, and most of them are rather conservative in making investments. (On the other hand, some insurance companies, having made bad high-risk investments in search of substantial profits, have gone bankrupt, leaving their clients without coverage.) As a consequence, you are likely to fare no better if you buy the whole-life policy in the hope of a return than if you were to buy the cheaper term policy and periodically invest the premium difference yourself.

The more expensive whole-life policy is preferable only as a form of "forced savings"—for people who will pay the monthly premium regularly under threat of cancellation but who lack the discipline to invest a surplus each month when there is no threat involved. But the long-run cost of this attitude can be high—not only because the yield from the policy may be lower than they could earn through do-it-yourself investment of the premium difference but because the higher premium is likely to force them to buy less coverage than they need.

Endowment Policies

Like a term insurance policy, the endowment policy offers you protection for a specified period—10 or 20 years, for example, or until age 65. Should you die during this term, your survivors will be paid the full face value. But unlike the term policy, it pays you its face value when it terminates—either in a lump sum or in installments. If you anticipate, 15 years from now, a substantial outlay for college tuition for one of your children, you could schedule an endowment to mature when you need the money. But endowment policy premiums are high, because they must pay for your life insurance as well as for the endowment, and many independent experts believe that if you were to buy a term policy at far lower cost and use the premium difference for investments of your own choosing, you might not only achieve as good a result but also you would be able to use the accumulation at any time instead of having it locked up until the policy matured.

Family Income Policies

Adopting some of the features of the decreasing term policy, the level-premium family income policy insures the life of the major breadwinner for his entire life but adds an income supplement for a specified number of years. Thus, for example, on a policy with a face value of $100,000, the income supplement might be 1% or $1,000 a month if the policyholder should die within 15 years.

After the 15th year the supplement is no longer payable but the face value continues until death.

Other Types

In recent years a number of life insurance companies have devised policies that stress their investment function at least as much as their basic function of providing income protection through life insurance. These policies, described as "universal life insurance" or "variable life insurance," offer a wide range of options that are intended to make their premium payments and their face value more flexible and to increase their "cash value" in one way or another. The brochures that describe them, however, relegate to the small print such matters as administrative charges, load charges for each premium payment, and surrender charges. More important, there is no guarantee of a specified return—or that your entire investment may not drop in value, in which case your survivors would get less than you had hoped.

Here, again, you need to decide whether you prefer to hand over most or all of your investment decisions to someone else and, if you do, whether a life insurance company is your best choice. An alternative might be to budget life insurance as a separate item, buy maximum coverage through term insurance, and invest whatever surplus you have in other ways.

WHO SHOULD NOT BE COVERED

Once they have sold you as much coverage as you can possibly afford, ambitious insurance agents are likely to try selling you policies for other members of your family. These should be scrutinized skeptically. Your spouse should be covered sufficiently to compensate for her earnings if she is employed or to replace her with paid help if she is a homemaker and the mother of young children. Insuring the children makes no sense at all, because they earn no income, because the death rate in children beyond the age of one is very low, and because money would not compensate you for your loss in the highly improbable event that your child should die before you.

SOURCES OF INFORMATION

As we have noted, insurance agents, regardless of their qualifications, are likely to be both overeager to earn commissions and biased toward certain products. If, however, you need to use an agent, select one who is entitled to use the letters C.L.U. (Chartered Life Underwriter) after his or her name. This indicates that the agent has passed a fairly rigorous examination, is reasonably well informed, and has demonstrated some degree of professionalism. The agent may be biased, but he is less likely to mislead you deliberately—especially if you are prepared to ask knowledgeable questions.

Consumer Reports periodically publishes sophisticated and unbiased evaluations of life insurance policies which may help you select not only the best policy type but also the most reliable company. *Best's Insurance Reports*, available at many public libraries, periodically rates individual companies on the basis of financial stability.

If it is aggressively consumer-oriented, your state insurance commission may be a useful source of information, since it regulates the industry within your state and handles consumer complaints. In addition, some states publish detailed evaluations of companies and policies, and these can be useful to consult before making a final decision. In general, no matter how attractive its premiums or its policy, it is unwise to buy life insurance from a company not authorized to do business within your state—or from one about which the state commission has a significant number of complaints.

COMPARING POLICY COSTS

Comparing the actual costs of two policies of the same type on the basis of their premiums can be very difficult, because the true costs may be distorted by differences in the premium schedules, dividend payments, the accrual of cash surrender value, and other factors difficult to identify or calculate.

Fortunately, many states now require life insurers to present to the potential customer, along with each policy, a figure known as the "interest-adjusted cost index" together with instructions for using it. Although this index may sometimes be preceded by a dollar sign, it is not a premium figure but simply an index that provides for an accurate comparison of two seemingly identical policies. In connection with term policies, for example, indexes are available for 5-, 10-, and 20-year terms. Other things being equal, the policy with the lower index is the less expensive one.

Cost comparisons between whole life policies require the use of two cost indexes. The "net cost" or "surrender" index reflects the cost if you hold the policy for a specified number of years and then surrender it for its cash value. The "net payment" index reflects the cost if you hold the policy until you die without cashing it in. In comparing two or more policies, both indexes should be used because they may not be consistent for each policy.

Although these indexes are useful, bear in mind that a small index difference between two policies may not be significant and may be offset by differences in the financial strength of the company, the services promised by the agent, or small differences in features of the policies themselves.

DESIGNATING YOUR BENEFICIARIES

If you are buying your own life insurance coverage, your application will not be processed until you have designated the policy's beneficiaries. But if you get coverage as part of your employment fringe benefits, your employer's personnel or human resources department may neglect to ask you to specify beneficiaries or to record your designation. If the policy is to benefit the persons you have chosen, the beneficiaries must not only be specified but also must be kept up to date as your family situation changes—when, for example, a spouse dies or a child reaches the age of majority.

Your choice of beneficiaries will depend on whether you are married or single and whether your children are minors or adults. Most parents designate their spouse as primary beneficiary and their children as alternates but setting up a trust and designating its trustee as the primary or alternate beneficiary may be a sounder arrangement. For more on designating life insurance beneficiaries, see chapter 2.

≈ 6 ≈
GIFT AND ESTATE TAXES

If you give someone money or property while you are alive, you may be subject to the federal gift tax. And when you die, the property you transfer to survivors may be subject to the federal estate tax. The following discussion will give you a general understanding of how much money or property you can give away tax-free during your lifetime and how much you can leave tax-free to your survivors at your death.

Under the 2001 Tax Law, most lifetime gifts are not large enough to be subject to the federal gift tax and most decedent's estates (98%) are not large enough to be subject to the federal estate tax. There is no tax on lifetime gifts you make to your spouse and no estate tax if you leave your entire estate to your spouse. If you make lifetime gifts to others, the gift tax does not apply to the first $12,000 you give that person each year, and you have an additional lifetime gift tax exemption of $1 million.

THE FEDERAL GIFT TAX

Federal law imposes a gift tax on very large gifts made by you during your lifetime. And if your gift is substantial enough to be subject to this tax, then you as the donor (giver), not your donee (recipient), are responsible for filing a federal gift tax return. The purpose of the gift tax is to prevent people from giving away all of their property during their life and thus avoiding the federal estate tax at their death. The federal estate tax is discussed later in this chapter. As a result, gift tax rates are the same as estate tax rates.

As noted in table 6.1, you have a lifetime gift tax exemption which remains at $1 million while your estate tax exemption increases over the next few years. As a result, you cannot give away during your lifetime as much property free of gift tax as you can if you transfer your property at death.

If during your life, you make a taxable gift exceeding your annual $12,000 annual exclusion plus your lifetime $1 million exemption, you need not pay any gift tax at that time. Instead, the amount of your taxable gift is deducted from your estate tax exemption.

There exist several significant exceptions to the gift tax: the annual exclusion, the lifetime exemption, the marital deduction, the charitable deduction, and an exemption for gifts for medical bills and school tuition.

THE ANNUAL GIFT TAX EXCLUSION

Federal law excludes from the gift tax a specific dollar value of gifts per each donee per calendar year. For 2005, the annual exclusion amount was $11,000. For 2007, the annual exclusion amount is $12,000. This exclusion amount is indexed annually to the cost of living. As the cost of living increases, the annual gift tax exclusion will increase in increments of $1,000 rounded down to the lower thousand.

Both members of a married couple each have separate $12,000 annual gift tax exclusions. So, if you are married, you and your spouse can gift off a combined total of $24,000 per donee per calendar year, to as many donees as you wish, free of the federal gift tax. Combining the annual exclusions and making annual gifts to several children, in-laws, and grandchildren, for example, can quickly reduce the size of one's taxable estate and thus minimize later exposure to the federal estate tax.

THE LIFETIME GIFT TAX EXEMPTION

In addition to the annual gift tax exclusion (currently $12,000), there is a $1 million cumulative lifetime gift tax exemption. In addition to the annual exclusion amount, you can give away during your lifetime a total of $1 million without exposure to gift tax. As noted in table 6.1, this $1 million lifetime exemption does not change over the next few years, while the amount of the estate tax exemption increases substantially through 2009. Even in 2010, the year in which the estate tax is currently scheduled to be eliminated, the gift tax will still exist but with the lifetime exemption amount remaining at $1 million. For 2010 and subsequent years (unless Congress amends the 2001 Tax Law), there will be a $1 million combined gift and estate tax exemption.

THE UNLIMITED MARITAL DEDUCTION

All lifetime gifts between spouses, no matter how substantial, are exempt from the federal gift tax. This rule is part of the unlimited estate tax marital deduction, discussed below. The marital deduction is available only to spouses and does not apply to unmarried cohabitants or other partners, or to gifts from a citizen spouse to a noncitizen spouse. But, lifetime gifts worth up to $117,000 can be made tax-free to a noncitizen spouse. In addition, the annual gift tax exclusion ($12,000 in 2007) applies to gifts to a noncitizen spouse.

THE CHARITABLE DEDUCTION

Lifetime gifts of money or property to tax-exempt charitable organizations, no matter their value, are exempt from the federal gift tax. In addition, such gifts will qualify for a charitable deduction for income tax purposes and therefore can be particularly valuable for persons in high income tax brackets.

EXEMPT GIFTS FOR MEDICAL BILLS AND TUITION

If you pay another person's medical expenses or school tuition, no matter how large the payment, your gift is exempt from the federal gift tax. In order to take full advantage of this exemption, however, there are stringent requirements. First, you must pay the money directly to the health care provider or the school. If instead you give the money to the ill person or the student (who then pays the bills), your gift is not tax exempt. And you do not get this gift tax exemption by simply reimbursing someone who has already paid a medical bill or tuition expense. Lastly, the gift tax exemption for tuition payments is for just that, and does not apply to your payments for other educational expenses, such as room, board, and books.

PAYMENT OF THE GIFT TAX

If you make a lifetime gift that is subject to the federal gift tax, you need not pay the tax until and unless your total taxable gifts exceed the amount of the estate tax exemption for the current year. See table 6.1. Instead, any tax charged on the taxable gifts you have made during your lifetime uses up some of your estate tax exemption and reduces the amount you can distribute tax-free upon your death. So, the good news is that people with estates valued below the estate tax threshold ($2 million during calendar years 2006–2008) need not worry about having to pay federal gift tax or estate tax. Nevertheless, you must file a federal gift tax return for any lifetime gift exceeding the annual exclusion, which is $12,000 during 2007 or $24,000 if your spouse joins in the gift.

THE FEDERAL ESTATE TAX

Under the 2001 Tax Law, most decedent's estates (98%) are not large enough to be subject to the federal estate tax. No estate tax is assessed if the net value of your taxable estate is worth less than $2 million in calendar years 2006 through 2008. This exemption amount will increase to $3.5 million in 2009. And in 2010 (unless Congress amends the 2001 Tax Law), there will be no estate tax no matter how large your estate. But in 2011, the estate tax is scheduled to return with an exemption amount limited to only $1 million. If your estate is currently large enough to be subject to this tax, the rate for 2007 can be as high as 45%. Exemption amounts and tax rates for subsequent years are shown in table 6.1.

YOUR TAXABLE ESTATE

Although for most people it is unlikely the federal estate tax will apply to their estate at death, your "taxable estate" is what the IRS deems to be your "gross estate" less allowable deductions. Your gross estate includes the value of all property in which you had an interest at the moment of your death. Your gross estate may encompass far more property than is in your "probate estate" and includes the following assets:

- Property owned in your name alone, including cash, securities, real estate, etc;
- One-half of all property that you owned jointly with your spouse;
- The portion of any jointly owned property that you owned with a nonspouse that is attributable to your contributions to the acquisition of that property;
- Property in a revocable living trust that you established during your lifetime;
- Proceeds from life insurance on your life, if you owned the insurance policy;
- Assets in a pay-on-death bank account and in a transfer-on-death securities account;
- Real estate subject to a transfer-on-death deed (in those few states that recognize this form of ownership);
- The value of your interest in IRA, 401(k), and other retirement, profit-sharing, and pension plans;
- Partnership and business interests, even though they may not be included in your probate estate.

Tallying up the value of the above items will produce the amount of your gross estate for estate tax purposes. From the gross estate, your survivors can subtract several available exemptions and deductions. The result is that you can transfer at death substantial amounts of property free of the federal estate tax. The most important exemptions are the estate tax exemption, the unlimited marital deduction, and the charitable deduction.

THE ESTATE TAX EXEMPTION

The most important estate tax reducer is called the "exemption equivalent" or simply the "exemption amount." For 2001, the exemption amount was $675,000, which meant that if you died in 2001 and made no taxable lifetime gifts, the first $675,000 of your estate could pass free of the federal estate tax, leaving aside all other available credits and deductions. Under the 2001 Tax Law, the exemption amount for estate tax purposes is different from the exemption amount for gift tax purposes. The exemption amounts for each are shown in table 6.1.

TABLE 6.1
Federal Gift and Estate Tax

Year of Death	Estate Tax Exemption	Gift Tax Exemption	Maximum Estate/ Gift Tax Rate
2002	$1 million	$1 million	50%
2003	$1 million	$1 million	49%
2004	$1.5 million	$1.5 million	48%
2005	$1.5 million	$1.5 million	47%
2006	$2 million	$1 million	46%
2007	$2 million	$1 million	45%
2008	$2 million	$1 million	45%
2009	$3.5 million	$1 million	45%
2010	Estate tax eliminated	$1 million	35%
2011 and thereafter	$1 million		55%

THE UNLIMITED MARITAL DEDUCTION

Aside from the estate tax exemption noted above, the most significant deduction against the federal estate tax is the unlimited marital deduction which shields from estate tax all property transferred at death to your surviving spouse. This deduction, when applied with other available deductions, will reduce the gross estate to the "taxable estate." Since the marital deduction is unlimited, you can use it to transfer millions to a surviving spouse.

But for the very wealthy, care must be taken not to transfer too much to a surviving spouse by use of the marital deduction. If too large an estate is left to a surviving spouse, then it will later be included in the surviving spouse's estate at his or her death. A frequently used estate planning strategy to avoid federal estate tax on the "second death" is to set up what is called an "AB Trust," where each spouse transfers all or most of his or her property to a trust. The surviving spouse has the right to all income from the trust property, the use of the trust property during life (for example living in the home), and can even spend trust principal for certain essentials, but he or she never becomes the outright owner of the trust property left by the deceased spouse. In this way, spouses can combine their individual exemption amounts ($2 million in 2006 through 2008) and effectively transfer much larger estates (for example, $4 million in 2006 through 2008) to their survivors.

A significant limitation on the marital deduction is that it is not available for property left by one spouse to a surviving spouse who is not a U.S. citizen. A surviving spouse must be a U.S. citizen to be eligible for the marital deduction. Fortunately, you can still leave a noncitizen spouse a substantial amount of property free of estate tax. The exemption amount ($2 million in 2006 through 2008), can be used for estates left to a noncitizen spouse, as well as to anyone else.

THE CHARITABLE DEDUCTION

All transfers on death to tax-exempt charitable organizations are exempt from the federal estate tax. A charitable deduction is available to a deceased's gross estate for transfers made at death to organizations operating exclusively for religious, charitable, scientific, literary, or educational purposes, trusts that use contributions only for such purposes, and certain other entities that qualify as charities for these purposes.

PAYING THE FEDERAL ESTATE TAX

A decedent's gross estate that exceeds the available exemption amount ($2 million in 2006 through 2008) must file a federal estate tax return, even if deductions and other tax-avoidance methods mean the estate ultimately owes no tax. Federal estate taxes, if any, are due nine months from the date of death.

If an estate does owe estate tax, and nothing in the decedent's will or trust specifies which assets must be used to pay the tax, state law usually provides that the taxes must be paid by the surviving beneficiaries on a proportional basis. Stated another way, the more a beneficiary inherits from an estate subject to the estate tax, the more tax the beneficiary will have to pay out of the assets that he or she inherits, unless the decedent's will or trust specifies otherwise. Some people, however, provide in their wills and trusts that certain funds must be used specifically to pay taxes. Wills and trusts often specify that taxes and debts are to be paid first and then the balance of the estate is to be divided among the surviving beneficiaries in accordance with the decedent's instructions.

STEPPED-UP INCOME TAX BASIS

Although not part of the federal gift and estate tax law, federal *income* tax laws offer a particularly valuable death benefit to those who own property that has appreciated in value during their ownership, for example, real estate and securities. For federal income tax purposes, appreciated property that is transferred at death acquires a new "stepped-up" tax basis to its value in the decedent's gross estate as of the date of death. For example, suppose A purchased a rental house in 1978 for $50,000 but it is now worth $200,000. If A now sells the house, he would realize a capital gain of $150,000 and must pay federal income tax approximating 15% ($22,500). Similarly, if A now gifted the rental house to B, who in turn immediately sold it for $200,000, she would have the same taxable gain . . . because when a donee receives gifted property, the donee takes the donor's same tax basis in that property.

But if instead A transferred the rental house to B by use of a will, revocable living trust, or transfer-on-death deed (in those few states where this is allowed), B gets the property with a new tax basis, stepped-up to the property's value as of the date of A's death. If B then sells the house at $200,000 with its stepped up tax basis of $200,000, B realizes no taxable gain and pays no capital gains tax on the transaction.

Under the 2001 Tax Law, as part of the phase-out of the federal estate tax, the stepped-up basis at death regarding federal income tax is scheduled to end in 2010.

STATE DEATH TAXES

Some states impose a state tax on inheritances (payable by the beneficiary) or a state tax on estates (payable by the estate). A state estate tax is imposed on the privilege of transferring property at death, whereas a state inheritance tax is imposed on the beneficiaries' privilege of receiving property. Generally, the closer that the beneficiary is related to the decedent, the lower the rate of tax and the greater the number and size of available exemptions.

States that levy an inheritance or estate tax do so on all persons domiciled in the state. Domicile is a legal term referring to the state where you maintain your permanent residence, that is, where you intend to make your home. Generally, it is the state where you live most of the time, own a home, work, and vote.

STATE INHERITANCE TAXES

As of 2007, nine states impose an inheritance tax levied on all or part of on the following:

- All real estate owned in the state, no matter where a deceased resided, and
- All personal property owned by a deceased state resident.

State inheritance taxes are imposed on the people who receive an inheritance (the beneficiaries), rather than on the deceased's estate itself. Generally, beneficiaries are divided into different classes, such as "Class A: Husband or Wife," "Class B: Immediate Family," and "Class C: All Others." Each class receives different tax exemptions and is taxed at a different rate. Generally, the largest exemption and smallest rate is available for surviving spouses and other relatives within "Class A."

TABLE 6.2
State Inheritance Tax Rates and Exemptions[1]

State	Exempt Amount	Tax Rates
Indiana	See[2,8]	1%–20%
Iowa	See[2,3]	5%–15%
Kentucky	See[2,6]	4%–12%
Louisiana	See[2,4]	2%–10%
Nebraska	See[2,5,7]	6%–18%
New Jersey	$25,000[2,3,7]	11%–16%
Oklahoma	See[2,7]	0.5%–15%
Pennsylvania	See[2,7]	4.5%–15%
Tennessee	$1 million[2,3,7]	5.5%–9.5%

1 Rates and exemptions as of January 1, 2006
2 Exempts any amount passing to a spouse
3 Exempts any amount passing to parents, grandparents, and descendants
4 Exempts any amount passing to lineal ascendants and descendants
5 Exempts up to $10,000 passing to parents, grandparents, children, grandchildren, and siblings
6 Exempts up to $100,000 passing to parents and lineal descendants
7 Exempts any amount passing to governmental, educational, and charitable entities

If you reside or own real estate in one of the above states that impose an inheritance tax, you need to consider the impact of this tax. In some instances, the amount of the tax is relatively small and doesn't create a problem. In some other states, however, the tax may be larger, particularly for inheritances left to nonrelatives.

STATE ESTATE TAXES

Even if your state does not impose an inheritance tax, your estate may still be subject to a state estate tax. As of 2007, four states impose a state estate tax—and several other states are considering the adoption of such a tax. In states that impose an estate tax, the executor of a decedent's estate may be required by law to file a state estate tax return, even though no estate tax is payable.

TABLE 6.3
State Estate Tax Rates and Exemptions[1]

State	Exempt Amount	Tax Rates
Connecticut	$200,000[2,3]	12.87%–20.02%
Ohio	$338,333[2,4]	2%–7%
Oklahoma	See[2,6]	.05%–15%
Washington	$2 million[5]	10%–19%

1 Rates and exemptions as of January 1, 2006.
2 Exempts any amount passing to a spouse.
3 Exempts any amount passing to parents, grandparents, and descendants.
4 Exempts up to $1 million passing to parents and descendants.
5 Deduction allowed for several items plus qualified farm property passing to a family member.
6 Exempts up to $1 million passing to parents and lineal descendants.

STATE GIFT TAXES

As of 2007, four states (Connecticut, Louisiana, North Carolina, and Tennessee) impose a gift tax on lifetime transfers of property. The methods used to compute state gift taxes fall into two main categories. The first is a tax on total taxable gifts in a manner similar to the federal gift tax discussed above. The second is a tax on each gift separately, with the tax rate being based on the relationship between the gift's donor and the donee. Typically, the closer the donee is related to the donor, the lower the tax rate and the greater the size and number of exemptions.

☙ 7 ☙

SPECIAL SITUATIONS

A sound estate plan will address your typical needs, depending on whether you are young and single, married with or without minor or adult children, approaching your retirement years, in good or poor health, and of modest or substantial means. Estate planning tools to be considered include wills, trusts, beneficiary designations, the several different forms of ownership, and financial and medical powers of attorney. In addition, you may face one or more *special situations* that warrant carefully tailored estate planning. Such special situations include protecting a disabled child, addressing a second marriage or unmarried cohabitation, passing on a vacation home, and providing for the family pet.

PROTECTING A DISABLED CHILD

Parents who wish to protect and provide for a minor or adult child who is physically or mentally disabled require special estate planning. As a parent, you can of course provide for your disabled child while you are alive. The big question is how can you be sure that your disabled child receives adequate support and care after you are gone. And, if your disabled child receives a substantial inheritance, she may lose eligibility for Medicaid or SSI (Supplemental Security Income) benefits. You may have considered the following strategies:

1. Disinherit the disabled child, hoping that her siblings will use their inheritance to care for the disabled child. This will likely

protect against loss of governmental benefits—but can you really be sure that siblings will always provide for the disabled child?

2. Establish a trust to provide for the support and maintenance of the disabled child. Although this plan sounds fine, it will surely cause the disabled child to lose entitlement to governmental benefits, unless special provisions are made.

The question then is how can you provide for your disabled child without causing her to lose eligibility for governmental benefits? The answer is to set up a *special needs trust*, sometimes called a "supplemental needs trust," which ensures that the inheritance will be used for your disabled child while she is alive, and later can be distributed to other survivors. Your assets transferred to the special needs trust are used merely to supplement, not to replace, governmental benefits by providing, for example, drugs, medical procedures and equipment, and nursing care, not provided by Medicaid. In addition, the trustee of the trust could use trust funds to provide travel, entertainment, home equipment, and other amenities for the child.

Under Social Security guidelines, the property in a special needs trust will not affect one's eligibility for SSI benefits if the beneficiary cannot:

- Control the amount or frequency of payments from the trust, or
- Revoke the trust and use money or property from the trust.

The beneficiary of the governmental benefits must have no legal right to direct and receive money from the special needs trust, either income or principal. Nor can the trust's beneficiary be authorized to amend or revoke the trust and acquire the trust assets. All control over the trust's principal and income must rest exclusively with the trustee. Generally, the trustee is given power to spend trust funds for specifically defined needs of the beneficiary that are not met by the governmental benefits.

You can fund a special needs trust with any type of assets, including cash, securities, real estate, and life insurance. If, for example, you estimate that your disabled child's monthly expenses will be $2,000, and that she will receive $500 monthly from SSI, you may conclude a need for a trust fund of $1 million to cover the child's life expectancy—which could be provided by purchasing life insurance on your life.

You can establish a special needs trust within a revocable living trust where, typically, a part of your estate would be set aside for your disabled child upon your death. Or, if you don't wish to set up a revocable living trust, you could include special needs trust provisions in your will. In either case, you may choose any adult, bank, or other entity as your trustee to manage and distribute the trust funds to the disabled child. The legal requirements governing special needs trusts are both complex and stringent. Therefore, the attorney you choose to set up this type of trust should be experienced both in estate planning law and in the regulations governing benefits available for your disabled child.

THE SECOND MARRIAGE

For many courting couples, only one subject remains taboo: money. It seems indelicate if not downright greedy to ask one's mate-to-be, "How much do you own and what do I get if we split?" Nevertheless, more prospective couples are overcoming their inhibitions and engaging in estate planning to establish who owns what property—and what becomes of it in various contingencies, such as divorce or death. The types of romantic relationships involving older Americans most often include a second marriage, unmarried cohabitation, or simply maintaining a steady relationship with a special person.

The kind of second marriage most likely to present a special situation for estate planning is that between two middle-aged widowed or divorced persons, either or both of whom already have children. In such a special situation each partner may be torn between a concern for the security of the other and a desire to leave at least some property to his or her own children.

Joint ownership as a planning tool must be used with caution if at all in this situation, because on the death of one joint owner, the surviving joint owner automatically inherits all jointly held property with no legal obligation to share it with the children of the deceased spouse. (See chapter 3.) A will can, of course, provide for each spouse's children, but only to a limited extent. A will cannot disinherit a spouse in the event that the marriage proves unhappy and short-lived. Worse yet, even if spouses agree to will their joint property to the children of each of them after both die, if one parent dies first, the surviving parent is free to change his or her will so as to disinherit the deceased spouse's children.

Two alternatives deserve consideration. First, a *prenuptial agreement* signed by both partners can specify precisely how the assets of each spouse are to be divided in the case of divorce or death. Although such agreements are legally binding assuming full disclosure of assets by each partner, most couples are reluctant to use them on grounds that they introduce a grossly materialistic note into what—at least at the time when they are signed—is a highly romantic situation.

The second alternative, a revocable living trust, may provide a more satisfactory solution. If before the marriage each partner transfers all his or her property into a trust in his or her own name alone, each partner retains full control of his assets, the children of each are protected, and the other spouse can be left with nothing if the marriage terminates, whether by divorce or by death. There is no need for either partner to disclose to the other the existence of the trust, although in the eyes of most couples such deception may be every bit as anti-romantic as the prenuptial agreement.

UNMARRIED COHABITATION

When a man and a woman live together without marriage—a status legally called "unmarried cohabitation"—the law distinguishes their relationship from marriage in ways that reflect society's traditional disapproval of it despite its increasing prevalence. In general, both while their relationship persists and after it terminates, cohabitants have none of the protections the law provides for married couples. For this reason, unmarried cohabitation presents a special situation that warrants careful estate planning.

Cohabitants, for example, are not entitled to file a joint income tax return, and neither of them may claim the other as a dependent or purchase life insurance on the other's life. Although one partner may acquire property from the other if they owned it jointly or in a living trust, the law does not entitle a surviving partner to any inheritance should the other die without leaving a will. And, or course, cohabitants cannot claim the unlimited marital deduction with respect to the federal gift and estate tax or the exemptions often granted to surviving spouses regarding state inheritance and estate taxes.

The Social Security Administration will not provide unmarried cohabitants the same old-age pension that it provides a married couple, nor is a surviving female cohabitant entitled to a widow's pension, death benefit, or any other benefits to which widows are often entitled. In fact, even while living with her partner, a cohabitant mother of children is, in the eyes of the law, in much the same position as a single parent.

When the cohabitation terminates, each partner is fully entitled to the property that he or she owned before the relationship began. Gifts exchanged between cohabitants belong legally to the recipients. Problems often arise, however, in connection with jointly owned property and child support. If the relationship has endured for several years, and especially if it has produced children, a few courts recently have regarded cohabitation as based on an implied contract and have used contract law to compensate the woman for her services and to require a minor child's father to provide child support. But this principle is not yet embodied in any laws related specifically to cohabitation.

Because a couple's preference for cohabitation instead of marriage is so variously motivated, no advice about estate planning is likely to be universally acceptable. All cohabitants would probably do well to prepare and sign a *cohabitation agreement* that specifies property division, financial support, and inheritance rights in the event that the cohabitation is terminated by separation or death. But most cohabitants, like many premarital couples, are likely to shun such an agreement as too materialistic and unromantic, while others may reject it as excessively restrictive. Several gay-rights organizations offer information about the legal rights of persons in nontraditional relationships including Lambda Legal Foundation (http://www.lambdalegal.org) and the Equality in Marriage Institute (http://www.equalityinmarriage.org).

In the absence of a cohabitation agreement, cohabiting couples should be aware of the options open to them. If they see their relationship as permanent, a house can be purchased and titled in joint ownership to ensure the survivor's inheriting it; otherwise, sole ownership or tenancy in common may be preferable. (See chapter 3.) An apartment can be leased jointly or only by the partner who intends to retain occupancy and the responsibility for future rent payments. Shared bank and brokerage accounts and property purchased with shared funds, also can be held individually, in tenancy in common, in joint ownership, in pay-on-death or transfer-on-death accounts, or in a revocable living trust. (See chapter 2.) In addition, if each cohabitant intends that the other should inherit at death, each should prepare a will, as well as durable financial and medical powers of attorney, all of which can be altered unilaterally if the relationship changes or terminates.

Many older persons, as well as their younger counterparts, maintain a series of short-term romantic relationships lasting, for example, one to three years. If such a person owns property and desires to provide for whomever might be his lover at the time of death, he could sign a will—and make new codicils (amendments) corresponding to his current relationship. However, if probate assets are to be passed on at death, a will, as well as its codicils, would ultimately need to be probated. A better solution may be to set up a revocable living trust and then transfer all assets to such a trust. (See chapter 4.) Thereafter, all that is required to conform the trust provisions to one's current relationship would be a simple amendment to the trust. This plan would accomplish probate avoidance while at the same time establishing a means of managing one's property in the event of later incapacity.

PASSING ON A SECOND HOME

Many families own a second home or vacation property that may include a cottage up north, a chalet in Colorado, a condo in Florida, a cooperative apartment in Manhattan, or a modest fishing cabin in Canada or Minnesota. If you are fortunate enough to own such a vacation property, perhaps you have memories of you, your children, or your grandchildren swimming, skiing, hiking, generally communing with nature, or simply cuddled up by the fireplace with a good read. And if you are like many vacation home owners, you have dreams of keeping the place in the family long after your death.

The reality, however, is that unless you are a person of means and are willing to set aside a substantial fund to maintain your vacation home after you die, the economics of property ownership will surely create hardships for your survivors who inherit the place. Another problem associated with your survivors being partners in owning a vacation home is the need for someone to be in charge—

to manage finances, to oversee the place, to parcel out periods of use, and to assign responsibilities for upkeep.

In addition to the time commitment of managing a second home, a big concern can be ongoing taxes, utilities, and maintenance costs. Do you want family members to divide up these costs based on how often they use the place, based on their individual share in the property's value, or based on their contributions to an operating fund? And to help pay the bills, should the home be rented during in-season or off-season? Things get more complicated when a vacation home passes to a third generation (your grandchildren), spreading the ownership and management among an even larger group with even more opinions on how it should be managed and possibly less attachment to the property.

At a minimum, you should discuss your vacation home plans with your adult children and determine if there is a mutual interest in keeping the place in the family. If so, consider setting up a *cottage trust* and either now deeding the vacation home, or later willing it, to the trustee of the trust. The cottage trust can be structured to address all of the concerns noted above, and also establish a means for selling the property in cases where some or all of the owners lose interest or have other financial commitments. And if your vacation home is located in another state, a trust can be used to avoid your survivors having to undergo what is called ancillary probate administration in the other state in order to transfer title to the property, a process that can be both expensive and time consuming.

PROTECTING FAMILY PETS

Approximately 65 million U.S. households include dogs or cats. Since many pet owners consider their pets to be members of the family, they wish to take steps to protect and provide support for their pet after their death. Informal arrangements for a pet caregiver can be established without the need for sophisticated estate planning. But if you wish to establish and fund a *pet trust* to care for your pet, this is a special situation that calls for careful planning.

One option is to select a pet caregiver who is willing and able to take in your pet if you should predecease your pet. Before selecting a caregiver, however, you should consider the following factors:

- Does the caregiver have the time and energy to care for your pet? Consider whether the caregiver already has young children or other pets, has allergies to pets, or has obligations that keep her away from home most of the day.

- Is the caregiver's home appropriate for your pet? For example, if you own a large german shepherd that requires much exercise, is it wise to select a caregiver who lives in a small apartment in the city?

- Avoid selecting a caregiver who will also be the beneficiary of funds left to support your pet after you die. Otherwise your pet may die prematurely.

Once you have selected a caregiver, prepare an information card including the pet's name, species, and location; the caregiver's name and telephone number; special care information (including medications) and your veterinarian's name and telephone number. Maintain copies of the card with your pet's important papers and with your caregiver. Some humane societies offer free wallet-size identification cards for pets, which include some or all of the above information.

Another more formal option is to set up a pet trust for your pet. Approximately 25 states currently have laws that allow you to create trusts for pets. A pet trust should designate a trustee who will oversee the pet's trust fund and make distributions to the pet's caregiver. The trust should expressly authorize the trustee to remove the pet from the caregiver if the trustee determines the pet's care is not appropriate. The structure of a pet trust depends on the pet and of course its state of residence. Some states limit the term of pet trusts to 21 years, which makes them unsuitable for long-lived pets, such as parrots.

Providing for a pet to be supported by a trust fund is not cheap. It may take several thousand dollars to care for a dog throughout its lifetime. And that is assuming the dog doesn't have any unusual allergies or illnesses. Any money left in a pet trust at the end of the pet's life can be distributed from the trust to family members or donated to a charity. Lawyers who draft pet trusts may recommend separating the pet care from the money. One strategy is to set up the trust and specify that the trustee gets both the money and the pet and then promptly delivers custody of the pet to a separate caretaker. The trustee controls the purse strings, and can make sure the pet is being treated well.

8

PREPARING FOR INCAPACITY

Although no one expects to become seriously injured or critically ill, each of us is likely, if we live long enough, to become incapacitated to some extent before dying. Physical incapacity through injury or illness can occur at any time. Mental incapacity generally occurs later in life, although it too can occur at any time. Both possibilities require advance planning, because, once the incapacity has occurred, planning is impossible. In this chapter we discuss the appointment of a surrogate to handle financial and health care decisions if and when you are no longer able to make or communicate such decisions. We also describe alternatives for paying for long-term health care.

MANAGING YOUR FINANCES DURING INCAPACITY

If you become incapacitated you will need someone who can act on your behalf in handling your financial affairs—bank deposits and withdrawals, bill paying, check cashing, investment management, the buying, leasing, and selling of property, and other transactions. The various techniques discussed below allow you to name a person who will take responsibility for your assets should the need arise. It is important to note that arrangements must generally be completed before the onset of your incapacity. Most of the procedures discussed, although widely used, have some limitations. Nevertheless, each offers a degree of comfort and protection.

GUARDIANSHIPS AND CONSERVATORSHIPS

When a person is already incapacitated, a guardian can be appointed to manage his or her personal affairs. If the assets are substantial, a conservator can be appointed for purposes of financial management. Such appointments can be made only by petition to a court, usually the probate court. The petitioner—often your spouse, adult child, a close friend—must file a petition with the court for the appointment. In most cases a lawyer must be retained and compensated to see the process through to completion. If the person for whom the guardianship is sought objects to the appointment, he or she may contest it, usually with the assistance of yet another lawyer. The court may also require the testimony of a physician, who must also be compensated, to establish the patient's lack of capacity. The process can be expensive and time consuming, and if the allegedly incapacitated person contests the appointment, emotionally devastating for everyone involved.

Once a guardianship or conservatorship has been established, it is subject to stringent and continuous supervision by the probate court. Guardians are required to report any major decisions relating to the welfare of the person under their supervision. Conservators must report every financial transaction carried out on behalf of the person whose assets and affairs they are managing. Although there may be good reason for this supervision by the court, most people find the entire arrangement bothersome and expensive. More importantly, a person under a guardianship or conservatorship may automatically surrender most of his fundamental rights.

REPRESENTATIVE PAYEESHIPS

Several states have established a procedure for the management of money known as "representative payeeship," to be used in connection with state and federal government benefits programs. The appointed representative can be a spouse or adult child of the recipient. The representative payee receives and manages the money on the recipient's behalf, applying it to the cost of support and health care, and investing any balance.

Representative payeeships are attractive because, compared to conservatorships, they are relatively easy to establish. The government agency making the payment determines whether the representative payeeship should be created, avoiding the need to employ a lawyer and petition the probate court. On the other hand, the representative payeeship is strictly limited in scope, since it applies to one benefit only. Thus, it is useful when the beneficiary is relying entirely on veterans' or Social Security benefits, for example, but not if the beneficiary has one or more sources of nongovernmental income.

If you have signed a power of attorney designating someone to manage your finances or you medical care, that person does not automatically become qualified as a representative payee regarding Social Security benefits. You must still contact the Social Security Administration and sign its required form in order to establish the payeeship.

SHARED OWNERSHIP

Some people concerned with the possibility of future incapacity convert their solely owned property into shared ownership with a family member, or other person. A bank account, a brokerage account, or even a home can be transferred into joint ownership for its management when incapacity occurs. But creating joint ownership of assets is difficult to unwind and has several significant limitations, detailed in chapter 3. In general, shared ownership is not a desirable option if its major purpose is merely to have someone act on your behalf in the event of your incapacity.

REVOCABLE LIVING TRUST

The revocable living trust, described in chapter 4, is especially useful in cases of incapacity because the trustee or successor trustee of the trust can immediately manage, invest, and reinvest trust assets without prior court approval or intervention. However, the incapacitated person must have established and funded the trust *before* the onset of incapacity, particularly in cases of mental incompetence. Finding a suitable trustee may also be a problem, and if the assets are modest, the expense and time involved in establishing and maintaining a living trust may not be worthwhile.

DURABLE FINANCIAL POWER OF ATTORNEY

A more useful and flexible alternative, the durable financial power of attorney, has none of the limitations of guardianships, conservatorships, representative payeeships, shared ownership, or revocable living trusts. In this context, the word "attorney" is a misnomer, since the empowered person designated to act on your behalf can be any adult—a relative, a close friend, or even a bank—and need not be (and rarely is) an attorney. Hence, in the discussion that follows, we will refer to the "attorney" as the "agent."

Once signed by you—the "principal"—the power of attorney document authorizes your designated agent to take virtually any action with respect to financial and property management on your behalf except the signing and revocation of your will.

Obviously, then, your choice of an agent is critical. The person selected must be trustworthy and have good business sense, and should be available and willing to serve over what may be an extended period of time. The agent, unless it is a bank, serves without compensation. For this reason an adult family member, a friend, or any potential beneficiary of your estate may be a good choice. You should also designate a successor agent in case your first choice is unavailable or unwilling to serve when the need arises. It is possible to select two persons to act as co-agents, but doing so can lead to problems if the two individuals cannot agree on a particular course of action, unless the document authorizes each agent to act independently.

One advantage of the power of attorney is that, unlike a guardianship or a conservatorship, its use does not require court approval or supervision. A power of attorney also offers both the principal and the agent a greater degree of control. The principal can choose his own agent and specify when and in what circumstances the agent can act. He can revoke the power of attorney document at any time. And while the power of attorney is in effect, the principal can handle his financial affairs however he likes for as long as he remains competent.

Unlike joint ownership, the power of attorney retains for the principal the exclusive ownership and control of the principal's assets. And, unlike a revocable living trust, there is no need to retitle assets from your name to the trustee's name. Moreover, power of attorney forms are available at most office-supply stores and usually can be prepared without the assistance of a lawyer. A power of attorney document can be signed by any adult who is mentally competent and free of duress or undue influence. It represents a private agreement between the principal and his designated agent and need not be filed with a court or otherwise made public. See figure 8.2.

Until recently a financial power of attorney was revoked automatically when the principal became mentally incompetent. Today, however, all states recognize what is called a *durable* power of attorney, which, if it expressly recites that it will continue in effect after you become incapacitated, will survive incompetence until the principal later revokes it or dies.

LIMITED POWER OF ATTORNEY

The limited of power of attorney restricts the agent's authority to a specific activity—the sale of a house, for example, or the management of a checking account. (See figure 8.1.) Limited powers of attorney are useful even in the absence of incapacity—when, for example, you are out of the country. The limited power of attorney is durable in that it survives incompetence (if it includes the required terminology) and at the same time temporary since it expires when the specified transactions have been completed.

GENERAL POWER OF ATTORNEY

The general power of attorney gives your agent the right to handle all your financial affairs and is available in two forms, the present power of attorney, and the "springing" power of attorney. The present power of attorney (see figure 8.2) takes effect as soon as the document is signed. It is useful for anyone who needs immediate management of his or her financial affairs. The springing power of attorney, on the other hand, is written so that it becomes effective only after the principal becomes incapacitated. Because the springing power of attorney gives the agent no immediate authority, the document should recite that the principal's incapacity is to be determined by a specified physician. Once a physician certifies that the principal can no longer manage his financial affairs, the power of attorney then takes effect.

Since springing powers of attorney can result in expensive and emotional disputes (or even lawsuits) over whether and when they become effective, they are not widely used. If you wish to sign a financial power of attorney but you are not comfortable with it being immediately effective, consider signing it and placing the document in escrow with your attorney, instead of presently delivering it to your designated agent. In this way, your agent does not have access to the document and therefore cannot use it prematurely. But if you adopt this strategy, be sure to tell a family member or friend that you signed a power of attorney and where the document is located.

Figure 8.1

DURABLE LIMITED FINANCIAL POWER OF ATTORNEY

I, _____ , the principal, of _____ make this power of attorney revoke any prior power of attorney I may have made dealing with my financial affairs as described below.

1. APPOINTMENT OF AGENT.

I appoint _____ of _____ as my agent. If that person fails, for any reason, to serve as my agent, I appoint as successor agent _____ of _____ .

2. DURATION. This power of attorney shall take effect when I sign it. The power of attorney shall not be affected by my disability.

3. POWERS OF AGENT. The agent can do the following thing(s) for me:

_____

_____

If I have given the agent the power to transfer real property, the property may be described in an attachment to this form, which may be revised from time to time.

5. COMPENSATION OF AGENT. The agent may receive reimbursement for actual and necessary expenses incurred in carrrying out the above powers. Otherwise, the agent shall not receive any compensation.

6. RELIANCE BY THIRD PARTIES. Third parties can rely on this power of attorney or the agent's representations about it. Anyone who does shall not be liable to me for permitting the agent to exercise powers under the power of attorney, unless they have actual knowledge that the power of attorney has terminated.

7. MISCELLANEOUS. This power of attorney shall be governed by Michigan law, although it may be used out of state. Photocopies of this document shall have the same legal authority as the original.

Date: _____

_____

Principal

Witnesses:

_____   _____

STATE OF MICHIGAN
COUNTY OF _____ } SS

This instrument was acknowledged before me on _____ , _____ by

_____

Figure 8.1

DURABLE LIMITED FINANCIAL POWER OF ATTORNEY *(continued)*

_____

Notary Public

_____County, Michigan

My commission expires_____

Prepared by:

_____

_____

Figure 8.2

DURABLE FINANCIAL POWER OF ATTORNEY

I, _____ , the principal, of _____
make this power of attorney revoke any prior power of attorney I may have
made dealing with my financial affairs as described below.

1. APPOINTMENT OF AGENT.

I appoint _____ of _____ as my agent.
If that person fails for any reason to serve as my agent, I appoint as
successor agent _____ of _____ .

2. DURATION. This power of attorney shall take effect when I sign it. The
power of attorney shall not be affected by my disability.

3. POWERS OF AGENT. Except as stated in paragraph 4, the agent can
do anything with regard to my financial affairs that I could do, including powers to:

(a) Property management. Buy, sell, give (outright or in trust),
hold, convey, exchange, lease, partition, improve, mortgage, option,
insure, invest or otherwise deal with my real or personal property
(my real property may be described in an attachment to this form,
which may be revised from time to time). Make deeds, bills of sale,
purchase agreements, land contracts, sales contracts, listing agreements, easements, mortgages, leases, options, security agreements
or other documents with regard to my real or personal property.

(b) Investment. Invest or reinvest in stocks, bonds, loans, U.S. government obligations (including savings bonds and treasury bills) and
other securities; receive dividends or interest from the securities; vote
stock in person or by proxy; deal with the securities directly or through
a brokerage firm; make any documents with regard to the securities.

(c) Manage business. Operate, participate in, reorganize, recapital-
ize, incorporate, sell, consolidate, merge, close, liquidate or dissolve

---

Figure 8.2

DURABLE FINANCIAL POWER OF ATTORNEY *(continued)*

a business that I might be engaged in; employ agents, officers or directors for the business; make contracts with regard to the business, including buy-sell or partnership agreements.

(d)   Borrowing. Borrow money, unsecured or secured by my property; make promissory notes, mortgages, security agreements, guaranties or similar documents in connection with any borrowing.

(e)   Debts and expenses. Pay bills, loans, notes or other debts owed by me or incurred by the agent on my behalf; pay all expenses for the support and maintenance of me or my dependents; pay all expenses for the management of my property.

(f)   Financial institutions. Open or close an account at a bank, savings and loan association, credit union or other financial institution; make deposits or withdrawals from the account, and make drafts, checks, receipts, notes or other instruments for that purpose; lease, discontinue, enter or withdraw contents from a safe deposit box at a financial institution; carry on any other transactions at financial institutions.

(g)   Taxes. Pay federal, state or local taxes I owe, or any interest or penalty on them; make and file tax returns, reports, forms, declarations or other documents for these taxes; claim and cash any tax refund; handle any and all federal, state and local tax matters.

(h)   Employee benefits. Exercise all rights, options, powers or privileges for any pension, thrift, stock option or ownership, profit-sharing or other employee benefit plan for which I am eligible.

(i)   Government benefits. Apply for and receive any government benefits, including social security, that I am eligible for; receive and cash or deposit any benefit check or draft.

(j)   Legal and administrative proceedings. Begin, continue, defend, appeal, settle or compromise any legal or administrative proceedings involving me or my property

(k)   Insurance. Obtain, redeem, borrow against, amend, cancel, convert, pledge, surrender or change any insurance I have; make any documents, forms or affidavits in connection with any insurance.

(1)   Motor vehicles. Apply for or transfer the certificates of title to automobiles or other motor vehicles.

(m)   Agents and employees. Employ and compensate real estate brokers, stockbrokers, investment advisers, accountants, lawyers, or other agents and employees.

(n)   Other powers. I also give the agent powers to:

_____

_____

Figure 8.2

DURABLE FINANCIAL POWER OF ATTORNEY *(continued)*

4. RESTRICTIONS ON POWERS OF AGENT. The agent shall not have the power to do any of the following: a) make a will or codicil for me, b) change the beneficiary of any life insurance, c) have any power or incidents of ownership over life insurance I own on the agent's life, d) exercise any powers that would make my property taxable to the agent for income, gift, estate or inheritance tax purposes, e) other:

_____

_____

5. COMPENSATION OF AGENT. The agent may receive reimbursement for actual and necessary expenses incurred in carrying out the above powers. Otherwise, the agent shall not receive any compensation.

6. RELIANCE BY THIRD PARTIES. Third parties can rely on this power of attorney or the agent's representations about it. Anyone who does shall not be liable to me for permitting the agent to exercise powers under the power of attorney, unless they have actual knowledge that the power of attorney has terminated.

7. MISCELLANEOUS. This power of attorney shall be governed by Michigan law, although it may be used out of state. Photocopies of this document shall have the same legal authority as the original.

Date: _____ .

_____
Principal

Witnesses:

_____   _____

STATE OF MICHIGAN   } SS
COUNTY OF _____

This instrument was acknowledged before me on _____ , ____ by

_____
Notary Public

_____ County, Michigan

My commission expires_____

Prepared by:
_____

_____

ACCEPTABILITY OF THE POWER OF ATTORNEY

A power of attorney is useless unless the bank, insurance company, brokerage firm, or other third party is willing to accept and act upon it. Acceptance of a present power of attorney is likely to be routine if photocopies of the document are distributed to the parties involved and if the document contains a clause releasing these persons or entities from any liability they might incur by relying on it. It should also contain a statement that photocopies are valid, although some third parties will accept only the original document. In addition, it should be witnessed and, if real estate is involved, notarized and recorded in the register of deeds office where the property is located.

Copies of a springing power of attorney should not be distributed except possibly to your personal physician who, when the time comes, will be asked to sign a statement certifying your incapacity. In all cases, your designated agent should receive a photocopy and be informed about the location of the original.

REVOKING A POWER OF ATTORNEY

A power of attorney, because it is a voluntary arrangement, can be revoked by the principal at any time prior to his or her mental incompetence or death. Revocation requires nothing more than the signing of a form called "revocation of power of attorney," which need not be witnessed (see figure 8.3). If the original power of attorney document was recorded with the register of deeds, a witnessed and notarized revocation should also be recorded.

Copies of the revocation should be submitted promptly (by certified mail, if necessary) to the agent and to any third parties who honored the original power of attorney. The original document should be retained with your records. If you revoke a power of attorney in order to appoint a new agent, the new power of attorney document should contain a clause reciting that your previous power of attorney is revoked and that the current version is effective.

Just as it is required to sign a valid power of attorney, mental competence is required to revoke a power of attorney. If the principal becomes mentally incompetent, subsequent revocation requires an interested person to petition the probate court for the appointment of a conservator, who may then, depending on state law, be authorized to sign a revocation on behalf of the principal.

Figure 8.3

REVOCATION OF POWER OF ATTORNEY

I, _____, the principal, of _____ revoke my power of attorney dated _____ [and recorded on _____, at Liber _____ Page _____, in the office of the Register of Deeds, _____ County, Michigan], and all the powers given to my agent _____ in such power of attorney.

_____   _____
           Date   Principal

Witnesses:

_____   _____

STATE OF MICHIGAN   } SS
COUNTY OF _____

This instrument was acknowledged before me on _____ , ____ by

_____
                         Notary Public

_____County, Michigan

My commission expires_____

Prepared by:

_____

_____

TERMINATING A POWER OF ATTORNEY

Aside from revocation by the principal, there are several ways in which a power of attorney can terminate. A power of attorney terminates automatically on the death of the principal, or when the principal's agent and any third parties involved receive news of the principal's death. A springing power of attorney that went into effect when the principal became incapacitated terminates automatically if the principal's physician certifies that the principal has regained capacity. A power of attorney automatically terminates if the agent resigns or dies and no successor agent was named in the document. A power of attorney can be terminated by court order if a claim is made and proven—by a beneficiary, for example—that the principal was mentally incompetent or was under duress when the power of attorney was signed.

Although a power of attorney generally avoids probate court intervention in order to deal with incapacity, it cannot prevent disaffected family members from later seeking appointment of a guardian or a conservator to manage the principal or his assets. (In selecting a guardian or conservator, the court may, however, give priority to the agent named in the power of attorney.) Despite this limitation, though, a durable financial power of attorney is a useful, effective, and inexpensive means of preparing for possible incapacity.

CUSTOMIZING A FINANCIAL POWER OF ATTORNEY

A durable financial power of attorney, although relatively inexpensive, can prove extremely useful to you and your family in the event of your incapacity. Indeed, some estate planning attorneys consider this document just as important as your will. If properly drafted, a financial power of attorney can authorize your agent to perform a multitude of important tasks, including making gifts of property, transferring funds in and out of custodial accounts and trusts, and engaging in estate tax, gift tax, and Medicaid planning. If you don't sign a financial power of attorney or, if the one you did sign is too limited or otherwise deficient, then upon your incapacity, your family may need to employ an attorney to petition the probate court for appointment of a guardian or a conservator to handle your affairs—a process that can be expensive, time-consuming, and emotionally draining.

For these reasons, preparing and signing a durable financial power of attorney is not a do-it-yourself project in which you should feel confident using a form purchased at an office supply store, copied from a self-help book, or downloaded from the Internet. Instead, you would be better advised to retain the services of a skilled estate planning lawyer.

ISSUES OF LIFE AND DEATH

There are two documents that can express your preferences about medical treatment or its cessation: the living will and the medical power of attorney. The living will explicitly states your preferences about medical treatment should you become unable to express them when suffering from a serious illness. The medical power of attorney names another person who will have the authority to make medical decisions for you if you become incapable of making them yourself. Both of these documents are called *advance directives*.

THE RIGHT TO DIE

Most of us hope our death will be swift or painless, but not everyone will be that lucky. Accidents or diseases like cancer, Alzheimer's disease, and AIDS may lead to physical or mental deterioration. Increasingly sophisticated life-support systems intended to maintain a patient's vital processes during major surgery or while diseases run their course can be used to prolong by days, months, or even indefinitely the lives of patients whose condition is obviously hopeless—sometimes extending the agony of the patient, and nearly always resulting in high health care bills. Many individuals, if faced with such a situation, would prefer a quick and relatively painless death.

The law distinguishes between active and passive euthanasia. Active euthanasia—the deliberate administration of lethal doses of medication or any other intentional act undertaken to end a terminal patient's life—is illegal everywhere. (Oregon law permits physician-assisted suicide in limited circumstances.) Because humanitarian motives are not a defense, imploring a doctor or friend to end your suffering by killing you, constitutes soliciting the commission of an illegal act, though your request will not necessarily go unheeded.

Passive euthanasia involves the refusal of treatment. It is well established that all patients have the right to be fully informed of the risks and outcomes of every medical procedure, and to refuse treatment. This is known as "informed consent." Thus, if a doctor tells you that you have cancer and suggests that radiation or surgery can prolong your life, you may, provided you are mentally competent, decline the suggested treatment. The right of a patient to refuse medical treatment, even when such refusal means certain death, is absolute.

The right to refuse treatment, however, is useless if the patient is comatose or otherwise mentally incompetent. In all states such cases are covered by "right to die" laws, which specify the circumstances under which treatment may be withheld and designate individuals empowered to make the decision to withhold treatment.

Right-to-die laws, though they differ from state to state, are designed to protect both the patient and the doctor. They protect the patient's right to a dignified death by permitting the refusal of further medical treatment—essentially a reiteration of the principle of informed consent. And they protect the doctor who authorizes passive euthanasia from criminal or civil liability that might otherwise result from his decision. All states require consensus by a group of physicians as well as the patient's family before treatment may be withheld.

LIVING WILL

Regardless of the laws of your state, if you would prefer to have your life terminated by passive euthanasia, the most effective instrument available to you is a *living will*, a document that expresses your preference clearly and formally. In most states, a properly executed living will is legally binding on your survivors and your doctor. Moreover, in these states, the execution of a living will cannot be interpreted as suicide—important because insurance policies often contain a clause rendering the policy void if the insured commits suicide.

In a few states, living wills are not legally binding. Nevertheless, a living will clearly expresses your preferences to your family, your close friends, and your doctor. This can be extremely important because in some cases both the soon-to-be survivors and the doctor would prefer to discontinue life support but feel restrained by their uncertainty as to the preference of the now-incompetent or comatose patient.

SIGNING A LIVING WILL

Although required terminology for a living will varies from state to state, the following instructions should produce a legally acceptable document. The wording should generally follow the sample shown in figure 8.4.

Your living will should be dated, and the signing should be witnessed by two persons who are not your beneficiaries or related to any of your beneficiaries and who are not your physician or employees of your physician.

Some states do not regard a living will as legally binding unless executed after the patient has been diagnosed as terminal. Thus, it may be wise to change the date on your living will annually and then initial the change.

Many hospitals urge patients to sign a living will on admission for almost any but the most routine surgical procedures. In any event, copies should be given to your doctor for filing with your medical record, to one or more members of your family, to your spouse or domestic partner, and perhaps to a trusted (and younger) friend. The original document, along with a list of all persons who have received copies, should be kept with your will, your letter of instruction, and other important papers.

Figure 8.4

LIVING WILL

I, _____ , being of sound mind, make this statement as a directive to be followed if I become unable to participate in decisions regarding my medical care. These instructions reflect my firm and settled commitment to decline medical treatment under the circumstances indicated below:

I direct my attending physician to withhold or withdraw treatment that merely prolongs my dying, if I should be in an incurable or irreversible mental or physical condition with no reasonable expectation of recovery, including but not limited to: (a) a terminal condition; (b) a permanently unconscious condition; or (c) a minimally conscious condition in which I am permanently unable to make decisions or express my wishes.

I direct that treatment be limited to measures to keep me comfortable and to relieve pain, including any pain that might occur by withholding or withdrawing treatment.

While I understand that I am not legally required to be specific about future treatments, if I am in the condition(s) described above I feel especially strongly about the following forms of treatment:

I do not want cardiac resuscitation.
I do not want mechanical respiration.
I do not want tube feeding.
I do not want antibiotics.

However, I do want maximum pain relief, even if it may hasten my death.

Other directions (insert personal instructions):

Figure 8.4

LIVING WILL *(continued)*

These directions express my legal right to refuse treatment under federal and state law. I intend my instructions to be carried out, unless I have revoked them in a new writing or by clearly indicating that I have changed my mind.

Signed: _____ Date: _____

Address: _____

I declare that the person who signed this document appeared to execute the living will willingly and free from duress. He or she signed (or asked another to sign for him or her) this document in my presence.

Witness: _____

Address: _____

Witness: _____

Address: _____

MEDICAL POWER OF ATTORNEY

According to the laws of many states, in the absence of a living will, the termination of life support measures requires written consent, which obviously cannot be obtained from a patient who is comatose or otherwise incapable of communicating his wishes. Some states delegate decision making in such instances to the patient's parents or next of kin—a classification that does not include friends, no matter how close or long lived the relationship. Therefore, many people choose to sign a medical power of attorney.

A medical power of attorney authorizes a person of your choice to make all medical decisions for you in the event you become incapable of communicating such decisions yourself. The document, which goes into effect as soon as it is signed and witnessed, retains for you the right to make medical decisions as long as you are competent and then transfers this right to the person of your choice if and when you become incapacitated. (See figure 8.5.)

The living will, although a useful document, deals only with the question of life or death, and not other medical issues. The medical power of attorney, on the other hand, can deal with a wide range of medical issues. Moreover, it puts the decision-making in the hands

Figure 8.5

MEDICAL POWER OF ATTORNEY

I, _____, the patient, of _____
make this power of attorney and revoke any prior power of attorney I may have made dealing with my health care as described below.

1. DESIGNATION OF PATIENT ADVOCATE.

I, _____ designate _____
of _____ as my patient advocate.

If that person fails, for any reason, to serve as my agent, I designate as successor patient advocate _____ of _____.

2. DURATION. This power of attorney shall take effect only when I am unable to participate in medical treatment decisions. That determination shall be made, in writing, by my attending physician and another physician or licensed psychologist. This power of attorney shall not be affected by my disability

3. POWERS OF PATIENT ADVOCATE. Except as prohibited by law or as restricted in paragraph 5, the patient advocate shall make all decisions about my care, custody and medical treatment, including powers to:

(a) have access to medical records and information; give medical waivers and authorizations.

(b) authorize admission to or discharge from health care facilities, including hospitals, hospices and nursing homes

(c) employ or discharge medical caregivers, including physicians, nurses and therapists, and pay them reasonable compensation from my funds

(d) consent to or refuse any medical treatment, including diagnostic, surgical and therapeutic procedures

4. FOREGOING LIFE-SUSTAINING TREATMENT (OPTIONAL). By signing below this paragraph, I give the patient advocate the power to decide to withhold or withdraw treatment that would allow me to die. I acknowledge that such a decision could or would allow my death.

_____
Patient

5. Exercise of Powers. In exercising the above powers, the patient advocate shall make decisions according to my best interests, or as instructed by me orally or in writing below:

_____

_____

6. RELIANCE BY THIRD PARTIES. Third parties can rely on this power of attorney, the doctors' statement or the patient advocate's representations about them. Anyone who does shall not be liable to me for permitting the patient advocate to exercise powers under the power of attorney,

Figure 8.5

MEDICAL POWER OF ATTORNEY *(continued)*

unless they have actual knowledge that the power of attorney has been revoked.

7. MISCELLANEOUS. This power of attorney shall be governed by Michigan law, although it may be used out of state. Photocopies of this document shall have the same legal authority as the original.

I am 18 years of age or older and of sound mind. I am signing this power of attorney voluntarily and without undue influence, duress or fraud.

I sign my name to this power of attorney on _____ , _____.

_____
Patient

STATEMENT OF WITNESSES

We are eligible to serve as witnesses. We have witnessed the patient's signature, and state that the patient appears to be of sound mind and under no undue influence, duress or fraud.

_____
Signature of Witness

_____
Name of Witness

_____
City   *State*   *Zip*

_____
Signature of Witness

_____
Name of Witness

_____
City   *State*   *Zip*

_____
Signature of Witness

_____
Name of Witness

_____
City   *State*   *Zip*

DOCTORS' STATEMENT

I, _____ of _____
am the patient's attending physician.

Figure 8.5

MEDICAL POWER OF ATTORNEY *(continued)*

I, _____ of _____ am either a physician or a licensed psychologist.

We have examined the patient and it is our opinion that he/she is unable to participate in medical treatment decisions.

_____	_____
Date	*Physician*
_____	_____
Date	*Physician*

ACCEPTANCE OF DESIGNATION

I have been designated as the patient advocate of the patient making this power of attorney. I accept that designation and agree to act as required by law and as stated below:

(a) This designation shall not become effective unless the patient is unable to participate in medical treatment decisions.

(b) A patient advocate shall not exercise powers concerning the patient's care, custody, and medical treatment that the patient, if the patient were able participate in the decision, could not have exercised on his or her own behalf.

(c) This designation cannot be used to make a medical treatment decision to withhold or withdraw treatment from a patient who is pregnant that would result in the pregnant patient's death.

(d) A patient advocate may make a decision to withhold or with-draw treatment which would allow a patient to die only if the patient has expressed in a clear and convincing manner that the patient advocate is authorized to make such a decision, and that the patient acknowledges that such a decision could or would allow the patient's death.

(e) A patient advocate shall not receive compensation for the performance of his or her authority, rights, and responsibilities, but a patient advocate may be reimbursed for actual and necessary expenses incurred in the performance of his or her authority, rights, and responsibilities.

(f) A patient advocate shall act in accordance with the standards of care applicable to fiduciaries when acting for the patient and shall act consistent with the patient's best interests. The known desires of the patient expressed or evidenced while the patient is able to participate in medical treatment decisions are presumed to be in the patient's best interests.

(g) A patient may revoke his or her designation at any time and in any manner sufficient to communicate an intent to revoke.

Figure 8.5

MEDICAL POWER OF ATTORNEY *(continued)*

(h) A patient advocate may revoke his or her acceptance to the designation at any time and in any manner sufficient to communicate an intent to revoke.

(i) A patient admitted to a health facility or agency has the rights enumerated in state law.

_____   _____

Date   *Patient Advocate*

---

of someone who knows you intimately and is presumably aware of your preferences. Although you should not designate more than one person as agent, it is wise to select an alternate should your original designee be unable or unwilling to serve when the need arises.

The person you designate, sometimes called a patient advocate or surrogate, can be most any adult. The person should clearly understand your wishes and be willing to defend them in the face of what may be strong opposition from family or physician. There is no prohibition against designating the same person named in your financial power of attorney. Most states prohibit the appointment of your physician and other health care providers. Some states extend that prohibition to anyone caring for you in a hospital or to any beneficiary named in your will. Thus, although a family member or close friend may be your preferred choice as patient advocate, in some states you are not permitted to make such a designation if he is a beneficiary of your will.

Because the medical power of attorney can be far more detailed than a living will, you should give your agent as clear an understanding as possible regarding what treatments you prefer to accept or reject in specific circumstances. If you have a massive stroke, for example, do you want to reject aggressive treatment (such as mechanical ventilation or tube feeding) immediately? Or would you prefer that your patient advocate allow such treatment initially, to be terminated later if ineffective? Or do you want to receive treatment for as long as possible? Because it allows you to make all sorts of specifications, the medical power of attorney is far more flexible than the living will.

If you are away from home, possibly in another state, your medical power of attorney and your living will may or may not be honored, depending on the laws of that state. They are almost never honored by emergency medical technicians, who by law must presume your consent, stabilize you, and get you to a hospital. Once you are there, however, your medical power of attorney can usually be relied on in the event you are unable to make or communicate health care decisions.

Although the legal requirements for a medical power of attorney differ from one state to another, you do not necessarily need the help of a lawyer in signing one. Forms are sometimes available from your hospital, your local bar association, or the state office on aging. Generic forms, which may not conform with your state's laws, should be avoided. Forms that conform with the laws of each state are available from Caring Connections, an organization concerned with end-of-life care (http://www.caringinfo.org) and from CCH Financial Planning Toolkit (http://www.finance.cch.com). The American Bar Association's Commission on Law and Aging offers a consumer kit for healthcare advance planning (http://www.abanet.org/aging).

Once you have signed a medical power of attorney, you should make several copies and distribute them to your physician and to anyone else with an interest in your welfare. Store the original in a safe place, making sure that your loved ones know where it is stored.

Unfortunately, there is no ironclad guarantee that either your living will or your medical power of attorney will be honored. In some states, health care providers are entitled to refuse to comply with it on moral or religious grounds. Some states require an objecting physician to remove himself or herself from the case and transfer it to someone willing to honor the documents, but this is not easily done. In some cases, the hospital's ethics committee may resolve the problem; in others, a lawsuit may be necessary. This is why your patient advocate should be someone who does not shrink from conflict.

FUNDING LONG-TERM NURSING CARE

The problem of paying for long-term nursing care in the event of a prolonged illness is one that everyone may face. Because eligibility for Medicaid-funded nursing care is uncertain, and because neither

Medicare nor the various Medigap policies cover all costs associated with a prolonged stay in a hospital, nursing home, or hospice, payment from other sources is almost essential.

MEDICAID

Medicare and Medigap do not pay for nursing home care beyond 100 days. Medicaid, a federal program administered by the states, is available for the payment of long term nursing care not covered by Medicare or Medigap. But eligibility for Medicaid requires a low net worth; the threshold is set by the state in which you reside. In general, you may own your house (regardless of value), one vehicle (regardless of value), household furnishings and personal goods (regardless of value), a prepaid irrevocable funeral contract, and funeral insurance. Medicaid's low net worth threshold has caused many people to rearrange their financial affairs to qualify. Medicaid planning may include converting countable assets into non-countable assets, spending down, and transfers to children or trusts.

The Medicaid Recipient

To become eligible for Medicaid, a person must reduce his assets to approximately $2,000. The person's income, including Social Security and pension, is paid over to the nursing home. The Medicaid recipient is entitled to a personal needs allowance that typically runs between $30 and $60 per month. By transferring assets to children, the Medicaid recipient builds a fund that can be used to pay for expenses that exceed the personal needs allowance. These typically include clothing, personal care and grooming, and certain supplies such as toothpaste.

The Community Spouse

The community spouse (i.e., the noninstitutionalized spouse) is permitted to keep one-half of the couple's countable assets with a cap that, for calendar year 2007, is set at $101,640. The community spouse may receive Social Security and sometimes a modest pension. The community spouse may receive a minimum income of $1,493 per month. For many families, this may be insufficient to maintain the community spouse in the family home. By paying off any debts that the community spouse may have, by making home improvements which have often been deferred, by replacing worn appliances, and by buying a prepaid funeral for the institutionalized spouse, the community spouse is able to reduce her anticipated future expenses. By buying a new or newer car, the community spouse can ensure that she will have transportation. By transferring assets to children, a fund can be established to meet the financial needs of the community spouse that are unable to be met through Social Security and pension income.

The Children

By transferring assets to children, a middle-class family is often able to ensure a modest legacy for survivors. Parents often feel that they have worked hard all their lives and lived frugally, and it is unfair that at the end of their lives they must lose everything because of unexpected illness.

For most families, the primary asset is the family home. This represents the largest single investment that most families have made during their lifetimes, and for many, there is a strong emotional tie because this is the place where many of the children were born and raised.

Disabled Children

Medicaid law permits transfers to or for the benefit of disabled children. These transfers could include a home or any other assets. The public policy reason behind permitting such transfers is that by transferring assets to the disabled child, that child's need for public benefits in the future may be reduced.

Caregiver Children

Medicaid law permits a person to transfer a residence to a child who has lived in the home of the parent for at least two years and provided a level of care sufficient to keep the parent out of an institution for that period of time. The policy behind this exception to the Medicaid transfer rules is to encourage children to care for parents in the parents' home and keep the parents out of a nursing home, which often results in significant savings of public funds.

LONG-TERM HEALTH CARE INSURANCE

When first sold a number of years ago, long-term health care insurance policies were generally unsatisfactory because insurers were uncertain about the extent of their payoffs and their exposure to liability. Recently, as a result of competition and government monitoring, benefits have improved significantly. But there is still no uniform format for these policies. Thus, any long-term health care policy should, before purchase, be closely examined with respect to the following issues.

Benefits "Trigger"

The benefits "trigger" is the event or condition that must occur before the benefits can begin. There are two approaches to triggering entitlement to benefits: functional and medical. The functional model identifies six activities of daily living and allows benefits to be paid when the insured can no longer perform a specified number—usually three of the six—without assistance. The medical model requires care to be "medically necessary" before benefits become payable.

Levels of Care

Long-term health care insurance policies generally offer three levels of care: custodial assistance; skilled care (daily care by professionals under a physician's supervision); and an intermediate level somewhere in between. Lower levels of care may be provided at the patient's home or in an institutional setting. Higher levels are almost always provided in a nursing home.

Any policy you choose should provide care at all levels, both at home and in a nursing facility. It should not require that you use a lower level of care before becoming eligible for a higher one. A good policy will offer access to any level of care at any time.

Daily Benefit Amount

The premium for a long-term health care insurance policy is based on the daily payment to which the insured is entitled when policy benefits are triggered. Before choosing the benefit amount, you should inquire about the cost of nursing home care and what contribution, if any, can be expected from Medicaid.

Duration of Benefits

Every policy sets a time limit on the payment of benefits, usually one, two, or five years, and sometimes a lifetime. The longer the benefit period, the higher the premium. Before making a choice, assess your personal situation. Bear in mind that the average length of nursing home care is between two and three years, and that only a small percentage of patients remain in nursing home care for more than five years.

OTHER ISSUES

Other policy conditions that need careful scrutiny are the waiting period—the length of time before benefits begin—and the existence of a medical condition prior to the purchase of the policy. A pre-existing condition should not postpone benefits for more than six months. An "excluded impairments" clause, on the other hand, denies benefit payments for any conditions that existed at the time the policy was issued. Unless the policy contains a "waiver of premium" clause, you will have to continue paying the premium even after benefits begin.

Helpful information on long-term healthcare insurance is available at the AARP Web site (http://www.aarp.org/healthinsurance/). In addition, a helpful publication "Guide to Long-Term Care Insurance" is available on the Health Insurance Association of America Web site (http://www.hiaa.org).

SUMMING IT UP

If you wish to authorize another person to deal with your possible future incapacity, a durable financial power of attorney and a medical power of attorney are generally the tools of choice. If your assets are substantial, complex, and likely to need management, the revocable living trust allows for flexible management during your life and is an excellent probate-avoidance device at your death. If extended nursing care seems possible, you should consider purchasing long-term health care insurance, particularly if the value of your non-exempt assets is likely to disqualify you from Medicaid-funded long-term care.

~ 9 ~
FUNERALS,
ORGAN DONATIONS —
AND SOME ALTERNATIVES

Unless you are on the verge of death, planning for the disposal of your body and for the rituals that will mark your death may strike you as futile if not downright morbid. And, to a large extent, you're right. Although some people plan their funeral service and their burial down to the smallest detail, there are several reasons why this doesn't make much sense.

To begin with, until you are terminally ill, the time, place, and circumstances of your death are uncertain. You may die while traveling, thousands of miles from home; or, years before you die, you may move far away from your preselected grave site; or the eulogist you have chosen may die before you do; or inflation may drive the cost of your plans far beyond the money you have set aside for them; or the membership of your survivor group may change through death or divorce. Moreover, if you die in certain kinds of accidents—fire, drowning, a plane crash—there may be no body for the survivors to dispose of.

There are other uncertainties, as well. Unless you donate your body for medical research or organ transplant (see p. 170), possession of it passes, on your death, to your next of kin, and with possession goes the right to decide about its disposal. Even if they know your preferences and want to comply with them, they may not be able to afford to. But, more important, they are under no legal obligation to comply, even if money is available.

Given these difficulties, it is not really practical for you to make advance arrangements with a funeral home, a cemetery, and perhaps even a monument firm, specifying exactly what you want from each. Because of continuous inflation, no reputable funeral home will write a future contract that specifies a price in current dollars. Even if you prepay a substantial amount for your funeral, your survivors may be faced with additional charges or, alternatively, with accepting a funeral much simpler than you had specified. It is also possible, of course, that by the time you die the funeral home with which you contracted may have gone bankrupt or out of business, in which case your repayment may be lost entirely.

Advance purchase of a cemetery plot or grave site also presents problems. Many people believe that the purchase of a cemetery plot represents a miniature investment in real estate that can yield a profit if it is not ultimately used. But this is not the case. Your ownership of a cemetery plot is not the same as your freehold ownership of your house and grounds. Ownership of a plot gives you the right to be buried there (in a casket or in a crematory urn), but if you move or change your plans, in some states you may not sell it at a profit, and some cemeteries restrict resale rights to themselves.

Monuments may also be purchased in advance, but what value will they have if you move before you die? They are very expensive to ship, and their resale value is low. As for caskets, not only can you buy one in advance, but you can also buy your choice of several models in kit form from the MHP Network at casketfurniture.com or (800) 789–9395, but even the most avid do-it-yourselfer would probably not want it in the house, even though the supplier points out that it has interim use as a blanket chest, a wine rack, or a coffee table.

Since most people don't enjoy contemplating their deaths in as graphic terms as funeral planning requires, you may feel that the arguments presented above relieve you of any need to think about the subject. But although it is inadvisable to try to formulate specific plans, it is crucially important, for several reasons, that you make some general decisions and share them with those closest to you.

To begin with, if your survivors have no idea as to your preferences, they are likely to put up little resistance to the arguments of a funeral director in favor of the most expensive funeral they can (or think they can) afford. These arguments center on three areas in which your survivors may be vulnerable: (1) social status and conspicuous display: the implication being that an elaborate funeral and expensive casket will impress the departed's friends and neighbors and express the survivors' love and respect; (2) an appeal to grief and guilt: "Your (parent, spouse, child) deserves the very best, doesn't he? And this is the last thing you can do for him"; and (3) a denial of the reality of death: "A very expensive casket will help protect the cremains against decay."

Now, if you yourself want an elaborate and expensive funeral, no harm will have been done by these arguments. But if you would have preferred something much simpler and less expensive but did not communicate your preferences, money that might have gone to the survivors may go instead to the funeral director.

A second reason for making and sharing your plans may be even more important. Your funeral is for the benefit of your survivors. It will be a significant event that at least some of them will remember for the rest of their lives. This is why it is crucial not only that *they* should be aware of *your* preferences but that *you* should be aware of *theirs*—and perhaps modify yours to accommodate theirs if there are differences. Obviously, if you are so concerned about their feelings that you don't express your own preferences candidly and if they, in turn, are inhibited by the same consideration, no communication will take place. But you may be able to achieve at least something more than polite evasiveness if you center your discussion not on specific funeral details but on the following four general questions:

What kind of ritual do I want to mark my death?
Do you want your family and friends to "pay their last respects" by filing past your open casket and joining a cortege to the cemetery? Or do you want a memorial service conducted by a close friend, without your body present? Or would you prefer a convivial party of your closest friends, with music, drinks, and whatever kind of merriment you usually enjoyed with them—the kind of ending described in the old song:

> See what the boys in the backroom will have
> And tell them that I'll have the same.

How concerned am I about keeping my body intact?
Your answer to this question will influence your decisions about donating your entire body or some of its organs, cremation, and other options described later in this chapter. It may also influence

your choice of casket and grave site, if you believe—against all scientific evidence—that the right choices can prevent decay. Lastly, your answer to this question is closely related to a third question:

How do I define immortality?
Although all of us have some concern with how—and how long—our survivors will remember us, our specific views vary widely. Some people, presumably believing that their physical remains are important, choose a memorably elaborate funeral and a conspicuous grave. (In some cultures a photograph of the deceased is embedded in the headstone, and some American funeral directors offer the survivors, at additional cost, a photograph of the deceased laid out in the casket.) Others, believing that their immortality depends on their works and acts, regard their physical remains as totally insignificant and may hasten the return of "ashes to ashes, dust to dust" by cremation. Still others believe that they achieve some degree of immortality by donating their corneas, kidneys, heart, lungs, and other body parts to prolong or enhance the lives of others or to assist medical education and research.

How much will the disposal of my remains cost my survivors?
Even if, allowing for inflation, you set aside enough money for a traditional funeral, cemetery burial, and perpetual care of the grave, some of this money could, if you made a less expensive choice, pass to your survivors. From this point of view, then, you are not really "paying your own way." At the time of this writing, the average funeral, including cemetery burial, costs between $6,000 and $10,000—and can escalate with elaborate caskets, mausoleums, and receptions. If this sum represents only a small fraction of your net worth, both you and your survivors may feel that it is well spent. But if, when you reach old age, your income diminishes and the cost of living goes up, your funeral expenses may be crippling to your survivors, and a less costly alternative may be desirable, if not, indeed, essential.

Once you and those close to you have reached some agreement—or at least compromise—on these fundamental questions, you can intelligently begin to examine specific alternatives. As you will have noted, some of your answers to the questions are related to actual disposal of the body; others are related to social rituals intended to mark your death. Usually, these two functions are independent of each other, but sometimes one places limitations on the other. A church service with the body present, for example, can be followed either by grave burial or by cremation, but usually not by donation of the whole body for education or research. Organ donation for transplant purposes can be followed by a viewing of the open casket, but body donation, of course, can be followed only by a memorial service. Since your body must ultimately be disposed of by one of only a few methods, whereas ritual is available in a wide variety of alternatives or can be dispensed with altogether, we shall review the disposal alternatives first and indicate any limitations they place on memorial rituals. Table 12.1 on page 229 provides a systematic overview of the alternatives.

DISPOSAL ALTERNATIVES

GRAVE BURIAL

Grave burial is so traditional in Western society that many people do not even consider the alternatives, and today approximately 70% of Americans choose this method of disposal. The arguments in its favor are so widely accepted that they need only the briefest mention. A grave is believed to provide a "permanent" resting place. A family grave plot, or even a pair of adjoining graves, offers eternal "togetherness" for family members or spouses. And a grave, especially if it is situated in serene and attractive surroundings, is an inviting place for memorial visits by survivors.

But none of these arguments is invulnerable. A grave is not, in fact, permanent. Cemeteries can be, and have been, moved or destroyed to make way for such public projects as reservoirs, hydroelectric plants, and even superhighways. Moreover, the togetherness provided by the family plot becomes less achievable in a society in which one out of every five families changes its address every year and in which divorce and other family changes inevitably reduce people's concern for their ancestors. And even if families remain in place and loyal to the memories of their forebears, many grave sites that were initially serene and inviting become unattractive as a consequence of overcrowding, surrounding urbanization, or sheer neglect.

Those who oppose grave burial offer additional arguments. Cemeteries, they point out, use land that might be put to more socially productive purposes. Cemetery plots are expensive, as are headstones. Cemetery burial usually, though not necessarily, is preceded by embalming, the purchase of an expensive casket, grave vault, and other elaborate and costly services. Many people feel, also, that burial concentrates attention on a person's physical remains rather than on the meaning of his life—and that, with respect to the body, a swift return to its original elements through cremation is preferable to what Robert Frost has called "the slow, smokeless burning of decay."

On the other hand, your own circumstances and feelings may render these counterarguments meaningless. If you have a family plot (or if you think your family is stable enough both structurally and geographically to justify one), grave burial may be a desirable alternative. If you are a veteran, you are entitled to free grave burial in a military cemetery, although it may be located at a considerable distance from your home—quite possibly in another state.

CREMATION

Cremation, although it is chosen by about 30% of Americans, is the most widely used method of disposal in a number of other countries—especially those, such as Japan and England, in where population density has made the use of land for cemetery purposes prohibitively expensive. According to the Cremation Association of North America, http://www.cremationassociation.org, as of 2003 the cremation rate in the United States was 28.46%. Washington had the highest cremation rate at 63%, Hawaii had 62%, and Nevada had 61%. The lowest cremation rates are Tennessee at 3%, Alabama at 7%, and Mississippi at 7%.

For some people, the very word "cremation" brings to mind the horrors of the smoking furnaces of the World War II death camps, but the modern crematorium bears no resemblance to this image. Often resembling a conventional funeral home, with rooms available for viewing the body and for conducting funeral or memorial services, the crematorium contains a high-temperature furnace that in a matter of two or three hours reduces the body to approximately eight pounds of ash. Temperatures are so high that there is no smoke, and the ashes produced by the container or casket are completely consumed. The remaining bones are pulverized and combined with the ashes, and these "cremains" are placed in an urn or other container.

The alternatives for actual disposal of the ashes are several. They may, of course, be buried in a conventional grave. Most cemeteries permit the interment of two cremated bodies in a single grave, and they charge less for the opening and closing of the grave than for a larger casket. Alternatively, the crematory urn may be kept permanently in a niche in a columbarium, usually operated by the crematorium. Some crematoria scatter the ashes in a memorial garden.

In some states commercial operators—who are often the owners of private aircraft or seagoing vessels—are permitted to charge fees for scattering the ashes from the air or on the waters at locations specified in your letter of instruction (see chapter 10) or by the survivors. Other states—presumably as a result of lobbying by cemetery interests—prohibit the scattering of ashes, but it is difficult to see how this prohibition can be enforced if survivors choose to do it privately and inconspicuously. None of these alternatives need be chosen before or immediately after cremation. Usually the survivors are given the cremains in a canister or urn, and their ultimate disposition can occur at any time after that.

Cremation is usually supported by either or both of two arguments—one philosophical, and therefore unresolvable; the other economic, and therefore testable. The philosophical argument is that the process is swift, clean, and final and that survivors are not stressed by thoughts about a body "amoldering in the ground." Obviously, this argument is entirely subjective.

The economic argument, on the other hand, is one whose validity you can check objectively. Cremation, its proponents argue, is far cheaper than grave burial because (1) no embalming is necessary, thus saving $500 to $1,000, (2) a simple, inexpensive container may be used instead of a casket, thus saving $500 to $25,000 or more, (3) no cemetery plot or monument is needed, and (4) if death occurs at some distance from home, it is far less expensive to ship "cremains," which can travel by parcel post or United Parcel Service, than to ship a body (which must first be embalmed) in a casket by air or rail.

But these economies are not inevitable, since some of them relate to the ritual rather than to the cremation process itself. If, for example, cremation is chosen in conjunction with a traditional funeral service, the full services of a funeral director may be required, and the only economy is the difference between crematorium and cemetery costs—a difference that may turn out to be negligible. On the other hand, grave burial, if you choose a simple graveside service, need not involve the full range of services offered by funeral directors as part of the "standard adult funeral."

To compare the costs of cremation with those of grave burial, you need to compare (1) the cost of cremation itself (currently $1,000) plus the cost of an urn and perhaps the placement of the urn in a columbarium or a grave against (2) the total cost of the cemetery plot, opening and closing costs, perpetual care or annual maintenance fees, plus the excess cost of a casket over a crematorium container.

If you have philosophical objections to cremation (only the Orthodox Jews have a religious prohibition against it), the economic argument will obviously leave you unmoved. If you have no particular preferences one way or the other, however, you might consider saying just that in your letter of instruction. (See chapter 10.) Giving your survivors this kind of discretion allows them to compare costs at the time of your death—or to take advantage of the substantial economy that cremation offers if you die away from home.

BODY DONATION

The donation of your body to a hospital or medical school for research or teaching purposes and the donation of certain of your organs for transplantation are often considered as essentially the same process, but they are not. Although both procedures are covered in the Uniform Anatomical Gift Act, a law adopted by all states, they are in some respects mutually exclusive. If you decide to give any of your organs except your corneas for transplant purposes, your body becomes unacceptable for use in research or teaching. On the other hand, if you give your body for research or teaching purposes, your specific organs cannot be used for transplantation. Hence, you need to consider each kind of donation separately.

People who intend to donate their bodies for research or teaching usually have one or both of two motives: to eliminate all funeral costs and to benefit humanity, usually by giving their bodies to a specific institution or for a specific purpose. Actually, neither of these intentions may ultimately be realized.

To begin with, not all bodies are acceptable, and no institution can be compelled to accept an anatomical gift. If your body has been mutilated by accident or surgery or emaciated by disease, it may not be usable for either research or teaching. For this reason alone, it is important that you have an alternative plan for disposal.

Giving your body to a specific institution is also somewhat uncertain. The need for bodies is by no means as great as it used to be, and it is not uniform in all parts of the country. In anatomy courses for medical, nursing, and dentistry students, sophisticated visual aids have reduced the need for bodies. And the cachet of being able to say, "I'm leaving my body to the Yale Medical School," has given high-status institutions more bodies than they need. As a consequence, reciprocity among medical schools has developed, and as a result of this very sensible arrangement, your body may not end up at the institution of your choice or be used for the purposes you'd prefer.

Although some medical schools will pick up and transport your body from the place of death at no cost to your survivors, others require that it be delivered, and none of them will pay transportation costs if you die in a distant place. And although you have the legal right to donate your body, most medical schools will nevertheless require written consent of your next of kin before making arrangements to accept your gift.

Thus, if you want to donate your body, you can indicate this preference on an Organ Donor Card (see figure 9.1), which must be signed by you and witnessed by two persons. But it is still advisable to choose an alternate method of disposal in case your wishes cannot be carried out for one of the reasons indicated above. If you are interested in arranging a body donation, the best place to contact is the nearest medical school. Information is also available from the National Anatomical Service, 800–727–0700.

Most medical schools require that your body not be embalmed—although some of them will accept a body that has been embalmed according to their instructions. This restriction on embalming usually precludes any kind of service with the body present, and the usual practice is for survivors to hold a memorial service shortly after the death. After the body has served its purposes in research or teaching, it can be returned to the survivors for burial or cremation; but in most cases it is disposed of, usually by cremation, by the institution to which it was donated, and the ashes are returned to the survivors, if they wish.

ORGAN DONATION

The donation of organs for transplant, in contrast to body donation, is not motivated by the desire to eliminate disposal costs, because it is not a method for final body disposal and in no way precludes a traditional service, including viewing of the body. And although the need for bodies fluctuates, the need for all transplantable organs always exceeds the supply, prompting one renologist to display a bumper sticker pleading, "Don't bury kidneys; transplant them."

Donating your organs will almost inevitably prolong or improve someone's life. Your corneas, transplanted, will restore the recipient's sight. Each of your kidneys can literally give an otherwise doomed recipient a new lease on life. Your skin can help the recovery of burn victims, and your bones, your pituitary gland, and other body parts can also be used in treatment or research. In fact, it is impossible to list organ donations exhaustively because the technology is evolving so rapidly that any list is likely to be incomplete within a year.

Although there are always more potential recipients than there are donors, organ transplant is beset by two problems: most organs must be removed very promptly after death, and a recipient who is biologically compatible with the donor must be readied for the transplant very shortly after the death of the donor. Obviously, this biological and chronological "match" isn't always easy to achieve. It depends not only on the circumstances of your death but also on the efficiency of an organ-transplant network in your community. Hospitals that are part of such a network can, when a donor's death is impending, alert a potential recipient in the community or plan for shipping the donation promptly to where it can be used.

One consideration that deters some people from becoming donors is the fear that their death will be hastened by physicians eager to get their organs for transplantation. This fear is groundless, because the code of ethics established for transplantation prohibits any physician involved in the transplantation from attending the potential donor. On the other hand, some people fear that they will be kept "alive" artificially until a recipient can be located and prepared. Whether you feel that this fear is justified depends on your definition of "death." Most states now accept the concept of "brain death"—a "flat electroencephalograph" taken several times and indicating irreversible inactivity in the brain. After death thus defined, it is possible to maintain circulation and respiration by artificial means, and this is sometimes done to keep organs in satisfactory condition for transplant. The individual thus maintained, however, is not being "kept alive." He is, in fact and in law, dead.

As you can see, just as it is difficult to donate your entire body to a specific institution for a specific use, so, too, it is difficult to donate specific organs. A better plan, if you intend to be a donor, is to sign a Organ Donor Card, indicating on it whatever options you prefer. Two of the options—body donation and organ donation—are mutually exclusive, but by checking both of them, you allow

Figure 9.1
ORGAN DONOR CARD

FAMILY NOTIFICATION CARD

This is to inform you that, should the occasion ever arise, I would like to be an organ and tissue donor. Please see that my wishes are carried out by informing the attending medical personnel that I have indicated my wishes to become a donor. Thank you.

_____

Signature   Date

For further information, contact:
NATIONAL KIDNEY FOUNDATION
800-622-9010 | www.kidney.org

ORGAN AND TISSUE DONOR CARD

_____
[print or type name of donor]

In the hope that I may help others, I hereby make this anatomical gift, if medically acceptable, to take effect upon my death. My wishes are indicated below.

I give: ☐ any needed organs or tissues
         ☐ only the following organs or tissues

_____
[specify the organ(s), tissue(s)]

for the purposes of transplantation, therapy, medical research or education;
         ☐ my body for anatomical study if needed

Limitations or special wishes, if any: _____

Figure 9.1
ORGAN DONOR CARD *(continued)*

THIS IS YOUR DONOR CARD FROM
THE NATIONAL KIDNEY FOUNDATION

Here's all you have to do:

1. **Designate your wishes by completing the card, and sign it in front of two witnesses.**
2. **Discuss your wishes with your family and give them the top half of the card.**
3. **Carry the bottom half of the card in your wallet.**
4. **Tell someone else about organ and tissue donation.**

DONATE LIFE

Signed by the donor and the following two witnesses in the presence of each other:

_____   _____
Signature of Donor   Date

_____   _____
City and State   Date of Birth of Donor

_____   _____
Witness   Witness

This is a legal document under the Anatomical Gift Act or similar laws.

☐ Yes, I have discussed my wishes with my family.

For further information, consult your physician or

NKF National Kidney Foundation®
Making Lives Better

800-622-9010 I www.kidney.org   13-10-0602

---

the ultimate decision to be determined by the circumstances of your death and thus ensure that your gift will be used optimally. State laws typically require the donor card to be witnessed by two persons.

The National Kidney Foundation's Web site (http://www.kidney.org) provides an organ and tissue donor card (see figure 9.1) plus an excellent publication "The Organ and Tissue Donor Program." Some state motor-vehicle departments offer all licensed drivers a press-on donor label that can be attached to the reverse side of their driver's license—thus ensuring that the intention to donate will be noticed promptly in the event of accident or death away from home. No matter which form of donor card you use, you can always change your mind: simply deface or tear up the card, or peel the label off your driver's license.

RITUAL ALTERNATIVES

TYPE AND LOCATION OF SERVICE

Unlike the alternatives for body disposal, which are clearly limited, the alternatives for rituals marking your death are virtually limitless, and their various features can be combined in a variety of ways. A religious service, for example, can be held in a house of worship, a funeral home, your own home, a crematorium, or at the grave site. It can be held with an open casket, a closed casket, or with no body present. A memorial service, too, can be held anywhere and at any time after the death, since it usually takes place with no body present. As in the case of body disposal, it is difficult to make precise arrangements before death occurs, but you and your next of kin can and should reach some agreement on a number of preferences.

Although the choice between religious and secular services may seem to depend very simply on the nature of your own religious beliefs, problems can arise if funeral arrangements are left in the hands of children who may have a more secular outlook than you do. In such a situation, the lack of open discussion can cause your children—in an attempt to please you or to please themselves—to err in either direction.

CHOICE OF CASKET

Because the cost of the casket is the largest single component in the total funeral costs and because the price of a casket ranges from under $500 for a simple pine box to $10,000 or more for an elaborate engraved container, your choice becomes especially important if you are concerned with sparing expenses for your survivors. There are two bases for choice of a casket: social display and the hope of preserving the body against decay.

Social display is so personal a consideration that no "objective" advice is possible—other than the sometimes overlooked fact that simplicity is always in good taste, whereas ostentation rarely is. On the question of whether an expensively durable casket preserves the body, however, the objective answer is clear: it does not. Enough exhumations have been conducted to support the firm conclusion that no casket can prevent decay and that sealed metal caskets, which are sold on the grounds that they postpone decay, often hasten it.

OPEN- OR CLOSED CASKET

Viewing of the body, as we have noted, has been the subject of considerable debate. Those who favor it argue that it convinces the survivors of the reality and finality of the death and that many friends as well as relatives want the opportunity of a "last look." Those who oppose it point out that it places undue emphasis on the physical remains and that it indirectly increases funeral costs because it usually requires embalming and cosmetic restoration and may induce the survivors to choose a more elaborate casket.

If you are considering an open casket, bear in mind that at your death emaciation or disfigurement by accident or disease may make you look somewhat less than presentable. Some morticians, working through photographs, create admirable restorations; others produce grotesque and irreparable caricatures.

FLOWERS OR OTHER TRIBUTES

You may also want to discuss with your survivors the question of whether the mourners should send flowers. This, of course, is the traditional way in which mourners can express their sympathy—and flowers can be used to make a minimum-price casket look somewhat less austere. On the other hand, you may feel, as many people do, that flowers are a waste of money and that your obituary notice should include the phrase "No flowers, please"—and possibly the suggestion that mourners might instead make a contribution to your favorite charity, church, hospice or research foundation.

GRAVESIDE AND CREMATORIUM RITUALS

If you have chosen a ritual, religious or secular, to which all your friends and acquaintances are to be invited, you may prefer that the ultimate disposal process be attended by your family only. Thus, after the service in a church or funeral home, only the few people you have chosen will accompany your body to the grave site or watch it moved into the crematorium furnace. The addition of the phrase "Interment private" to the usual obituary notice will make your preference clear.

POSTFUNERAL RITUALS

Although it is not an integral part of the funeral, a post-funeral gathering of mourners, usually with food and drink, has become traditional. Its primary purpose is to provide support to those who are most severely bereaved, but another is to offer an opportunity for relatives and friends who have not met in a long time to come together in a social way. Because there is no prescribed format for these occasions, you may wish to lay out some specifications of your own—for food, drink, music, etc.

SOME MODERN ALTERNATIVES

The various disposal and ritual alternatives described above are chosen so commonly that they are likely to be available in almost every part of the country. Two further alternatives are not yet available everywhere, but both are likely to proliferate because they appeal to an increasing number of people on both philosophical and economic grounds.

DIRECT DISPOSAL

If you are not concerned with how your body is disposed of or with a ritual that involves the presence of the body, you may be interested in the process called *direct disposal*. Under this procedure, a commercial firm specializing in the process collects your body from the place of death and transports it directly and immediately to a cemetery or a crematorium. Because many of the usual services provided by a funeral director are entirely eliminated (e.g., embalming, viewing, and cosmetic restoration) or provided at lower cost (e.g., the use of minimal-cost caskets), these firms can provide complete service for about one-fourth the cost of a standard adult funeral. Memorial services or any other rituals remain the responsibility of the survivors.

Not surprisingly, the funeral industry, perceiving the direct-disposal firms as a serious threat to profits, has lobbied strenuously— and to some extent successfully—for legislative restrictions against them. In California, for example, direct-disposal firms are required to employ licensed morticians even though they provide no professional services. Nevertheless, perhaps as a consequence of the growing secularization of the American public, such firms seem likely to proliferate—not merely because of the substantial economy they offer but also because of the philosophy underlying the entire procedure.

MEMORIAL SOCIETIES

Far more widely available than the direct-disposal firm is the memorial society, which originated some fifty years ago as a consumer cooperative aimed specifically at reducing the high costs of funerals and providing its members with dignified funerals at minimal cost. Although, like the direct-disposal firms, memorial societies have aroused the hostility of the funeral industry, its opposition has not been effective enough to prevent their spread, and today several hundred such societies exist throughout the United States and Canada.

All memorial societies are devoted to public service and are operated almost entirely by volunteers, but they differ somewhat in the way they function. Some of them have formal contracts with one or more funeral homes that offer special prices—as much as 50 percent below the typical cost of a funeral—in return for the volume of business assured by the society. Others have no formal contract but deal on an informal cooperative basis with one or more commercial funeral homes, continuously monitoring their services and charges. Still others simply provide their members with advice and alternatives when the need arises. A lifetime individual or family membership, usually for $20 to $40, entitles you to the society's services, and since there is reciprocity among societies in various parts of the country, you do not necessarily lose the benefits of membership if you move.

When these societies originated, the membership they attracted tended to be above the average in income, education, and occupational prestige. Because people with these characteristics tend to prefer the simplest possible alternatives for both body disposal and ritual, the memorial societies initially stressed a rather austere style at minimal cost. As they attempted to extend their membership beyond this relatively small group, however, they recognized that members of other cultures and other income groups had very different preferences. As a result, many memorial societies have broadened the range and style of service they can suggest. But the common denominator remains protection of the member against exploitation and a reasonable assurance of minimal cost for whatever style of disposal the member chooses.

You may be able to find your local memorial society by checking in the yellow pages of the telephone directory under "Memorial Societies," in the white pages under the name of your community (e.g., Rochester Memorial Society), or by consulting a local clergyman. A centralized source of information is the Funeral Consumers Alliance, 800–765–0107, http://www.funerals.org, which also offers a variety of publications on the subject.

PLANNING TENTATIVELY

In this chapter we have attempted to present not a detailed description of "how to shop for a funeral" but, instead, a broad overview of current practices and alternatives. Our purpose is to help you make very general decisions rather than negotiate for "prearrangements." If you are seriously concerned about the costs of the kind of funeral you prefer, you might consider setting up an investment account or a savings account of some sort specifically earmarked for your funeral expenses. Such an account may, in fact, keep pace with inflation. A life insurance policy bought for the same purpose will not keep pace with inflation but may net a "profit" if you die before your premiums equal its face value. See chapter 5

In general, however, the actual negotiations for funeral arrangements are best left to your survivors, and for this reason we deal with them in chapters 12 and 13. The decisions you make on the basis of this chapter should be tentative, because many unforeseeable changes may occur before you die—changes in your place of residence, in your family structure, in the composition of your survivor group, and even in your religious or philosophical beliefs. Nevertheless, because death may occur at any time, making some general decisions after thoughtful discussion with your spouse and children will inevitably, sooner or later, make the planning of your funeral arrangements easier for them and thus relieve them of some of the stress occasioned by your death.

One final caution. Some people think that once they have made decisions about organ donations, burial or cremation, and funeral ceremonies, their last will is the best place to specify these details. On the contrary, a will is a poor place to note these preferences. Wills are often not located or read until days or weeks after death—long after the time in which organ donation and body disposal must occur, and long after decisions are made about funeral and memorial ceremonies. A far better place to specify your wishes on these matters is in your letter of instruction. (See chapter 10.) And if you wish to make an organ or body donation, a donor card should be properly signed and witnessed. See chapter 9.

≈ 10 ≈
YOUR LETTER
OF INSTRUCTION

As we have noted in chapter 1, your will, because it is an important legal document, must be prepared, signed, and witnessed carefully in accordance with stringent legal formalities. This means that revising it each time the nature or value of your possessions changes is likely to be inconvenient and somewhat expensive. For this reason, your will should dispose of your assets in rather general terms and should not attempt to enumerate everything you own. Your will may, of course, bequeath certain personal items (a piece of jewelry, for example, or an antique desk) to a specific person, but it should not attempt to specify the disposition of every stock, bond, savings account, vehicle, household item, or other possession, because these change continuously over time.

Yet it is extremely important that you maintain a current record of everything you own so that your survivors will not overlook assets of value simply because they don't know of their existence or whereabouts. It is all very well to assume that your spouse or partner is fully aware of your assets and your liabilities—especially if most of your possessions are owned jointly—but if you both die in an accident your survivors will be unlikely to know what you own and what you owe, unless you have provided them with a current inventory. Such an inventory is known formally as a letter of instruction. (See figure 10.1.)

There are two further purposes that can be served by your letter of instruction. First, it can express your wishes about funeral arrangements and body disposal. Embodying these wishes in a will

Figure 10.1

LETTER OF INSTRUCTION

This version of a letter of instruction, adapted from a form provided by Citibank, suggests the various items and the level of detail that should be specified, but you should feel free to adapt it to your own situation and the nature of your assets. People who make frequent changes in their securities or their insurance policies may find that a loose-leaf binder or a box of index cards is more convenient and more flexible.

Name _____

YOU CAN EXPECT

From my employer: _____
(Person to contact, dept., phone)

_____
(life insurance)   (profit sharing)

_____
(accident insurance)   (pension plan)

_____
(other benefits)

From insurance companies _____
(total amount)

From Social Security _____
(lump sum plus monthly benefits)

From the Veterans Administration _____
(you must inform VA)

From other sources: _____
UPDATED _____
(date)

FIRST THINGS TO DO

1. Call _____ to help.
(relative or friend)

2. Notify my employer: _____
(phone)

3. Make arrangements with funeral home. See page _____.

4. Request at least 5 copies of the death certificate. (Usually, the funeral director will get them.)

5. Call our lawyer: _____
(name, phone)

6. Contact local Social Security office.

7. Get and process my insurance policies.

8. Notify bank that holds our home mortgage.

Figure 10.1

LETTER OF INSTRUCTION *(continued)*

SOCIAL SECURITY

Name _____ Soc. Sec. number:_____

Location of card: _____

File a claim immediately to avoid possibility of losing any benefit checks. Call local Social Security office for appointment. They tell you what to bring. _____

(phone)

Expect a lump sum of about $ _____ plus continuing benefits for children under 18, or until 22 for full-time students.

A spouse may receive benefits until children reach 18, between ages 50–60 if disabled, or if over 60.

SAFE DEPOSIT BOX*

Bank: _____

Address: _____

In whose name: _____

Location of key: _____

List of contents: _____

_____

Number: _____

POST OFFICE BOX

Address: _____

Owners: _____

Number: _____

Location of key/combin. _____

*In the event of death, the bank may be required by state law to seal the lessee's box as soon as notified, even if jointly leased.

LOCATION OF PERSONAL PAPERS

Last will and testament: _____

Birth and baptismal certificates: _____

Communion and confirmation certificates: _____

School diplomas: _____

Marriage certificate: _____

Military records: _____

Naturalization Papers: _____

Other (adoption, etc.): _____

Figure 10.1

LETTER OF INSTRUCTION *(continued)*

CHECKING ACCOUNTS

Bank: _____

Address: _____

Name(s) on account: _____

Account number: _____

Kind of account: _____

Repeat to cover all accounts of husband and wife.

Canceled checks and statements are in: _____
                                                    (location)

SAVINGS ACCOUNTS AND CERTIFICATES

Bank: _____

Address: _____

Name(s) on account: _____

Account number: _____

Kind of account: _____ Type: _____

Location of passbook (or certificate receipt): _____

Any special instructions: _____

_____

Repeat for each account.

DOCTORS' NAMES/ADDRESSES

Doctor(s): _____
                    (name, address, phone, whose doctor)

Dentist: _____

Pediatrician: _____

Children's dentist: _____

CREDIT CARDS

All credit cards in my name should be canceled or converted to your name.

Company: _____ Phone:_____

Adress: _____

Name on card: _____ Number: _____

Location of card: _____

Repeat for each card.

Figure 10.1

LETTER OF INSTRUCTION *(continued)*

LOANS OUTSTANDING
(OTHER THAN MORTGAGES)

Bank: _____

Address: _____

Name on Loan: _____

Account number: _____

Monthly payment: _____

Location of papers: _____
(and payment book, if any)

Collateral, if any: _____

Life insurance on loan? ❑ Y   ❑ N

Repeat for all loans

DEBTS OWED TO ME

Debtor: _____

Description: _____

Terms: _____

Balance: _____

Location of documents: _____

CAR

Year, make, and model: _____

Identification number: _____

Location of papers: _____
(title, registration)

Repeat for each car.

INCOME TAX RETURNS

Location of all previous returns—federal, state, local: _____

_____

Our tax preparer: _____

_____
(name, address, phone)

Check: Are estimated quarterly taxes due?

SPECIAL WISHES

1. _____

2. _____

Figure 10.1

LETTER OF INSTRUCTION *(continued)*

PERSONAL EFFECTS

I would like certain people to be given these personal effects:

                                                         Person

My white jade pendant _____

My camera _____

My photography books _____

All my other books _____

Other items _____

INVESTMENTS

Stocks _____

Company _____

Name on certificate _____

Number of shares _____

Purchase price and date: _____

Location of certificate(s): _____

Repeat for each investment

Bonds/Notes/Bills _____

Issuer: _____

Issued to _____
                          (owner)

Face amount: _____ Bond number: _____

Purchase price and date: _____

Maturity date: _____

Location of certificate(s): _____

Mutual Funds _____

Company: _____

Name on account: _____

No. of shares or units: _____

Location of statement(s), certificate(s): _____

Other Investments (U.S. savings bonds, etc.) _____

For each, list amount invested; to whom issued; issuer; maturity date and other applicable date; location of certificates and other vital papers

CEMETERY AND FUNERAL

Cemetery Plot: _____

Location: _____

Figure 10.1

LETTER OF INSTRUCTION *(continued)*

When purchased: _____

Deed number: _____

Location of deed: _____

Other information: _____
(perpetual care, etc.)

Facts for Funeral Director (Bring this with you, and bring cemetery deed, if possible)

My Full Name: _____

Residence: _____ Phone: _____

Marital status: _____ Spouse: _____

Date of Birth: _____ Birthplace: _____

Father's name and birthplace: _____

Mother's maiden name: _____

Length of residence in state: _____ In U.S.: _____

Military service: ❑ Y ❑ N When: _____

(Bring veterans' discharge papers if possible.)

Social Security number: _____ Occupation: _____

Life insurance (bring policy if proceeds will be used for funeral expenses):

_____
(company names and policy numbers)

LIFE INSURANCE

Location of all policies: _____

To collect benefits, a copy of the death certificate must be sent to each company.

Policy: _____
(amount)

Whose life is insured: _____

Insurance company: _____

Company address: _____

Kind of policy:_____ Policy number: _____

Beneficiaries: _____

Issue date: _____ Maturity date: _____

How paid out: _____

Your other options on payout: _____

other special facts: _____

_____

Figure 10.1

LETTER OF INSTRUCTION *(continued)*

Repeat information above for each policy.

For _____ in veterans' insurance call
   (amount)
local Veterans Administration office: _____
                                           (phone)

OTHER INSURANCE

Accident

Company: _____

Address: _____

Policy number: _____

Beneficiaries: _____

Coverage: _____

Location of Policy: _____

Agent, if any: _____

Car, Home and Household

Give information below for each policy.

Coverage: _____

Company: _____

Address: _____

Policy number: _____

Location of Policy: _____

Term (when to renew): _____

Agent, if any: _____

Medical

Coverage: _____

Company: _____

Address: _____

Policy number: _____

Location of Policy: _____

Through employer or other group: _____

Agent, if any: _____

Repeat for all medical insurance policies.

Mortgage Insurance: _____

HOUSE, CONDO, OR CO-OP

In whose name: _____

Address: _____

Figure 10.1

LETTER OF INSTRUCTION *(continued)*

Lot: _____ Block: _____ On map called: _____

Other descriptions needed: _____

Our lawyer at closing: _____
(name) (address)

Location of statement of closing, policy of title insurance, deed, land survey, etc.: _____

Mortgage _____

Held by: _____
(bank)

Amount of original mortgage: _____

Date taken out: _____

Amount owed now: _____

Method of payment: _____

Location of payment book, if any (or payment statements): _____
_____

Life insurance on mortgage: ❑ Y   ❑ N

If yes, policy number: _____

Location of policy: _____

Notify bank of my death; the unpaid amount will be paid automatically by the insurance, and the house is owned free and clear.

Veterans' exemption claim, if any: _____

Location of documentation papers: _____

Annual amount: _____

Contact local tax assessor for documentation needed or more information.

House Taxes

Amount: _____

Location of receipts: _____

Cost of House

Initial buying price: _____

Purchase closing fee: _____

Other costs to buy _____
(real estate agent, legal, taxes, etc.):

Improvements as of _____ come to _____
(date)   *(total so far)*

Itemized House Improvements

Improvement: _____ Cost: _____ Date: _____

Location of bills: _____

Figure 10.1

LETTER OF INSTRUCTION *(continued)*

If Renting: ❑ Y   ❑ N

Lease location: _____ Expires: _____
                                                          (date)

HOUSEHOLD CONTENTS

Names of owners: _____

Form of ownership: _____

Location of documents: _____

Location of inventory: _____

IMPORTANT WARRANTIES, RECEIPTS

Item: _____

_____   _____
(warranty location)   *(receipt location)*

is not a good idea, because often the will isn't read until after the funeral. The letter of instruction, on the other hand, can be more readily accessible and is more likely to be read immediately after death. Second, the letter of instruction is the appropriate place for the expression of any personal wishes or messages to your survivors. Your will, if it should require probate, will become a public document, accessible to anyone who is curious about its contents, and for this reason it should not contain any information that you'd prefer to keep private.

Unlike your will, your letter of instruction is not a legally enforceable document, and the instructions it contains are merely advisory and are not binding on your survivors. (As we shall see, your survivors are not legally bound to carry out your funeral and burial preferences, whether you include them in your will or in your letter of instruction.) Your will is likely to contain such phrases as "I direct that . . .", but your letter of instruction, despite its name, merely *informs* your survivors and cannot legally *command* them to do anything.

The letter of instruction may take any of a number of forms. It can, for example, consist of an informal letter to survivors, a file of index cards, a looseleaf notebook, or a computer disk, all of which are relatively easy to update. *The Beneficiary Book, A Family Information Organizer* (P.O. Box 500028, San Diego, CA 92150, 1-800-222-9125 or http://www.active–insights.com) offers a comprehensive fill-in-the-blanks letter of instruction in looseleaf form. *Personal Record* (Nolo Press, 950 Parker St., Berkeley, CA 94710, 1-800-992-6656, http://www.nolo.com) is a software program compatible with almost any computer.

Whatever the form you choose, the location of your letter of instruction should be known to those who are closest to you—your spouse or partner, your children, perhaps a close friend, or your lawyer. This does not mean that they need have access to it or knowledge of its contents while you are alive; you can, for example, keep it in a locked desk drawer to which only you have the key, in a bank safety deposit box, or in some other location that is private. But it should be easily and readily accessible so that you can keep it up to date regularly—every time you buy or sell a stock or open or close a bank account—and so that it can be found by your survivors within hours of your death.

Because the letter of instruction is a highly personal document, it is impossible to specify what the "ideal" letter should contain. The following listing, therefore, is suggestive rather than prescriptive. You may not need to include every item, but you should review it to make sure that you have not overlooked anything.

FUNERAL AND BURIAL PREFERENCES

If you already own a cemetery plot, the letter should indicate the plot number, the name and location of the cemetery, and the location of the cemetery deed. Similarly, if you have made advance arrangements with a funeral home, the location of the contract should be specified. Figure 10.2 illustrates a sample form.

If you have made no advance arrangements, you may want to express a wish to donate one or more organs or your entire body, or a preference as to the type of funeral service, the person you would like to serve as your eulogist, and the method of body disposal. Although these preferences are not legally binding on your survivors, there is no reason why they should not comply with them if they are reasonable; most survivors are grateful for this information, especially if you have been reluctant to discuss them openly during your lifetime.

Figure 10.2

FUNERAL AND BURIAL PREFERENCES

Check the following Yes/No spaces as they pertain to your wishes.

Yes   No

____ ____ 1. I direct that my body be used for medical purposes as follows:

_____

_____

____ ____ 2. I request postmortem examination be made if desirable.

____ ____ 3. I direct cremation of remains.

      a. Ashes to remain

      b. If (a) is yes, then the disposition of ashes should be as

      follows: _____

_____

____ ____ 4. I request burial in the following manner:

      a. Place of burial: _____

      b. Address: _____

____ ____ 5. I want a memorial service with no casket present.

____ ____ 6. I desire a funeral with remains present.

      a. Closed casket.

      b. Open casket.

      Funeral Home: _____

      Address: _____

      Phone: _____

____ ____ 7. Service:

      a. House of worship: _____

      b. Clergy: _____

      c. Prelude: _____

      d. Solo: _____

      e. Hymns: _____

      f. Special scripture or poems: _____

_____

      g. Other instructions: _____

_____

_____

____ ____ 8. I request that memorial gifts be given to the following organi-

      zations: _____

_____

____ ____ 9. Other information: _____

_____

Date _____   Signed _____

BODY AND ORGAN DONATIONS

If you have made arrangements and signed a donor card making anatomical gifts of either your whole body or individual body organs (see chapter 9), be sure to tell your loved ones. Anatomical gifts must be acted upon very quickly after death, otherwise your preferences may be frustrated. In addition, your letter of instruction can be used to inform survivors of these gift arrangements, particularly if you intend to distribute your letter to family or friends prior to your death.

YOUR ASSETS—LIQUID AND OTHERWISE

Liquid Assets

Although your letter need not account for every penny of your net worth, it should list each bank or credit-union account, certificate of deposit, U.S. savings bond, money-market account, and any other instrument that represents cash. Each year millions of dollars in unclaimed bank accounts revert to state treasuries simply because the original owners or, more often, their survivors have lost track of them.

Because the past decade has seen dramatic fluctuations in interest rates, many people have shifted their cash back and forth among savings accounts, money market funds, certificates of deposit, government bonds, mutual funds, brokerage accounts, and other investments, and some people have hedged by keeping part of their assets in several of these. This is why it is extremely important to pass on to your survivors a complete inventory of your current investments, including the schedule of interest payments and the physical location of the passbook, certificate, statement, or other document.

Stocks and Bonds

If your stock and bond transactions have been handled by one brokerage firm and if your securities are registered in the broker's street account name, your letter of instruction should include (or specify the location of) your most recent monthly statement. If, on the other hand, you have been using several brokers and the stock or bond certificates are in your possession, your letter should include a complete inventory and a schedule of dividend due dates, along with an indication of whether the dividend checks are addressed directly to you or are deposited automatically in a bank or money-market account.

Other Assets

Your letter should include a listing of all other moneys due you—from loans you have made, from rents, royalties, promissory notes, land contracts, etc.—and information as to where the contracts, notes, and other documents are located.

Insurance Policies

Each of your current life insurance policies should be inventoried by company, policy number, face value, and beneficiary designation—with a schedule of premium payments and dividend dates. The location of the policies themselves should be specified. Any loans you have taken against their cash value should be noted.

Medical Benefits

If you are covered by some kind of medical plan, your letter should identify the provider or insurer, the coverages, and the location of the policy. This is important to your survivors not only for the collection of possible benefits resulting from your terminal illness but also for the continuation of coverage for themselves.

Death Benefits

In order to collect your death benefits, your survivors will need your Social Security number, possibly your birth and marriage certificates, and evidence of your discharge from military service. Your letter should indicate the location of all these documents. In addition, it should specify any union death benefits or mortgage or credit life insurance that pays off your indebtedness on your death.

Tangible Property

Your letter should also list all of your possessions that involve some form of registration, deed, or title: real estate, motor vehicles, boats, snowmobiles, etc. Because your survivors will need the registration document in order to transfer its ownership, the location of each document should be specified. If these items are covered by insurance policies, the letter should identify the insurer, the policy number, location, and expiration date of each policy, and the schedule of premium payments. This is especially important with respect to automobile and homeowner's insurance because a lapse in premium payments, which can occur all too easily when your survivors are distracted by your death, can leave important assets completely unprotected.

YOUR LIABILITIES

Although a painstaking review of your checkbook can help your survivors identify your recurring financial obligations, you can make their task much easier by listing in your letter of instruction all your current financial obligations: mortgage payments, loan payments, charge accounts, installment payments on cars, boats, and major appliances. In addition to listing each of these obligations, your letter should note whether you alone are responsible for the indebtedness or whether someone else (perhaps your spouse) cosigned for the loan. As we shall see in chapter 15, outstanding debts on cosigned notes or other agreements remain the responsibility of the cosigner after your death, but debts incurred by you alone may not have to be paid by your survivors if there is insufficient money left in your estate. This listing will, in addition, help your survivors decide which of your obligations must be paid promptly in order to prevent foreclosure, repossession, or the cutting off of essential utility or other services—and which can be delayed until final settlement of your estate.

Your letter should also list any major payments you have made or documents you have signed for goods to be delivered or services to be performed in the future: airline tickets you have bought in advance, tour reservations, a purchase agreement on a car not yet delivered, taxes paid in advance of the due date in order to gain an income-tax deduction. Many of these items represent cash that can accrue to your survivors if the agreements or reservations can be canceled promptly.

MISCELLANEOUS

No matter what your lifestyle, you carry around "in your head" many facts that will not be in the heads of your survivors. You should include in your letter of instruction, therefore, any information that you cannot assume your survivors know. The following suggestions should lead you to think of other items:

Keys

Nothing is more frustrating to survivors than encountering a locked drawer or cabinet for which they can't identify a key—or a key for which they can't identify the lock. You yourself have no difficulty in identifying your keys by shape or color, but you can't expect your survivors to do the same. Your letter should specify the location of all important keys and combinations (safe-deposit box, desk drawers, file cabinets, office, safes, vehicles), and each of those keys should be somehow identified. All keys for long-discarded suitcases, padlocks, or typewriter cases should be immediately discarded.

Hiding Places

Even people who rent bank safe deposit boxes often have secret hiding places at home—to foil burglars or simply to avoid frequent treks to the bank. For example, some people store the sterling tableware in a cranny behind the furnace, or they cache precious jewelry at the back of the third shelf of the linen closet.

If these hiding places are ingenious enough to fool burglars, they are just as likely to be overlooked by your survivors. Your letter, therefore, should specify their location(s). Of course, if a burglar finds your letter, your hiding place is no longer secure, but since burglars rarely spend time reading private documents, you would do well to avoid the far greater risk that your survivors will overlook some of your highly valued possessions.

Inconspicuous Valuables

The value of some antiques and collectibles is apparent at a glance, but this is not true of others, especially those that require a certain amount of expertise. Your survivors, especially if they don't share your enthusiasm or knowledge, may discard as junk or send to the local thrift shop some highly valuable old clocks, china, paintings, first editions, guns, antique woodworking tools, or other items that you have painstakingly and lovingly acquired over many years.

Your letter, therefore, should identify each of these items and indicate their approximate value and the location of any documents (bills of sale, receipts, customs declarations, etc.) that provide evidence of their provenance. This listing, if it is done with care, can serve a second purpose: by omitting certain items, it can prevent your survivors from assuming that the omitted items have high value as antiques and taking them, with high hopes, for appraisal by antique dealers or auctioneers, only to be told that they should be consigned to the local thrift shop.

On the other hand, certain items with no value as antiques may nevertheless have high personal value: a four-generation family bible, for example; a century-old daguerreotype of an ancestor; a set of metal working tools crafted by a grandfather as part of his blacksmithing apprenticeship; a type cabinet handed down by a great-grandfather who was a printer. Sketching the history of such items in your letter may not only increase their value in the eyes of your survivors but also strengthen their feeling for the family's history.

YOUR "LETTER TO THE WORLD"

Your letter of instruction also gives you an opportunity to communicate to one or more of your survivors some feelings or ideas that, for one reason or another, you are unable to express in a face-to-face situation. You may, for example, want to use your letter to heal a longstanding breach in a relationship or to explain its causes or origins. You may want to express affection or respect that you are reluctant or embarrassed to express while you are alive. You may want to explain or apologize for certain of your own actions that at one time or another created problems or raised questions for your survivors.

Because this is *your* letter, there are no prescriptions or proscriptions as to its contents. One principle, however, might be worth following: in general, it is wise to avoid vindictiveness or to express hopes or expectations that are unlikely to be fulfilled. No purpose is served by a posthumous revelation that you have always resented your brother because your parents sent him, but not you, to college or by a hope that your thirty-five-year-old daughter will abandon her homosexual relationship and find herself a husband. If you would like to be remembered fondly, it is better to err on the side of tolerance and charity.

KEEPING UP TO DATE

Even if your affairs are quite complicated, completing a letter of instruction involves no more than a couple of evenings of concentrated work. This effort will be entirely wasted, however, unless you continue updating the letter at regular intervals: monthly if you shift your investments frequently; not less than twice a year to account for insurance premiums, automobile changes, and other shifts in your assets and liabilities.

Such changes can, of course, be combined with your other household accounting chores, especially if you keep at least part of your letter of instruction in the form of a ledger or loose-leaf account book. A good deal of its contents will be useful to you during your lifetime in budgeting and in calculating state and federal income tax, and the more carefully you maintain your letter the more time you are likely to save on these other chores.

◈ 11 ◈
WHEN DEATH SEEMS IMMINENT

If you die suddenly—as a result of an accident, a heart attack, or a massive stroke—whatever estate plans you have made or funeral arrangements you have made will obviously be unchangeable. But the majority of people don't die suddenly or unexpectedly; either they die of "natural causes" at an advanced age—an age at which death within a few years is reasonably predictable—or they die of a terminal illness such as cancer, liver disease, or kidney failure, from which death may be predictable within a matter of weeks or months.

Learning that you have only a few more months of life is, of course, a devastating experience, but psychologists and others who have studied people in such situations report that after a period of severe emotional upset a state of tranquil resignation almost inevitably evolves. Having reached this stage, the dying person often uses his remaining time not only to "put his house in order" with respect to family relationships but also to fine-tune his estate plan and to make last-minute property transfers or beneficiary changes that will reduce probate assets and death taxes and minimize red tape for survivors. Often, too, he can relieve his family and friends of some responsibility by making decisions about future medical treatment (or its withdrawal) and by planning his funeral more precisely than was practical when the time of his death was remote and its place uncertain.

If you are stricken with a terminal illness, however, the likelihood that you will be able to take advantage of these last-minute opportunities will depend on your relationship with your doctor and with your family, your domestic partner, and your lawyer. According to recent studies of death and dying, doctors are notoriously reluctant to tell a patient that death is approaching—in part because they see such a statement as an admission of personal defeat, in part because such predictions occasionally turn out to be wildly inaccurate, and in part because they believe that such a warning will demoralize the patient.

Some doctors inform the family of a patient's imminent death, but families may be just as reticent as doctors to convey this information to the patient, especially if they share the doctor's concern about the patient's morale. And even if both they and the patient know that life is about to end, they may feel that any discussion of medical treatment or funeral details will somehow hasten the patient's death or that any reference to estate planning or property distribution is in poor taste if not downright ghoulish.

This reticence on the part of doctor and family is not easy to overcome. But if you have signed a living will (figure 8.4) or medical power of attorney (figure 8.5), convinced your doctor, throughout your relationship, that you want to be told the truth at all times, and generally responded rationally to bad medical news in the past, you have at least some possibility of being forewarned of your imminent death.

Once you know that death is imminent, the advantage you can take from this knowledge is considerable, but your own reactions may create problems. The awareness that you are going to die can turn your thoughts so thoroughly inward that you may have none for the welfare of your survivors. Or you may become too depressed or angry to be able to function rationally. (Some individuals never attain the stage of resignation that psychologists have identified.) But most people do eventually become reconciled, and many of them derive considerable comfort from the opportunity for last-minute decisions that will either benefit their survivors directly or, at the very least, reduce the number or the difficulty of the tasks that will face them immediately after your death.

Not everything that is suggested in the following pages may be appropriate for you or, for that matter, feasible. Setting up a trust or writing a will for the first time, for example, involves at least one session with your lawyer, which may have to take place at your bedside. On the other hand, given some degree of cooperation from your family members, your doctor, and your lawyer, you will probably be able to accomplish more than you may expect.

MATTERS OF LIFE AND DEATH

YOUR WILL

If the value or the kind of property you own has changed significantly since you signed your most recent will or if the membership of your survivor group has changed, now is the time to review and update your will. At this time you may want to reconsider the dollars-versus-percent question (see p. 24) and to make sure that all the provisions of your will dispose of your property completely and according to your wishes. Before making or amending your final will, however, you need to consider the advantages of making some lifetime gifts—a procedure described later in this chapter. Other last-minute revisions of your will might include a change in your designation of executor, guardian of your minor children, conservator, or trustee of any trust created in your will.

If all the revisions you plan to make are few and simple, there is no need to have the will entirely redrawn. Signing an amending codicil (see p. 28) will serve the purpose just as well.

Changing the beneficiaries in order to take account of changes in the membership of your survivor group (the death of a child who was childless, for example) is obviously sensible. But changing beneficiaries on an emotional basis is unwise. True enough, people who know they are terminally ill often review their entire lives and achieve a more balanced perspective of their relationships with friends and relatives—a perspective that may lead to the forgiving of old injuries, real or imagined, and to a more rational view of old feuds and grudges. On the other hand, if the terminally ill person becomes embittered about his fate and reviews his life in terms of slights, feuds, and failed relationships, he may well express his unhappiness vindictively in his will, since this is now his only means of "getting back" at people. He may, for example, disinherit a favored relative for failure to visit him in the hospital as frequently as he thinks is proper.

Perhaps the only counsel one can give the terminally ill person is to make any beneficiary changes from charitable rather than vindictive motives. But this advice may not prevent an impulsive and excessively generous gift to a nurse or housekeeper for personal services that a more objective observer would consider entirely routine, but it will prevent disinheritances or slights that the dying person would otherwise regret.

HOLOGRAPHIC AND ORAL WILLS

Revising your will or signing an amending codicil usually involves a lawyer and the presence of witnesses. If circumstances make this difficult or impossible, you might consider signing a holographic will, which is recognized currently in 28 states (see table 1.2). This informal will must be written entirely in your own handwriting. You must sign and date it, but your signature need not be witnessed. (See figure 11.1.)

If you live in a state that does not recognize holographic wills, don't prepare one with the thought that it might be "better than nothing." It will not be valid, and you will be regarded as having died intestate. Oral wills or deathbed statements have even weaker legal standing than holographic wills (see table 1.2).

The problem with holographic and oral wills, even though they may be recognized in some states, is that they may invite later legal challenges, risk expensive will contests, and may end up being totally ineffective. A safer approach is to use the services of a lawyer skilled in estate planning.

YOUR LIVING WILL

This is also the time to sign or revoke a living will or medical power of attorney (see chapter 8). The approach of death may very well change whatever decision you might have made earlier with respect to the prolongation of your life by heroic measures or life-support systems. The pain you now suffer may be greater than you anticipated—although for most terminal patients it is apparently less. Or you may decide that the cost of your continued hospitalization may cause your survivors more deprivation than a few weeks or months of prolonged life are worth to you. On the other hand, if each day seems precious to you and you now want to remain alive as long as possible, you may decide to revoke the living will you made when you were in good health.

If your imminent death persuades you to sign a living will, all you need do is copy the sample form shown in figure 8.4 and sign it in the presence of two witnesses—assuming this form complies with your state's law. Whether or not your state recognizes the living will,

Figure 11.1

HOLOGRAPHIC WILL

Will of John J. Jones

I, John J. Jones, declare this to be my last will. I revoke all previous wills.

First: I leave my art collection to my son, William B. Jones.

Second: I leave the rest of my property to my wife, Mary M. Jones, if she survives me. If she does not survive me, I leave the rest of my property to my children, in equal shares. If any of my children die before me, then that child's share shall go to that child's children by right of representation.

Third: If it cannot be determined if my wife died first, then it shall be presumed that my wife survived me.

Fourth: I nominate my wife as Personal Representative. If she does not act, I nominate my son, William in her place. My representative need not post bond.

Fifth: If my children need a guardian, I nominate my brother, Richard J. Jones.

Dated: January 15, 2007

John J. Jones

the document communicates your wishes to your physician and your family. If, on the other hand, you decide to revoke an existing living will, the procedure is even easier: simply destroy the original and notify your physician and your family that you have done so.

Obviously, any such decisions need to be made carefully—over a period of weeks. For terminally ill people, the sudden discovery of a miracle cure—an argument sometimes advanced by opponents of euthanasia—is too remote a possibility to deserve serious consideration. On the other hand, the decision to hasten your death should not be made during what may be a transitory condition of severe depression or pain.

Cashing in Life Insurance

If you have life insurance, you may want to consider cashing in or selling your policy to pay medical bills or provide immediate funds that are otherwise needed. Under what is known as a viatical settlement, insurance companies, and brokers (who sell the policies to investors) will buy your policy for a substantial fraction of its face value once a doctor certifies your illness is terminal. The advantages of such an arrangement are that you, rather than your survivors, collect the proceeds and that you pay no income tax on the money you receive.

Selling your policy is essentially a bet. The purchasing company is betting you will die quickly (thus ensuring a profit for the company, which, on your death, gets the face value of your policy) and you are betting you will live long enough to use the money for whatever purpose you need or want. Although viatical settlements were primarily developed for persons with AIDS, they are also available to patients suffering from other potentially terminal illnesses such as cancer, Alzheimer's, and Lou Gehrig's disease.

The percentage of the face value you can collect on your policy varies widely but can be as high as 85%. Initially, when death from AIDS was likely to occur a very short time after diagnosis, the collectible percentage tended to be high. The percentage has dropped, however, as new and more effective drugs have been introduced, prolonging the lives of AIDS victims. Currently the rates vary sufficiently to justify shopping around. This can be done by contacting either the National Viatical Association (1-800-741-9465; http://www.nationalviatical.org) or the Life Insurance Settlement Association (407-894-3797; http://www.lisassociation.org).

The average life expectancy of people utilizing viatical settlements is about 20 months, and those individuals may receive up to 70% of their policies' death benefit. Someone diagnosed as having 12 months to live might collect as much as 85%, whereas someone with a life expectancy of five years might collect only 50% or less. As tempting as the prospect of immediate cash may be, you need to be very careful before committing to a viatical settlement. You should have a clear idea of whether you really need the money now and what you will do with it.

Viatical companies are obligated to inform you of your options, including one called accelerated death benefits—an arrangement made with the life insurance company. Because viatical companies operate on a "buyer beware" principle, it is wise to consult with your state insurance commissioner to make certain that any company you deal with is licensed in your state. Before signing any viatical contract, you should seek advice from a lawyer skilled in estate planning.

For some patients, viatical payments are a godsend—funding, for example, the purchase of expensive drugs. For others they may be nothing more than a way to diminish the size of their estate at a considerable discount.

FUNERAL PLANNING

When death is imminent and the prospect of a funeral becomes a reality, people tend to react in widely different ways. Some find the notion of making specific plans even more grotesque than they might have when younger or in better health. Others, however, derive comfort from the opportunity to plan every detail of their obituary and funeral service and the disposal of their remains.

As death approaches, detailed planning becomes much more feasible than it was earlier in life. You are unlikely, at this time, to move to another community or to die far from home. You can now negotiate funeral and burial (or cremation) arrangements in terms of their dollar costs, since inflation is unlikely to change them appreciably. And you now know which of your survivors will take responsibility for the final arrangements and how much money will be available to pay for them. Hence, you can, if you like, call to your bedside your clergyman or other eulogist, a representative of the funeral home or memorial society, or anyone else involved in your plans and, with their advice, make plans covering every detail.

(If you decide on this kind of prearrangement, you will find further information in chapter 13.)

If, on the other hand, you feel repelled by this procedure, there is no reason why you shouldn't leave it in the hands of whichever survivor will be ultimately responsible. This does not mean, however, that the subject should be regarded as taboo—never to be mentioned or discussed by you. If you ignore planning entirely, your survivors are very likely to overspend on your funeral. A major reason that funeral directors are able to exploit their customers is that the customer is not only grief-stricken (and hence unable to make rational decisions) but also under enormous time pressures (and hence unable to do any comparison shopping). If, however, your imminent death is openly acknowledged, you can urge your survivors to begin making arrangements in a more leisurely and rational way.

If you have expressed your preferences in your letter of instruction (see chapter 10), there is no need to do anything more than give it (or at least the part dealing with funeral arrangements) to your likely survivors along with the suggestion that the time has come for making definite plans. On the other hand, you may, since writing the original letter, have changed your mind about either the funeral ritual or the method of body disposal. If so, now is the time to make your plans final and if necessary, amend your letter of instruction.

You may also have changed your mind about body or organ donations. Your own illness may have heightened your sympathy for people with illnesses that your anatomical gifts might alleviate or for the needs of medical schools and scientists for bodies in their research on certain diseases. Making a body or organ donation is a simple process that can be done at any time (see chapter 9).

MATTERS OF MONEY

With respect to your estate, there are five steps you should consider taking as death draws near.

1. Revise your letter of instruction or make an inventory of your current assets and liabilities, as both may have changed significantly during the past few months.

2. Review the various probate-avoidance and tax-avoidance tactics described in chapters 2, 3, 4, and 6. If you have already utilized some of them, now is the time to consider transferring additional assets into such arrangements as joint ownership, pay-on-death bank accounts, transfer-on-death security registration and trusts or to shift assets from one to another to maximize the advantages each provides.

3. Consider the possibility of now disposing of part of your estate, by giving away some assets before your death, including transfers to custodial accounts or trusts for minors—an effective way of avoiding probate and federal estate taxes.

4. Take care of any administrative details that can be handled more easily while you are alive than by your survivors at a later date.

5. Review your will, your trust, and your financial power of attorney, to see whether their provisions have been significantly mooted or otherwise affected by anything you may have done in steps 1–4.

The following pages describe steps 1–5 in detail. Although not every suggestion will be relevant to your situation, a careful reading is almost certain to uncover some simple, practicable measures that can save your survivors time, trouble, lawyer's fees, court costs and taxes.

INVENTORY YOUR CURRENT ASSETS AND LIABILITIES

If you have never prepared a letter of instruction (see figure 10.1), now is the time to do it. If you already have one, it needs to be updated—especially with respect to the listing of your current assets, debts, and insurance benefits. If your illness has been lengthy, some of your assets may have been used to pay medical bills or to meet household expenses if the illness interrupted your earnings. Perhaps your stockbroker, if he has discretionary power, may have bought or sold securities since you became ill. You may also have some assets that you have hitherto concealed from your family or your domestic partner—a secret bank account or perhaps a security bought abroad on which you have never paid income tax. Your list of assets is likely to change, too, if you follow some of the property-transfer procedures outlined later in this chapter.

Because your life insurance proceeds may represent a major portion of your total estate, you should make certain that your survivors know where each of your policies is located and whether they are still in force. Sometimes survivors discard an old policy that looks as though it has lapsed, not realizing that the premiums paid earlier may have kept it in force (though at a reduced face value) or that the premiums were paid in full many years ago.

It is also important, too, to make sure that your designation of life insurance beneficiaries—both primary and contingent—is up to date. If you would like to place some conditions or limitations on their access to the proceeds, there may still be time for you to set up a life insurance trust and name its trustee the beneficiary of all your life insurance proceeds. The trust can not only designate the beneficiaries but also set whatever conditions and timetables you choose with respect to their receiving the money. Be sure, however, not to name your own estate or executor as the beneficiary of your life insurance, because this makes all insurance proceeds subject to probate (and possibly to state estate tax, if applicable), whereas naming the trustee of a trust as the beneficiary does not.

If you live in a state that permits the purchase of life insurance policies without medical examination or if you belong to a credit union that schedules open-enrollment periods for group life insurance, also without medical examination, you may be able to buy more coverage, even in your present condition. If this is possible, don't let your conscience trouble you on grounds that you think you are committing fraud; you can be sure that the premiums are calculated to take your kind of situation into account.

LAST-MINUTE PROBATE AVOIDANCE AND TAX AVOIDANCE

Updating the inventory of your assets can help you determine whether they will require probate administration (see chapter 2) and whether your estate will be subject to federal estate tax (see chapter 6). If you classify all your assets as either probatable or nonprobatable and if the total value of your probatable assets exceeds the maximum figure for "small estate" transfers in your state (see tables 16.1 and 16.2), now is the time to consider transferring these assets to forms of ownership that make them nonprobatable, such as the revocable living trust, the pay-on-death bank account, or the transfer-on-death securities account. These devices (described in detail in chapter 2) remove assets from probate but do not remove them from your control—an important point if there is any possibility that you might yet recover from your present illness.

Although your inventory of assets is very likely to disclose some probate assets, it is far less likely to disclose whether your estate is subject to federal estate tax. To begin with, the current estate and gift tax exemption is so high ($2 million in 2007) that only 2 percent of all estates are currently exposed to the federal estate tax. Second, the unlimited marital deduction permits you to transfer to your spouse your entire estate tax-free regardless of its value. If, however, you cannot or choose not to take full advantage of the marital deduction, you should calculate the entire value of your taxable estate (which may *not* be the same as your probate estate) to determine whether this total, plus the total of all taxable gifts you have made during your lifetime, exceeds the maximums shown in table 6.1.

GIVING AWAY YOUR ASSETS

If you discover that your taxable estate is large enough to be subject to the federal estate tax, you can reduce its total below the taxable minimum by making lifetime gifts (within the $12,000 annual gift tax exclusion) or by transferring some of your assets to a custodial account for minors, an irrevocable trust, a family annuity, or some other form of irrevocable transfer described in chapter 2. These transfers (of $12,000 to *each* recipient) enable you to avoid both probate administration and federal estate taxes (see chapter 6), but their great disadvantage is that they are irrevocable; hence, if you transfer your assets beyond your control and subsequently recover from what was thought to be a terminal condition, you could find yourself penniless and financially dependent on your donees.

Giving away your assets removes them from undergoing probate administration, may reduce the value of your estate below the estate tax exemption, and usually does not require the paperwork involved in setting up a trust. In addition, the recipients will be able to express their gratitude to you while you are still able to enjoy it, and you may derive additional pleasure from witnessing the uses to which they put your gifts.

THINK BEFORE YOU GIVE

The procedures we have described above can offer you a good deal of satisfaction from both an economic and a psychological point of view. In economic terms, they enable you to maximize the effectiveness of your estate planning for the benefit of your survivors by minimizing the erosion of your estate by probate costs and death taxes. But the psychological advantages may be even more substantial. When death is imminent, a review of one's life is almost inevitable—and the quality of one's life is measurable not only in terms of the personal relationships one has established but also (in our society, for better or for worse) by the material assets one has acquired. For some people on the verge of death, the revision of their wills and the making of lifetime gifts constitute a very real reassurance that their lives have been worthwhile.

On the other hand, as we have noted earlier, the prospect of imminent death can easily distort one's perspective and precipitate a number of actions that are ill-advised. Thus, the prospect of giving your assets away while you are still alive and can experience the recipients' gratitude, not to mention the added pleasure from avoiding taxes, may tempt you to reduce your estate to almost nothing. But bear in mind though that it may be better for you to retain control of your estate and to reserve the opportunity to change your mind—even if this may result in your beneficiaries' eventually having to pay some probate costs and death taxes.

In addition, the recommendations in this chapter are based on the assumption that, when death is near, your family relationships are stable and your family structure is unlikely to change. But this may not always be the case. And so, before transferring ownership of the bulk of your assets to anyone, you must be totally confident that he or she will not use them in ways that would violate your wishes or your standards.

Lastly, as we pointed out at the beginning of this chapter, the doctor who predicted that you are to die shortly may just possibly be wrong. Completed lifetime gifts are legally irrevocable, and unless your beneficiaries are totally trustworthy, you may find yourself restored to good health but financially destitute as a consequence of your own generosity. For this very reason, you may be well-advised to use a revocable living trust or one of the other techniques discussed in chapter 2 as a means of avoiding probate while at the same time reserving your right to revoke or modify the entire arrangement at any time before you die.

MAKING THINGS EASIER FOR YOUR SURVIVORS

A number of matters that will become the responsibility of your survivors after your death can be attended to more easily and more flexibly while you are alive.

The ownership of your motor vehicles, for example, is more easily transferred by you than by your survivors. Most states permit the after-death transfer of the deceased's vehicles without probate, but these transfer procedures place a maximum limit on the value of the transferred vehicle, restrict the transfer to members of the deceased's family, and require an affidavit of heirship and a certified copy of the death certificate. If you make the transfer while you are alive, however, there is no limit on the value (other than gift-tax concerns) of the vehicle, nor is there any restriction on your relationship to the recipient. You can give the vehicle to anyone you please by signing the certificate of title and delivering it to the recipient.

Transfers of some assets while you are alive may save your survivors time and trouble. If, for example, you own some stock certificates, whether in your own name alone or jointly, it would make sense to have a broker place them in a "street account." Once he does this, you need merely change the ownership of the account instead of having to go through a separate change-of-ownership procedure for each of the several securities.

If you rent a safe-deposit box, whether jointly or in your name alone, the bank, on hearing of your death, is sometimes required to seal the box and prevent further access to it until a representative of the state treasury arrives to inventory its contents for tax purposes. At that time, all the unregistered contents may be presumed to belong to you (and hence be subject to probate administration and estate tax) unless there is evidence to the contrary (see p. 274). For this reason, it may now be advisable for your co-lessee to empty the box of all contents not registered in your name and perhaps to rent another box under his or her name alone into which the valuables may be placed for safekeeping until they are disposed of. If the box you now have is leased in your name alone, a trusted friend can get access to it while you are alive if you provide him or her with a power of attorney or with an authorization form that some banks use for this purpose.

Although the avoidance of probate is generally advisable, there are some situations in which passing assets through probate has desirable tax consequences. If, for example, you own jointly with your daughter a hundred shares of a stock for which you paid $10 a share, the shares will pass to her automatically on your death, but when she sells these shares, her capital gain will have to be calculated on their original cost of $10 per share, regardless of their value at the time of your death. If, on the other hand, the shares were worth $20 each at the time of your death, this would be her "cost" if she acquired the shares through inheritance. In short, the value of any inherited asset is calculated, for tax purposes, as its value at the time of the owner's death rather than its value at the time he or she acquired it.

Alternatively, this "stepped up" tax advantage basis can be achieved by transferring the securities by use of a revocable living trust or by a transfer-on-death securities account.

YOUR WILL—A FINAL REVIEW

If you have taken any of the actions suggested in the preceding pages, your will may no longer represent your intended disposition of your assets. If, for example, you have made a lifetime gift of your harpsichord to your elder daughter, there is no point in specifying this in the will as a bequest to her. Actually, this is of no great consequence, since a will cannot transfer property that the deceased did not own at the time of death. However, a final review and revision of your will to remove bequests that are no longer relevant may serve not only to prevent future disputes among beneficiaries but also to remind you of assets that you have overlooked or beneficiaries that you have neglected.

HOW IMPORTANT IS ALL THIS?

The suggestions and instructions in this chapter may well have given you the impression that the last days of your life should be spent with a calculator, tax tables, work sheets, and the company of your lawyer and accountant in a desperate effort to attain absolute perfection in your estate planning. This, however, is not our intent.

To begin with, if you followed the suggestions offered in chapters 1 and 2, your last-minute adjustments should involve only trivial odds and ends, which, even if neglected or mishandled, should not make an enormous difference to your survivors. Furthermore, in our society it is the responsibility of survivors to take care of both the physical and financial remains of their parents and other relatives. Just as you or your siblings may have had to cope with the problems created by the deaths of your parents or other relatives, so, too, your children or younger relatives can be expected to cope with yours. There is no need for you to be obsessively concerned with accounting for every last penny or every petty detail or to be conscience ridden by various bits of unfinished business.

The ending of life is a time for contemplation and for the repair or reinforcement of personal relationships. It would be unfortunate if you were to forego these important activities for the sake of a possible reduction in death taxes or the costs of probate administration.

Part II

COPING WITH A DEATH IN THE FAMILY

A NOTE TO SURVIVORS

The burden is borne by those that mourn.
—Christiaan Barnard

Even if it was expected, the death of someone who was close to you not only evokes strong feelings of personal loss but may suddenly confront you with an overwhelming array of unfamiliar responsibilities, all of which seem equally pressing. Not only must you make funeral arrangements with an eye to the emotional needs of the survivors, but you must also deal with banks, lawyers, life insurance companies, courts, and other government agencies with an eye to their financial needs.

This burden, coupled with your own grief and bereavement, may throw you into a state of depression or apathy that prevents you from doing anything at all. But if you recognize that the most meaningful way of "paying your respects" to the deceased is to make life easier for the survivors, you are likely to find that taking care of the deceased's unfinished business does not interfere with your grieving but, on the contrary, helps the process run its normal course. And if you can list your various responsibilities in order of their urgency—so that you take care of first things first and postpone the postponable—you are likely to find that what appeared to be overwhelming turns out to be quite manageable.

To help you rank your responsibilities in order of their urgency, we have arranged the chapters that follow in a sequence that reflects their priority for most survivors. Typically, arranging for a funeral service and disposal of the body is the first order of business, and this is discussed in chapters 12 and 13. Finding and reviewing the will (chapter 14) is next in urgency—especially if the will names a guardian for minor children who have been orphaned by the death. And, lastly, the deceased's assets and liabilities must be assembled and evaluated (chapter 15) in order to determine whether the estate requires administration by the probate court before it can be distributed to the beneficiaries or heirs, a topic discussed in chapter 16.

Because every death is a unique event and because every family is different, we feel it would be presumptuous to offer advice on coping with grief, on handling condolence calls and social activities among mourners, or on dealing with the family disputes that are often triggered by the stress of a death. Hence, we have limited our discussion to matters of fact and matters of law.

Two pieces of advice, however, are so universally applicable that we cannot refrain from offering them. First, don't be in a hurry, and don't let anyone press you for time. In making funeral arrangements, you can rest assured that nothing terrible will happen to the deceased or to you if you take all the time you need for a thoughtful decision, preferably in consultation with other survivors. The same holds true for financial matters. No matter how urgent the survivors' need for money, take as much time as you need to ensure that you are making the best possible decisions with respect to each of the deceased's assets.

Second, bear in mind that many of the tasks you face—especially those that are immediately pressing—can be delegated to relatives, friends, neighbors, even children. If you ask a neighbor, for example, to take responsibility for reserving accommodations for out-of-town mourners, he can use his own telephone and avoid tying up yours. Perhaps you can post an older child or a relative at your own telephone to handle the inevitable condolence calls and to give callers information about the funeral service. Someone not closely related to the deceased should be asked to remain at the house during the funeral and burial to receive deliveries of flowers and to protect the premises against burglars, some of whom schedule their activities by reading the obituaries to find out when survivors are likely to be away from home.

Above all, if you possibly can, ask a relative or a close friend for help in making funeral arrangements. Such a person can not only give you emotional support but can double your efforts to compare the services of several funeral homes and can restrain you from impulsive and costly decisions.

Help of this kind is easy to enlist, because many mourners—and even neighbors who knew the deceased only casually—are very eager to "do something to help out." Give them an opportunity and you are likely to find that their cooperation and competence make short work of what at the outset seemed almost insuperable.

⋙ **12** ⋘

BODY DISPOSAL
AND FUNERAL RITES

The first task facing you as a survivor—planning for the funeral ritual and the disposal of the body—is almost inevitably painful and difficult. Grief, inexperience, and the pressure of time may combine to impair your judgment and lead to a number of decisions you might not otherwise make.

Grief, especially if it is compounded with guilt and remorse—the feeling that "now it's too late" to do for the dead person all that you might have done—can cause you to compensate for your earlier failings, real or imagined, by overspending for a needlessly elaborate funeral, casket, and related services.

Inexperience—because a death in the family is, after all, a very infrequent event—can result in mistakes in buying funeral services that you would not make in buying something equally expensive but more familiar.

Time pressure, often exerted by a hospital or nursing home in its eagerness to get rid of the body, can lead you to make hasty arrangements with the first funeral home that comes to mind without considering alternative arrangements that might be less expensive or more satisfactory.

The stress you feel and the mistakes that result from it are to some extent unavoidable, but they can be reduced to a minimum if you follow the two basic principles we have mentioned earlier. First, don't allow yourself to be pressured into hasty decisions. Second, even if the major responsibility seems to be yours, try to involve other family members or friends in your planning. Decisions arrived at jointly are likely to be more objective and more rational and—perhaps more important—they can avert the arguments and long-term alienation among family members that often stem from disagreements over what should or should not have been done for the deceased.

RESISTING THE PRESSURES

If the death has occurred in a hospital or a nursing home, that institution may show indecent haste in urging you to remove the body. Indeed, the same telephone call that informed you of the death may have included a request that you "make arrangements" before the end of the day.

This urgency is understandable from the institution's point of view. Bodies, if they are awaiting autopsy or if they are to remain in an embalmable condition, must be refrigerated, and most hospitals, especially those that do autopsies for the county medical examiner as well as on their own patients, suffer a chronic shortage of refrigerator space.

But from your point of view this urgency is important only if the person who died left his body or specific organs as an anatomical gift or if you, as a survivor, are making the gift yourself in the deceased's behalf. In such circumstances, time is of the essence. The donated organs must be collected within a few hours of death, or the entire body must be promptly transported to the donee. In the absence of an anatomical gift, however, there is no need to feel pressed for time, because the institution is not permitted by law to dispose of the body without the consent of the next of kin. Keeping the body for a reasonable length of time may inconvenience the institution, but yielding to the pressure and, as a result, making arrangements that you have not thought out and discussed with others is a worse alternative.

Occasionally, nursing home or hospital personnel will suggest to you the name of a funeral home that can remove the body promptly. Although such a suggestion may be well-intentioned, you would not be paranoid if you suspected a financial arrangement between the funeral home and the "helpful" hospital employee. In most cases, you would do better to make your own choice.

In years past, it was not uncommon for hospital personnel to call a favored funeral home and instruct it to pick up the body without any authorization from the survivors—on the pretext that it had to be embalmed. This practice has presumably disappeared, because it is now strictly illegal. A funeral director who takes possessions of or embalms a body without authorization from the next of kin, or who refuses to release a body to the next of kin, faces immediate loss of license as well as a possible lawsuit brought by the survivors.

DEATH AT HOME

If a death occurs in a hospital or nursing home, the death certificate (which must be completed before the body can be moved to a funeral home) can be signed either by the deceased's attending physician or by any physician on the staff of the institution. If the death occurs at home, however, the certificate must be signed by the deceased's physician or by the county medical examiner (sometimes called the coroner).

In two sets of circumstances, involvement of the medical examiner is required by law. First, he must be notified if the deceased was not under the care of a physician. (The definition of "under the care of a physician" varies from state to state; in some it means having been seen by a physician during the forty-eight hours preceding death; in others the time limit is two weeks or more.) In most such situations the death is likely to have been sudden and the cause unclear. Second, the medical examiner must be notified of any death resulting from violence—not only possible suicide or homicide but also accidents of all kinds.

In some such situations the medical examiner may waive his examination, but the death should nevertheless be reported by a telephone call to his office, or to the police who will report the death to the appropriate authorities.

SOME LEGAL CONSTRAINTS

Before making any plans or decisions, you need to be aware of the state laws that relate to anatomical gifts and autopsies and that specify who has the final say about funeral arrangements, body disposal, and responsibility for the funeral bill. Although some of these laws are often violated and rarely enforced, a general understanding of them can help you avoid problems.

ANATOMICAL GIFTS

Under the Uniform Anatomical Gift Act, currently the law in all states, any gifts of organs or the entire body made by the deceased must be honored by the survivors. After the donor's death, the person in possession of the gift document, usually a donor card (see figure 9.1) but sometimes a will, is legally obligated to carry out the instructions it contains. However, the deceased's intent may be frustrated, deliberately or otherwise, by several circumstances.

To begin with, unless the body or any donated organs are in medically usable condition, the gift will not be accepted by the donee. Although the gift may be rendered unusable by disease or mutilation, the more common problem is delay: the body or organs must be transferred to the donee within a very few hours of death. If the body or organ donation is made by means of a will (always unwise) and if the will is not found or read until a day or two after the death, neither the organs nor the body will be medically usable, and the donee is likely to decline the gift.

The gift of a body may also be refused if, at the time it is offered, there is an adequate supply of bodies or if transportation from the place of death to the donee institution turns out to be impracticable or too expensive. The donee always has the right to decline a body or organ donation for any reason, or for no reason at all.

In all such situations, the survivors, having made good-faith efforts to comply with the deceased's wishes, are free to choose any alternative method of body disposal.

Even if the anatomical gift is made by means of a properly witnessed donor card, it may be frustrated by a reluctant survivor who conceals or destroys the card, refuses to sign the consent form that most donee institutions require, or fails to timely notify the donee. Although destruction of such a donor card is a clear violation of the law, it is altogether unlikely to result in court action, because the monetary value of the gift is too low to induce any prospective donee to file suit.

THE DECEASED'S WISHES

Aside from making an anatomical gift, the only other legally binding way in which a person can specify the disposition of his or her body is through a will. (Wishes expressed in a letter of instruction or in any other informal way, orally or in writing, have no legal standing.) But the instructions specified in a will are not always carried out—either because survivors ignore the will or the will is not discovered or produced before the disposal has taken place or because the survivors go to court to have the instructions set aside as unreasonable or unduly burdensome on them.

The person who has died may, of course, have negotiated a pre-need contract with a funeral home, specifying the kind of funeral wanted, stipulating the price to be paid, and setting aside a sum of money to pay for it. But even legal contracts of this kind have been successfully contested in court by survivors claiming that the money was more urgently needed for their own welfare.

WHO HAS THE RIGHT TO DECIDE?

One major problem, experienced by survivors and by funeral directors alike, stems from uncertainty as to who has the final say on all details of the ritual service and the disposal of the body. Survivors report that such issues as cremation versus burial or open versus closed casket have generated not only angry arguments at the time of the death but, occasionally, lifelong enmities within the family group. Funeral directors, in turn, complain that after they have set up painstakingly detailed arrangements with one member of the family, another arrives to countermand them and demand something entirely different.

Family conflicts of this kind often stem from intergenerational differences. At the death of a young man, for example, his widow may prefer a simple secular service followed by cremation, because both she and her husband had long ago abandoned formal religious observances. The husband's parents, on the other hand, still adhering to traditional religious practices, may insist on an elaborate religious service, a luxurious casket, grave burial, and an expensive grave marker—even though they have neither the intention nor the ability to pay the funeral costs, which may have to be paid from a pitifully small estate left to the widow.

Actually, the laws of your state specify, in priority sequence, the persons who have the right to make decisions about funeral arrangements. But, as we shall see, these laws are relatively easy to evade and difficult to enforce.

In general, the following people, in order of precedence, have the right to decide on all arrangements: the surviving spouse (if not estranged), an adult child, a parent, an adult sibling, a guardian of the deceased, or "any other person authorized or obligated to dispose of the body"—presumably a coroner or the administrator of a hospital or nursing home. But although the order of priority is clear and although it may be useful to cite in an attempt to settle family disagreements, it very rarely becomes the basis for a lawsuit—in part because disposition of the body usually must take place before court action is possible and because very few judges will order a body exhumed so that it can undergo an alternative method of disposal or be buried in a different place.

WHO PAYS THE FUNERAL BILL?

Under state law, all "reasonable" funeral expenses are chargeable against the estate of the deceased, even if the arrangements are made by a surviving relative rather than the executor. A relative who actually makes any payment for funeral services is entitled to reimbursement from the deseased's estate.

Often, however, there may be no probate estate, or it may be too small to cover the funeral bill, or the funeral director may have no idea of the financial situation of the person who has died. In such cases, the funeral director is likely to require the relative making the arrangements to cosign for the bill or to guarantee payment if the estate should prove unable to pay. For this reason, you should read very carefully any papers you are asked to sign in connection with funeral arrangements. In some cases, you will be asked to sign a contract authorizing certain services; in other cases, your signature also signifies your acceptance of responsibility for paying the bill. If you accept such responsibility, you will be legally liable for the entire bill or for whatever part of it the deceased's estate is unable to pay.

One way of reducing the direct charges against the estate (or against the cosigning survivor) is to sign over to the funeral director any Social Security or Veteran Administration death benefits to which the deceased is entitled (see p. 249). Taken together, these may cover the funeral director's basic costs and thus persuade him that cosigning is unnecessary. In addition, he, rather than you, will have to do the paperwork involved in applying for these benefits and endure the delay until they are paid. Some funeral directors are quite willing to do this because it assures them of at least some cash payment.

Under the law, the funeral director enjoys a preferred status among the estate's creditors; his bill must be paid by the estate before any other debts except administrative expenses (court costs, attorney fees, and personal representative fees) are paid, even though his charges may deplete the estate entirely. In return for this preferred status, the funeral director is expected to behave more ethically and more professionally toward his customers than are most other suppliers of goods and services, and the courts have frequently disapproved or reduced funeral bills that seemed exorbitant—not merely in absolute terms but in relation to the income level of the bereaved family. If a distraught widow is exploited by an unethical funeral director or even if the funeral director permits her to order an excessively expensive funeral, she may seek relief in the courts. Many, if not most, funeral directors are aware of this and govern their behavior accordingly.

AUTOPSIES

In all cases of violent death and in most cases of death under unknown or unusual circumstances, an autopsy to determine the cause of death is required by law. In such situations there is nothing that you can do except modify whatever arrangements you made to allow time for the autopsy to be completed.

Often, however, when the cause of death is known, the attending physician or the hospital will ask permission of the survivors to conduct an autopsy in order to learn more about the deceased's condition at the time of death or about the disease from which the patient died. There is no charge for this work.

Although the prospect of having the deceased's body mutilated and the organs removed and examined may be repugnant, you should carefully consider the possible benefits to society or to you personally. In addition to its usefulness to doctors, an autopsy can offer you considerable comfort if the results indicate that a death that seems sudden and inexplicable was, in fact, inevitable within days or weeks of its unexpected occurrence.

Autopsies do not, of course, preclude an open-casket funeral. Cosmetic restoration by the funeral director removes any indications that an autopsy has been performed.

WHOSE FUNERAL IS IT?

As our review of the legal situation indicates, the law is both specific and enforceable with respect to autopsies in certain cases and with respect to the payment of funeral bills. Most of the other legal provisions—those governing body and organ donations, compliance with instructions expressed in the will, the priority of persons making funeral decisions, and the validity of preneed contracts—can often be disregarded, circumvented, or contested. Thus, although you may wish to honor the deceased by carrying out his wishes, you can feel reasonably comfortable about disregarding them if they seem capricious, unduly burdensome to the survivors, or otherwise unreasonable.

Fundamentally, a funeral is for the benefit not of the deceased but of the survivors. It should, within the financial limits of the deceased's estate, be as satisfying as possible to all of them—emotionally, aesthetically, and socially. A young widow may be entirely justified in disregarding the expensive preferences of her in-laws if satisfying them would threaten the future welfare of herself and her children. On the other hand, you may feel that disregarding or rejecting a close relative's strong preferences isn't worth jeopardizing your relationship for a lifetime.

For all these reasons, even though the responsibility for choice of the arrangements and for payment of their cost is clearly specified by law, the most satisfactory funeral arrangements usually represent a compromise among the preferences of various family members. To achieve this compromise, your best plan is to arrange a meeting (or a long-distance conference call) among the next of kin in order to achieve some consensus on the following alternatives.

SOME BASIC ALTERNATIVES

As you begin formulating specific arrangements, you need to bear in mind that two separate procedures are involved: a ritual service of some sort and the physical disposal of the body. Although they are not entirely independent of one another—for example, the anatomical gift of an entire body precludes an open-casket ritual service—they can be put together in a large number of combinations. For this reason, you may want to make separate decisions about them.

In a few situations, simply following the wishes of the deceased—whether or not they are legally binding—may relieve you of all responsibility, or at least the responsibility for disposal of

TABLE 12.1

Funeral and Body Disposal Alternatives

Ritual	Body Disposal	Essential Costs[*]	Optional Costs[*]
Service with body present			
With casket open	Burial	1-10	11, 14, 15
	Cremation	1–4, 6–8, 12	9–11, 13–15
With closed casket	Burial	1, 3, 4,[a] 5–10	11, 14, 15
	Cremation	1, 3, 4,[b] 6–8, 12	9–11, 13–15
Graveside service only			
Closed casket	Burial	4, 5, 8–10	3, 11, 14, 15
Memorial service, body not present			
	Burial	[c]	14, 15
	Cremation	[c]	14, 15
	Body donation[d]	None[e]	14, 15

[*] Key to Costs
1. Transportation of body from place of death.
2. Embalming and cosmetic restoration.
3. Other professional services by funeral home staff.
4. Casket.
5. Vault or grave liner (not required by law but often required by cemeteries).
6. Viewing and/or visitation facilities at funeral home.
7. Chapel facilities at funeral home (or additional transportation charges to move body to house of worship).
8. Transportation of body to grave or crematory.
9. Cost of cemetery plot.
10. Opening and closing of grave.
11. Transportation of mourners by limousine to and from committal.
12. Crematory charge.
13. Columbarium charge for urn committal.
14. Clergy fee.
15. Classified obituary notices.

[a]A less expensive casket can be used, because it is not the center of attention and can be covered with flowers or a pall.

[b]Casket can be replaced by a much less expensive crematory container.

[c]One all-inclusive charge covers all costs of body disposal, but memorial service and applying for death benefits remain responsibility of survivors.

[d]For research or teaching and eventual cremation.

[e]The body (in a sealed casket) or the cremated ashes may be returned for disposal by the survivors, but this is rarely done.

the body. If, for example, a preneed arrangement was negotiated by the deceased with a funeral home, and if this arrangement strikes you as reasonable and appropriate, you need merely set it in motion by notifying the funeral home that the death has occurred. In such circumstances it is likely that the ritual service as well as the body disposal method has been specified.

If either the deceased or you, on his behalf, make an anatomical gift of the entire body, you are relieved of the problem of body disposal but not of the ritual service. If, however, the anatomical gift involves only one or more organs and not the entire body, you are faced with the responsibility of planning both the ritual service and disposal of the body.

One way to review and evaluate the alternatives available to you is to consult table 12.1, which presents the entire array of rituals and methods of disposal. The table is necessarily somewhat oversimplified, and it is not intended as a guide to detailed funeral arrangements, but a thoughtful reading of it can (1) make you aware of some alternatives you may not have considered, (2) give you a general notion of the procedures involved in—and relative costs of—the various alternatives, and thereby (3) immunize you against suggestions offered by a possibly greedy or unethical funeral director.

Although the table emphasizes costs, both the disposal of the body and the ritual service have not only economic consequences for the survivors but also profound social and psychological significance. It is important, therefore, that any decisions you make should not be based on cost alone. If, for example, direct disposal with cremation appalls you aesthetically or threatens the religious beliefs of close kin, the fact that it is the cheapest method—or even the fact that it represents the expressed preference of the deceased— probably should not sway your decision. On the other hand, it may be irresponsible to spend on unessential funeral services money that could make a significant difference in the survivors' standard of living.

The social and psychological significance of the various styles of ritual and the several methods of body disposal is so individual and personal a matter that little can be said about it in a book of this kind. Perhaps the most effective way for you to reach a satisfying compromise between the economic and the other considerations is to answer, together with the other involved survivors, the following questions. Although your answers will be determined largely by your collective feelings, the economic implications will be inescapable.

A Body-Centered or a Person-Centered Funeral?

If you focus strongly on the body of the person who has died, you will probably choose (as most Americans do) a service with an open casket, visitation and viewing of the body for one or two days, a cortege to the cemetery, grave burial, and a highly visible grave marker. Because an open casket funeral requires embalming and cosmetic restoration, an above-minimum-price casket, and a number of other goods and services provided by a funeral home (see table 12.1), this is by far the most expensive form of funeral.

If, on the other hand, you feel (as do an increasing number of Americans) that the body is less significant and that you want to focus on the individual's character and social relationships, then you may prefer direct disposal by cremation and a scattering of the ashes, followed by a memorial service at a later time. With this choice, many of the most expensive components of the traditional funeral service—embalming, cosmetic restoration, the casket, the use of a funeral home for visitation, the cemetery plot, and grave marker—are eliminated.

Although the cost differences between the two alternatives are obvious, the psychological differences are not. Some psychologists (and virtually all funeral directors) firmly believe that it is only after viewing the body that survivors accept the reality and finality of the death and that such viewing actually facilitates the grieving process. Some of them believe that even young children should view the deceased's body.

Other psychologists (and many clergymen), however, argue the opposite point of view with equal conviction. They do not feel that viewing a highly cosmeticized corpse helps the survivors accept the death, and they feel that in some circumstances viewing the corpse may be a traumatic experience. They point out that concern with the physical body may divert attention from the quality of the person's relationships, accomplishments, and personality.

There are, of course, no scientific data to support either position, but it is doubtful that such data would change people's convictions. Whatever your personal view, it is important that the choice resulting from it be acceptable to other survivors who may have been as close to the deceased as you were.

LARGELY PUBLIC OR LARGELY PRIVATE?

If the deceased was a public figure or simply a person with a vast number of friends and acquaintances, you may be obligated to give them an opportunity to mark his or her death, and this may require turning the funeral into a public event, complete with visitation and viewing, a large and elaborate ritual service, a cortege, a reception with food and drink, and other features that you personally might prefer to avoid.

In such circumstances, you can, of course, make compromises. Even if the ritual service is likely to attract large numbers of people, there is no need for the casket to be open, and it is quite possible for the committal (whether by burial or cremation) to be restricted to members of the immediate family. It is also feasible to keep the entire funeral simple and private and to hold a larger, more public memorial service at a later date. In general, the more public the funeral, the more expensive it is likely to be.

In thinking about the funeral in relation to people outside the immediate family, it is useful to distinguish between people with whom the deceased was socially *involved* and those whom the survivors would like to *impress*. As we've noted, your social obligation to the deceased's friends and acquaintances is both real and largely unavoidable. On the other hand, some survivors arrange expensive and elaborate funerals merely to impress neighbors with whom they have had no relationship. But a funeral seems a rather futile occasion for keeping up with the Joneses.

CREMATION OR EARTH BURIAL?

Because the aesthetic and philosophical aspects of cremation have been dealt with elsewhere (see p. 167), we shall restrict our discussion here to comparative costs. If you bear in mind that cremation is simply a method of body disposal that can be used with any style of ritual service—from a simple post–cremation memorial service to the most elaborate open-casket-with-visitation service—you will realize that its actual cost requires a rather careful comparison with earth burial (see table 12.1).

Cremation would seem to be cheaper than earth burial because, although ashes may be buried in a cemetery, this is not necessary. If no cemetery plot is used, there are no costs for a grave liner, a grave marker, or for opening and closing the grave. But this obvious saving will be reduced by the charge the crematorium makes for its service and possibly by additional charges if you want the ashes "inurned" and kept permanently in a columbarium, an urn repository usually operated by the crematorium.

Cremation can be cheaper because it requires, instead of a casket, only an inexpensive corrugated cardboard container—but this saving will not be realized if you choose an open-casket ritual service. Similarly, cremation does not require embalming or cosmetic restoration—but neither does earth burial if you decide on a closed casket or a graveside service.

It is likely that the cost difference between cremation and earth burial will increase as the prices of cemetery plots and caskets continue to rise. At the time of this writing, however, cremation is not as much cheaper than earth burial as many people believe, and the fact that it is chosen more often by people who are well-to-do suggests that the choice is made on other than economic grounds.

OBTAINING THE SERVICES YOU'VE CHOSEN

Once you and the other survivors have decided on the method of body disposal and the style of ritual service you prefer, you are ready to get in touch with one of the following organizations.

A DIRECT-DISPOSAL FIRM

Direct-disposal firms operate at present in only a few states, largely because the funeral-industry lobby has successfully opposed them in the others. These firms provide a minimal one-price service that includes removal of the body from the place of death and either burial (in a grave provided by the survivors) or cremation. The disposal is carried out so promptly that no embalming is required, and since there is no viewing of the body, neither is cosmetic restoration. Survivors who use this service usually plan a memorial service some time after the death. They take responsibility, also, for applying for death benefits and for other services normally rendered by the conventional funeral home.

Whether these firms appeal primarily to people seeking low-cost services or to people who take the person-centered rather than the body-centered approach to death is unclear, but the fact is that these firms are flourishing despite the persistent efforts of the funeral industry to place legislative or regulatory obstacles in their path.

If your state does not license direct-disposal firms, there is no reason why you should not ask for similar direct-disposal service from a conventional funeral home. Because the Federal Trade Commission's Funeral Rule requires funeral homes to publish an itemized price list of services, you should be able to order only those services that are absolutely necessary for prompt, direct disposal. You may meet with some resistance or downright refusals, but it is likely that at least one funeral home will quote you a price for exactly what you want.

A Memorial Society

Even if neither you nor the person who has died has a current membership, a local memorial society (see p. 177) may be willing to offer you immediate membership or refer you to a funeral home with which it has a contractual arrangement or an informal relationship based on satisfactory service and prices. Once in touch with a recommended firm, you can usually make whatever arrangements you prefer with reasonable confidence that you will be treated fairly.

A Funeral Home

If your state does not license direct-disposal firms, if your community does not have a memorial society, or if you prefer services that are not available from either, you will need to deal with a funeral home. Because this is the situation in which most survivors find themselves, we have devoted almost all of chapter 13 to this subject.

⚞ **13** ⚟
NEGOTIATING WITH FUNERAL DIRECTORS

Although most of this chapter is devoted to a discussion of the goods and services you will be offered when you shop for a funeral, you are likely to be in a stronger position to negotiate with a funeral director if you have some understanding of the current situation in the funeral industry as a whole.

During the past two decades, the rise of consumer activism generated an increasingly critical public attitude toward the suppliers of a vast array of goods and services, but few of them were attacked as sharply and persistently as the funeral industry. Responses to abuses perpetrated by funeral directors ranged from such exposés as Nancy Mitford's *American Way of Death* to the proliferation of memorial societies, whose fundamental purpose is to help funeral purchasers avoid exploitation. Although a number of states produced legislation intended to curb abuses, the major consumer victory occurred in 1984, when the Federal Trade Commission (FTC) implemented a set of regulations that offer survivors effective protection.

Because the Federal Trade Commission's Funeral Rule (see p. 238) is relatively recent, however, and because memories of earlier abuses are still vivid, many people regard funeral directors as only slightly less devious or dishonest than used-car salesmen.

Although serious abuses do occur, there is no evidence that the funeral industry attracts practitioners of poor moral character or that buyers of funerals are deceived or exploited more frequently than buyers of other goods and services. It is important, therefore, that you understand the relationship between the funeral director and the customer and something about the structure of the industry, because this understanding can help you avoid being exploited—or feeling convinced that you have been exploited, whether you have been or not.

To begin with, all of us share a fear of and a revulsion toward death. But since death itself is too abstract and remote to serve as a target for our feelings, we tend to shift our hostilities and anxieties to the people who deal with it, and thus the funeral director becomes a convenient scapegoat. Moreover, the funeral director sells us goods and services that we don't want to buy and that give us no joy and little satisfaction. And, lastly, the funeral director sells us goods and services with which we have had little experience and which, therefore, we are unable to evaluate critically. By virtue of our ignorance and inexperience, he is in a position to tell us what to buy and then to sell it to us—all this at a time when we are especially vulnerable. Given these circumstances, the funeral director, no matter what his ethical standards, is likely to be regarded with suspicion and hostility.

The structure of the industry also produces practices that disadvantage the consumer. Critics of the industry agree that it is overpopulated, that it could serve the public just as effectively if some 25 percent of funeral homes were to go out of business tomorrow—as indeed they might if they were to compete aggressively with one another on a price basis. It is for self-protective reasons, therefore, that the industry discourages (where it cannot prohibit) itemization of exact charges, price advertising, quotation of prices over the telephone, or any other practice that would encourage competition.

Price competition would, of course, threaten the existence of the small funeral home, because the home that handles one hundred funerals a week does not have fifty times the overhead—in land costs, payroll, preparation facilities, visitation areas, vehicles, or casket inventory—of the small firm that handles only two. But in the absence of price advertising, the customer who is unwilling or unable to do some comparison shopping has no way of knowing whether the price charged by the large firm reflects its relative efficiency or its maximization of profit or whether the price charged by the small firm reflects its inefficiency or the willingness of its owners to subsist on a minimal profit margin in order to survive.

This is why you cannot assume that the larger firm will necessarily quote you a lower price.

On the other hand, many funeral directors urge expensive and elaborate goods and services on their customers not merely to maximize profits but, rather, because they genuinely believe that an elaborate funeral is "better"—just as an automobile salesman genuinely believes that an Audi is better than a Volkswagen or as a university professor believes that a four-year degree is better than a two-year degree and that a doctorate is better yet.

Funeral directors point out in their own defense, moreover, that expensive and elaborate funerals often turn out to be "exactly what the customer wanted." Although this argument may often be disingenuous, there is evidence to indicate that some survivors do prefer to buy an expensive funeral.

Because the goods and services that make up a funeral are highly variable both in number and in price, funeral directors have been accused of sizing up each customer—in terms of severity of grief, level of affluence, and sophistication about funeral practices—and then adjusting services and costs to the maximum that each customer will be willing to pay. Funeral directors readily admit that they size up each customer, but their motive, they claim, is self-protection and not exploitation. They point out, quite correctly, that very few funerals are paid for in advance, that time does not permit a check on the size of the deceased's estate or the creditworthiness of the customer, and that payments are slow and often difficult to collect. Hence, they argue, a quick assessment of the customer is essential, and many of them pride themselves on their skill in making it.

Whatever its motivation, you can protect yourself against this assessment in several ways. First, if you are acutely grief-stricken—so much so that your normal good judgment and your usual consumer skills have deteriorated—have a friend who is emotionally less involved than you are accompany you and monitor all your discussions, decisions, and transactions. And, if you possibly can, give the friend veto power.

Your level of affluence cannot be entirely concealed from the funeral director, because it will be revealed in your clothing, your style of speaking, the car in which you arrive, and your address. But you can reduce the potential for exploitation by demonstrating, at the earliest possible moment in the discussions, that you are aware of the provisions of the FTC funeral rule as well as any additional regulations that may be in force in your state.

THE FEDERAL TRADE COMMISSION FUNERAL RULE

The FTC funeral rule, adopted in 1984 after several years of opposition from the funeral industry, governs several aspects of a funeral transaction including: prices, misleading or deceptive statements or behavior, and charges for the provision of optional services. Under the funeral rule:

- You have the right to choose the funeral goods and services you want;
- The funeral provider must state this right in writing on the general price list;
- If state or local law requires you to buy any particular item, the funeral provider must disclose it on the price list, with a reference to the specific law;
- The funeral provider may not refuse, or charge you a fee, to handle a casket you purchased elsewhere;
- A funeral provider that offers cremations must make alternative containers available for use in the cremation process.

PRICES

Perhaps the most important funeral rule provision—because it facilitates comparison shopping—is the requirement that in response to a telephone call the funeral director must (1) inform you that prices for individual components of a funeral are available by telephone and (2) answer any reasonable questions you raise in the course of your call. This requirement enables you to decide in advance precisely what you want and to telephone (or ask a friend to telephone) two or more funeral homes for information that will permit reasonably accurate price comparisons.

When you visit a funeral home in person, the funeral director is required to provide you with—and let you keep—a price list that itemizes the cost of every product and service offered. This price list must include the entire range of caskets available—from the most expensive to the cheapest—and if the funeral home offers cremation services, the list must include a plain wood box or a corrugated container (both of them much less expensive than a traditional casket).

Once you have chosen the casket and specified the services you want, the funeral director must give you an itemized statement with each of your choices priced separately and must offer you the option of adding or deleting items before making a final decision. Bear in mind that you are not obligated to buy anything you don't want, unless state law or cemetery regulations require it. A particular cemetery may, for example, require you to provide a grave liner, or state law may require embalming under certain exceptional circumstances, but in these situations the requirement must be cited specifically on the statement.

MISLEADING OR DECEPTIVE STATEMENTS

It is illegal for a funeral director to state or imply that any product or service—a special casket, for example, or embalming—will retard or prevent decay of the body or that a more expensive casket or a grave vault will protect the body from water seepage. Similarly, he may not state that embalming is always required by state law. In fact, he must inform you that embalming is not mandatory in any state except in special circumstances, although it is usually essential if the casket is to be open for viewing. If the funeral home offers cremation service, it must not insist that a conventional casket is mandatory and must offer you a less expensive container.

OPTIONAL SERVICES

Some of the details connected with a death—application for death certificates, purchase of obituary notices and flowers, provision of music, pallbearers, or a eulogist—can be carried out by the survivors, but they are often delegated to the funeral director. If these involve out-of-pocket disbursement by the funeral home and subsequent reimbursement by the survivors, the funeral home must inform you whether it adds a service charge to its cash disbursements or whether it receives a discount or rebate from the providers. Where the actual costs of some of these items cannot be precisely determined in advance, the funeral director must provide a reasonably accurate estimate.

DOES THE FEDERAL TRADE COMMISSION PROTECT YOU?

Our summary of the FTC funeral rule may reassure you, but during the years since its adoption, it has proved to be something of a paper tiger. As with other federal regulations, its effectiveness depends less on the stringency of the rule itself than on the resources devoted to its enforcement, and thus far there is no evidence that the FTC has mustered a police force. And even if you recognize that the funeral director with whom you are dealing has overcharged you through a clear violation of part of the rule, the FTC will not help you seek redress. In fact, the FTC's Consumer Protection Bureau states that it "does not resolve consumer or private disputes" but merely invites complaints that "may show a pattern of conduct or practice that the Commission may investigate to determine if any action is warranted." The FTC's Web site (http://www.ftc.gov) explains the funeral rule and includes a helpful publication *Funerals: A Consumer Guide*.

This does not mean, however, that the FTC funeral rule is valueless. Many laws that are poorly enforced (state seat-belt laws, for example) achieve a fair degree of compliance simply because people feel uncomfortable about breaking them. This is likely to be true of funeral directors—especially if you give them evidence, in the early stages of discussions, that you are fully aware of the FTC requirements. Furthermore, should you decide to take a funeral director to court over a dispute, evidence that he has violated the funeral rule will weigh heavily in your favor.

STATE REGULATIONS

Until the adoption of the FTC funeral rule, a number of states had adopted regulations governing funeral-home pricing practices and funeral and burial procedures. Many of these regulations have been superseded by the funeral rule, but those governing matters that are not covered by the rule remain in force.

These regulations are far too heterogeneous and complex to be dealt with on a state-by-state basis, but we can note that some states provide the consumer with significantly stronger protection than others. Oddly enough, the "good" states cannot be distinguished from the "bad" ones on the basis of their geographic location or the characteristics of their populations. Among the most protective states are such very different ones as Arizona, California, Colorado, Florida, New York, and Texas. The states that are least protective of the consumer—among them Iowa, Kentucky, Maryland, Massachusetts, and Tennessee—also appear to have little in common except, perhaps, a politically powerful funeral lobby. But survivors living in a "bad" state may need to be more cautious than those who are better protected by state law.

USING THE FEDERAL AND STATE REGULATIONS

As we have noted, the most effective way of using federal and state regulations to protect yourself against exploitation is to communicate to the funeral director—subtly if possible but emphatically if necessary—that you are aware of the several obligations that the regulations impose on him.

In addition, however, there are tactics and behaviors not prohibited by the regulations that can offer you some clue as to the funeral director's integrity. Does his showroom display of caskets, for example, feature the low-priced caskets as prominently as the deluxe models, or are the latter prominently floodlighted and the former tucked away in a dim corner? Tentatively select his lowest-priced model and note whether he disparages your choice, verbally or by facial expression. Ask to see his suppliers' catalogs and check whether the price range of caskets displayed in his showroom reflects the full price range of caskets available to him or only the more expensive models. Inquire about the lowest-priced model shown in the catalog and note his response about delivery problems—which in fact arise very rarely.

HOW FUNERALS ARE PRICED

The goods and services offered by the typical funeral home generally include the following:

Casket
Vault (unless a grave liner is purchased from the cemetery)

Professional services:
embalming
cosmetic restoration

Use of funeral home and facilities:
for visitation and viewing
for ritual service

Transportation:
for body, from place of death to funeral home
for body, from funeral home to disposal site (via house of
    worship if desired)
for mourners and pallbearers, to and from disposal site
for flowers, to disposal site (via house of worship if desired)

Other services:
professional pallbearers
visitors' register
acknowledgment cards
application for death benefits

Outlays on behalf of survivors:
crematorium charges or cemetery costs—grave, and opening
    and closing charges
copies of death certificate
newspaper obituary notices
flowers for casket
clothing for body (if not provided by survivors)
clergy fee
fee for music provided

Some of these services are, of course, optional, and not all of them are included in what is called, in the language of the trade, a "standard adult funeral." They are listed here simply to provide the context for the several pricing methods used by funeral homes.

More than half of all funeral homes currently use the *unit pricing system:* they quote a single price, which includes the casket and some of the services listed above, for a "standard adult funeral." Under this system, the price of the funeral depends on the price of the casket selected by the customer, but the services provided remain the same in number and quality regardless of the casket price. Outlays on behalf of the survivors—for cemetery plot, obituary notices, etc.—are not included.

Some funeral homes have adopted a *two-unit pricing system:* they quote one price for professional services and a separate price for the casket. Under this system, the various services provided are specified but are not itemized separately.

A third system (advocated by the Federal Trade Commission and currently used by a minority of funeral homes) involves *item pricing:* each component of the funeral, whether essential or optional, is priced separately, and the price list is offered to the customer before any arrangements are made.

Item pricing would seem to be the best system from your point of view. It enables you to compare prices not only among funeral homes offering item pricing but also with those using the unit or two-unit system. Armed with a printed list of item prices, you may be able to negotiate both services and prices with funeral homes offering the "standard adult funeral."

But item pricing is not widely used. Some funeral homes offer an itemized list but insert prices only after discussion with the customer. In such a situation, you can't know whether the prices are standard, whether the funeral director has adjusted them to what he perceives to be your income level, or whether he has raised them to compensate for your choice of a low-priced casket. Moreover, if you reject one of the items (embalming, for example), you may be forced to accept another item (refrigeration of the body).

If you are not overwhelmed by grief or by time pressures, the most effective way to buy funeral services is to decide in advance—at least tentatively—which services you want and to try to get itemized or comparable quotations from two or more funeral homes. You may be able to do this without going from one funeral home to another by yourself. Once you have the itemized list in hand, you may be able to get price information by telephone, even if your state law does not require the funeral home to provide it.

Most funeral directors are reluctant to quote prices by telephone because, they argue, misunderstandings are inevitable when customers do not know which services they want, which services are essential, and which services are included in the quoted price. Critics of the industry, on the other hand, maintain that this resistance to telephone quotation stems from the funeral director's desire to "get hold of the body" or at least the customer before discussing prices. But if you can communicate to the funeral director that you know precisely what you want and if you can imply that you plan to compare his quotations with those of his competitors, you may get results. If not, perhaps you can furnish one or two friends or relatives with your tentative list and have them visit two or more funeral homes to compare prices on everything except the casket, since this is a choice you probably want to make personally.

To help you prepare this tentative list, we shall describe briefly the goods and services offered by the typical funeral home.

CASKET

The casket—usually the most expensive component of the funeral and the most profitable for the funeral director—can range in price from less than five hundred to over ten thousand dollars. Prices are likely to rise sharply, because both wood and skilled labor are becoming more costly and because the rapid disappearance of small manufacturers will leave the market (and hence the control of prices) to a small number of large firms.

A casket is generally bought—or, more accurately, sold—on the basis of three kinds of appeal. The first of these fosters the illusion that the corpse is somehow alive and is therefore sensitive to physical discomfort and to the attitudes of the survivors. This explains the sale of luxuriously upholstered caskets based on the implication that they are more comfortable. It also justifies the argument that "this is the last thing you will ever be able to do for your father," the implication being that your dead father's feelings will be hurt if you choose a casket that is something less than luxurious.

A second appeal capitalizes on the survivors' fantasies about decay of the corpse. Expensive one-piece or hermetically sealed metal caskets are sometimes urged on the survivors with the implication that they will postpone decay. Exhumations have provided fairly conclusive evidence, however, that the construction of the casket has little or no effect on the rate of decay—even if this were a desirable goal. Casket manufacturers who offer a ten-year or twenty-year guarantee that their product will remain intact are quite safe in doing so because they are altogether unlikely to be presented with claims by unsatisfied customers. Both the FTC funeral rule regulations and some state regulations prohibit any claims that caskets postpone or prevent decay, and most funeral directors don't make them, but a good deal of casket salesmanship relies on this claim, which is usually subtly suggested rather than explicitly stated.

A third appeal implies that because it is the most conspicuous element in the funeral, the casket is an important indicator of social status—that a "quality" casket advertises the socioeconomic level of both the deceased and the survivors as well as the survivors' love and respect for the deceased. In actual practice, however, the price of the casket is often related inversely to the affluence of the deceased.

Your choice of casket may be influenced not only by your susceptibility to these appeals but also by your preferences for other elements of the funeral. If you plan to choose an open casket for viewing of the body, you may feel that the casket will be the focus of considerable attention. A closed casket, on the other hand, plays a less prominent part in any ritual, and an inexpensive model can be covered with a pall or with flowers. If you choose cremation, you will need only an inexpensive container; if cremation is to be preceded by a ritual service with the body present, it can, in some states, be placed in a rented casket; in others, the cremation container can be inserted in a rentable casketlike enclosure.

Entering the casket display room to make a selection is, for many survivors, one of the most traumatic episodes of the entire bereavement process, and their emotional state makes a rational selection difficult. Compounding the difficulty is the practice of some funeral directors of placing the less expensive caskets in inconspicuous, poorly lighted corners of the display room and, by subtle arrangements of lighting and room arrangement, focusing the customer's attention on the medium-priced and more expensive models. This wordless "bait and switch" strategy is sometimes reinforced by a display of the least attractive versions of the cheaper models (even though more attractive models are readily available) or by gestures, facial expressions, or even remarks of disapproval when the customer shows interest in the less expensive models.

The FTC Funeral Rule, as well as some existing state laws, require that a certain number of caskets in the lowest price range be displayed in every funeral home, but even in the absence of such regulations your persistent inquiry about minimum-priced models should yield results. If you don't like those that are on display, ask to see the manufacturer's catalog; any model it lists can usually be delivered promptly. If the style of the casket doesn't matter to you, inquire about the price of the Orthodox Jewish casket. Because religious law requires that this be a plain wooden box with no ornamentation whatever, it is likely to be inexpensive, and it is available almost everywhere. Many people like its simplicity and austerity.

VAULT OR GRAVE LINER

Once you have chosen a casket and decided on grave burial rather than cremation, you are likely to be offered a vault—a container in which the casket is enclosed in the grave. Although you may be told that the vault serves to "protect" the casket (and hence, presumably the body), its actual purpose is to prevent the ground level of the grave from sinking as the casket deteriorates with the passage of time. This purpose is served just as effectively by a cast-concrete grave liner, which can be bought from the cemetery at a substantially lower price.

Neither vaults nor liners are required by any state law, and you should be suspicious of any funeral director who implies that they are. Some states, however, give the individual cemetery the right to require a liner as a condition of burial. If you are concerned with the long-term condition of the grave, the liner may provide some protection against future maintenance problems.

EMBALMING

Embalming involves the replacement of the blood and other body fluids by a preservative solution in order to retard decay. If it is to be effective in preserving the body for purposes of viewing in an open-casket ritual, it must be done within about eight hours of death, by which time some deterioration has already begun. If the body is intended as an anatomical gift, however, embalming will render it unacceptable unless it is done under the supervision of the medical school or other recipient.

No state requires embalming in all cases, and some states (as well as the FTC Funeral Rule) prohibit it without the consent of a survivor, but all states require it in certain circumstances, such as death from a communicable disease, delay in body disposal, or interstate transportation of the body.

Embalming is not necessary if you choose direct disposal, and it is usually unnecessary if you choose cremation followed by a memorial service—although one state, presumably under pressure from the funeral industry, requires embalming if the body is held more than twenty-four hours but prohibits cremation sooner than forty-eight hours after death.

In some circumstances, deterioration of the body can be retarded by refrigeration instead of embalming, but refrigerator space is not always available, and the process is not inexpensive. If the body is to be viewed, it will require intermittent periods of refrigeration, and its low temperature is likely to shock mourners who want to touch or kiss it.

COSMETIC RESTORATION

Cosmetic restoration is unnecessary if a closed casket is used or, of course, if you choose direct disposal. But when an open casket is used, most survivors insist on it. An unrestored corpse is gray in color (because blood has left the surface capillaries), with open mouth and staring eyes, but these inescapable facts of death are likely to be traumatic to the survivors and other mourners who would like to see the deceased "as we remember him."

On the other hand, the quality of the restoration is always something of a gamble. Some funeral directors do a remarkable job of producing a likeness but, in the process, reduce the deceased's apparent age by ten to twenty years. Others produce a gross carica-ture that is a source of severe distress to the survivors and cannot be corrected to their satisfaction once the body is ready for viewing.

CLOTHING

For open-casket viewing, the body will, of course, have to be clothed, and many funeral homes offer a wide array of styles and colors. There is no reason whatsoever to buy this merchandise if you have access to a favorite dress or suit that belonged to the deceased.

VIEWING, VISITATION, AND RITUAL FACILITIES

If you choose an open casket, you will probably want to use the funeral home for visitation and viewing, and you will recognize that charges for the use of these facilities are legitimate. If you choose a closed casket, however, you may prefer to invite mourners to visit you at home, in which case the casket can be stored in the funeral home until committal, and the funeral-home charges are reduced accordingly.

The same holds true for the use of the funeral home for any kind of ritual service. If you plan to hold a memorial service at home or elsewhere after the body has been disposed of, or if you plan a service at a house of worship, there is no justification for a funeral-home charge for use of its chapel (although there will be a charge for transporting the body to and from the house of worship).

One alternative, which represents a compromise between direct disposal and a traditional funeral, is a graveside service with a closed casket. Although the funeral home may impose a charge for the additional time involved at the graveside, this should be more than offset by elimination of the charges for use of the chapel, for viewing, and possibly for embalming and restoration. The graveside service is commonly used when death has occurred elsewhere and the casket is brought directly from the airport to the cemetery.

TRANSPORTATION CHARGES

The "standard adult funeral" usually includes charges for transporting the body from the place of death to the funeral home, and thence to the cemetery or crematorium, and for one limousine to transport the principal mourners to and from the disposal site. Your decision to order additional limousines will be based, of course, on the number and the emotional states of the mourners, but usually such a decision can be made at the last minute—during the ritual service, if necessary. Generally, most mourners can be relied upon to drive their own cars and to provide space in them for those who don't.

If flowers are involved, there is likely to be an extra charge for the vehicle that transports them from the funeral home to the church or the cemetery but not for arranging them in the funeral home.

OTHER SERVICES

The traditional funeral home provides a number of miscellaneous services that should be specified when you make arrangements, whether or not their cost is itemized.

Death Certificates

In settling the estate, you will need a certified copy of the death certificate in order to transfer ownership of *each* piece of real estate, *each* stock certificate, and *each* motor vehicle; to collect the benefits payable under *each* insurance policy; to collect funds in retirement accounts and pay-on-death bank accounts; to retitle securities subject to transfer-on-death accounts; and to collect *each* death benefit; as well as for a variety of other purposes, such as gaining access to the deceased's safe-deposit box.

Virtually all funeral homes will offer to obtain these certificates for you from the local county clerk or the state health department. But there are two concerns connected with this offer. First, although some funeral homes provide this service at actual cost—the nominal fee charged by the county clerk or the health department—others add a surcharge, which you can easily avoid by the simple process of getting the copies yourself. Second, it is almost impossible for you to know, at the time you are making arrangements, precisely how many certified copies of the death certificate will be necessary in settling the estate, and consequently you are likely to order either too many or too few. The best solution may be to order only the minimum number that is needed immediately and to obtain additional copies yourself as the need arises.

Death Benefits

Funeral homes may offer to file applications in your behalf for any Social Security or Veterans Administration death or burial benefits to which the survivors are entitled, but often they will do this only if the benefits are applied to the funeral bill. Although this service may relieve you of responsibility for some or all of the funeral bill (see p. 226), and although it eliminates your having to file the applications yourself and waiting for payment, it has one disadvantage. If the funeral bill is presented to the executor with the death benefits already credited, the executor may regard the bill as reasonable, whereas the total bill may in fact be unreasonably high and hence challengeable. On the other hand, payment of the entire bill from the estate's assets reduces the net value of the estate and thus may eliminate the need for probate.

Pallbearers

Unless the funeral service takes place in a house of worship, pallbearers are unnecessary, because funeral-home employees will move the casket into and out of the hearse. If they are necessary, you can choose them from among the friends of the deceased, bearing in mind that carrying part of the combined weight of casket and body is not a task for the physically frail. An alternative is to ask the funeral home to provide professional pallbearers and to designate the deceased's friends as honorary pallbearers. You will, of course, be charged for the services of the professional pallbearers.

Crematorium or Cemetery Arrangements

If you do not own a cemetery plot and if you have not already made arrangements for disposal of the body, the funeral director can help you choose a cemetery or a crematorium and will add the charges to his bill. In some circumstances, this service can be very helpful, because funeral directors are usually well acquainted with all cemeteries and crematoriums within a reasonable radius of the community. As we shall see shortly, however, problems can arise when the funeral home advances substantial sums of money in your behalf.

Obituary Notices

The funeral director will usually offer to place paid obituary notices in the appropriate local newspapers and to help you with the wording of the notice. His experience can be useful, because grief-stricken survivors tend either to omit essential information from the notice or to overload it with unnecessary detail.

CASH OUTLAYS BY THE FUNERAL DIRECTOR

A number of the services described above—obtaining the death certificates, placing the obituary notices, buying a cemetery plot, or paying the charges for opening and closing the grave—involve cash disbursements by the funeral director in your behalf. In addition, the funeral director will also add to the bill gratuities for the hearse and limousine drivers and for the grave diggers.

At first glance, it would appear that the funeral director's willingness to take care of all these transactions spares you a good deal of effort and inconvenience at a time when you are under stress—and often this is the case. But critics of the funeral industry point out that this convenience is not always free of charge. Some funeral directors add to the bill an amount greater than the sum of the separate disbursements; others obtain discounts (for obituary notices, for example) that they fail to pass on to the customer. Worse yet, in some instances, clergy complain that they never receive the honorarium for which the funeral director has billed the customer.

There is something to be said, therefore, in favor of your handling some of these matters personally. Since you are not likely to select a grave or a crematorium sight unseen, you may as well make the financial arrangements at the same time that you inspect the site. You may want to see to it, also, that your honorarium for the clergyman reaches its intended destination, especially since, if you make your check payable to the church, mosque, or synagogue rather than to the individual, the amount becomes tax deductible as a charitable contribution.

WHEN TWO FUNERAL HOMES ARE INVOLVED

When a death occurs away from home—perhaps as the result of an automobile accident or a heart attack during travel—your best plan is to get in touch with a funeral director in your own community. He will make arrangements with a funeral director near the scene of death, and the two will collaborate on the services required to produce a complete funeral. You should not be charged more than the price of a "standard adult funeral" for their combined services, but you can expect to be billed for certain services you might not have required had the death occurred at home. Embalming, for example, is almost universally required if a body is to be shipped interstate, and airfreight charges for a casketed body are substantial. You can avoid the former and significantly reduce the latter by deciding on cremation where the death occurred and holding a memorial service locally at some later date.

SPECIFYING THE FINAL DETAILS

As we have noted, the funeral director is in the ethically difficult position of having to *advise* the customer which goods and services to buy and, at the same time, having to *sell* them to the customer. This is why customers who don't know what they want and put themselves into the hands of a funeral director whose entrepreneurial role requires him to maximize profit are rather likely to be exploited. After reading this chapter, however, you should have developed a reasonably clear idea of what you want and, more important, what you don't want. And just as you have learned to disregard or reject the suggestions of the automobile salesman who tries to sell you expensive options, so you should feel quite comfortable about rejecting funeral goods and services that strike you as inappropriate or unnecessary.

The funeral industry is, as we have noted, highly competitive, despite the absence of price competition in public advertisements. Every funeral director knows that an inexpensive funeral is more profitable than no funeral at all, and some may feel forced to forego any profit merely to pay their continuing overhead costs. Consequently, if you come to the funeral home with a set of clearly defined specifications, and if you can convey the impression that you are there to buy a funeral, not to be sold one, you are likely to get exactly what you want, and at a competitive price.

Although the funeral industry is, on the whole, probably no more dishonest than any other retail business, it has lobbied vigorously and successfully against regulation by both federal and state governments. Since regulation is often proposed in response to widespread or severe consumer abuse or exploitation, it is important that you be on your guard.

If you use our summary of the FTC funeral rule as a guide during your discussions, bear in mind that no funeral director is likely to comply with every one of its requirements. But if the funeral director with whom you are dealing violates a significant number of the more important provisions, you should probably visit one or more of his competitors.

DEALING WITH A CREMATORIUM

Unlike the funeral home industry, the crematorium industry is not overcrowded, and you are unlikely to have much choice among competing firms unless you live in a metropolitan area. And, again unlike funeral homes, crematoriums do not offer an essentially identical range of services. Some firms, catering mainly to survivors who choose direct disposal, provide only crematory service, which includes delivery of the ashes in a sealed canister to the survivors. Others provide, in addition, viewing and visitation facilities and a chapel for ritual services. Still others include facilities for the disposal of the ashes: a garden in which the ashes may be scattered or a columbarium, a building containing tiers of niches in which the ashes may be permanently inurned. All these differences in the range of services offered make price comparisons difficult.

In general, however, your guiding principle probably should be simplicity. The choice of cremation instead of grave burial is made more often by the deceased than by the survivors, and if the survivors disagree with it they can, as we have noted (see p. 225), disregard it. Hence, those survivors who comply with the deceased's wishes presumably share the philosophy underlying the decision: a lack of concern for the physical remains. With this in mind, they are less likely to seek preservation of the ashes in a decorative urn set permanently in a columbarium niche and more likely to see cremation as a method of swiftly returning the body to its basic elements.

SEEKING REDRESS

Because funeral negotiations usually take place under severe emotional stress and time pressure, you may, despite your best efforts, be misled, overcharged, or cheated. Although the FTC will not investigate or resolve individual complaints, you are not completely without resources.

Your first step (and the easiest to take) is to discuss the issue with the funeral director in the hope that the difficulty stemmed from a misunderstanding rather than any intent to defraud you. If this fails, the Better Business Bureau of your community may be helpful. But don't despair if the Better Business Bureau is of no use. Although in recent years this organization has strengthened its efforts on behalf of the public, some of its branches tend to retain their original function: protecting their merchant members from customers who feel that they have been victimized or treated unfairly.

Another possible resource is your state "mortuary board"—the administrative body that controls the licensing of funeral directors. As in the case of the Better Business Bureau, the degree of cooperation and support you'll receive depends on the state in which you live. Some states include on their mortuary boards not only licensed funeral directors but also "public" members, whose explicit function is to represent and protect the interests of the consumer; other state boards consist entirely of funeral directors. Some boards are concerned with professional ethics; others are concerned primarily with restricting entry to the industry and thus protecting current practitioners against newcomers and other competitors.

The Funeral Consumers Alliance (http://wwwlfunerals.org) a group "dedicated to protecting a consumers right to choose a meaningful, dignified, affordable funeral," offers helpful information and many links.

But before you take any action, you need to be as certain as you can that you are not directing against a perfectly honorable funeral director your very understandable anger or resentment over the death itself.

≈ 14 ≈

THE WILL: GUARDIANSHIPS AND OTHER FIRST STEPS

Although detective novels may have left you with the impression that an urgent search for the will immediately after a death is a mark of villainous greed, the fact is that a will should be located and read promptly because it is likely to contain information that may be needed immediately. Disposing of the deceased's property is only one function of a will, and often not the most important one. In addition, the will may:

Make anatomical gifts of the deceased's organs or entire body.

Express the deceased's preferences as to funeral rites or body disposal.

Nominate a guardian for minor children, and possibly a conservator for any assets inherited by them.

Nominate an executor (sometimes called a personal representative) to manage the deceased's assets and to settle the estate.

Identify specific assets owned by the deceased.

Not every will, of course, is likely to deal with all these matters, but most wills contain some instructions that require very prompt action as well as some that can, or must, be delayed. Organ or body donations, for example, or funeral preferences must receive immediate attention. And the appointment of a guardian for minor children is at least as urgent. The identification and disposition of the deceased's assets, on the other hand, may be a long-drawn-out process extending over several months at the very least. But since the survivors cannot be certain just what the will specifies, they should find it and read it without delay.

FINDING THE WILL

If the deceased was a person of orderly habits, he probably told one or more members of his family (or specified in his letter of instruction) that he had signed a will and perhaps had deposited it for safekeeping in the local probate court or left it in his lawyer's office or at his bank. In such cases, a telephone call to the court, the lawyer, or the bank can confirm the existence and whereabouts of the will and arrange for obtaining copies.

But because some people are not orderly and some die unexpectedly, it is not uncommon for survivors to be uncertain about the existence of a will and totally ignorant of its location if, indeed, one exists at all. In such circumstances the survivors may be tempted to conclude that the deceased left no will, since over half of all Americans die without one, but this statistic is misleading because it covers people of all levels of education and income. If the deceased was reasonably well educated and had even a moderate net worth, or left minor children, a search for a will should begin at once.

One common storage place for a will is a bank safe-deposit box rented by the deceased. Although, as we shall see (p. 274), access to the deceased's safe-deposit box may be restricted by state law, the probate courts of most states will permit access to the box for the express purpose of searching for a will (or a deed to a cemetery plot) and filing it with the court. Permission usually requires the filing of a petition with the court—a process that is simple but too slow to make anatomical gifts feasible.

If the safe-deposit box fails to yield a will or information as to its whereabouts, your next step is to find out from the deceased's bank whether he had nominated the bank as executor of the estate or as trustee of a trust. Often, in such cases, the lawyer who prepared the will sends a copy to the bank, along with information as to the whereabouts of the original documents. Indeed, some banks and trust companies provide safekeeping services for original wills, trusts, and related documents.

Another source of clues is the deceased's check register or file of canceled checks, which may yield the name of a lawyer who prepared a will. And in some cases it may be advisable to publish in a local newspaper a notice inquiring about the possible existence and whereabouts of a will signed by the deceased.

If these sources yield nothing, you will need to search the deceased's home, especially those places where he habitually kept personal papers—a desk, a filing cabinet, a strongbox, perhaps even a box stored in a closet or dresser drawer. However, although you ought to search conscientiously, there is no need to turn the house upside down. Most Americans, even some with considerable assets, *do* fail to make a will—or they sign an informal do-it-yourself document that has no legal standing in states that do not recognize holographic wills. In either case, the deceased will be regarded as having died intestate.

Intestacy can be inconvenient and sometimes expensive, but it should not be regarded as a disaster. In most cases, the probate court will comply with the wishes of the survivors with respect to the appointment of an executor or a guardian for minor children. It is only in connection with the disposition of the deceased's probate assets that the court is bound by state law rather than by the preferences of the survivors—and this becomes significant only if the deceased's probate assets are substantial.

Once you have found a will, open it and read it. Although movies and novels tend to depict the reading of a will as a formal and legalistic procedure, no formalities whatever are required by law. Some states require that the original will, upon its discovery, be promptly filed with the probate court—and this may be advisable for its protection even if it is not compulsory—but there is no reason why you should not make one or more photocopies for yourself and for any other interested party.

Your first reading of the will should enable you to classify its instructions into three categories: (1) matters that can be taken care of immediately by you or other survivors, (2) matters that involve the probate court but require prompt attention, and (3) matters that either can or must be delayed. The rest of this chapter will deal with the first two of these categories, because those in the third category cannot be attended to until you have read the next chapter.

STEPS YOU CAN TAKE BY YOURSELF

ORGAN AND BODY DONATIONS

If the will makes an anatomical gift of one or more of the deceased's organs or of the entire body, time is of the essence, but fortunately you often do not need prior court approval of the will in order to carry out the deceased's wishes. Simply get in touch with the donee specified in the will and make arrangements for the transfer, with a clear understanding as to who is responsible for any transportation costs. If no donee has been specified, you can usually find a willing recipient by getting in touch with a local hospital, organ bank, or medical school.

Don't blame yourself, however, if you discover the will too late to make such gifts possible. As we have noted, anatomical gifts should be made by means of a uniform donor card and not a will—because they must be carried out within hours of the death. Wills are all too often not found and read in time, especially by survivors who worry about showing indecent haste.

FUNERAL ARRANGEMENTS

The deceased's preferences for funeral rites and body disposal may also be found in the will, although the will is as inappropriate a vehicle for these preferences as it is for anatomical gifts—and for the same reasons. If the will is found in time, most survivors attempt to carry out the wishes of the deceased, but it is doubtful that the will is legally binding on them if the deceased's preferences will seriously deplete the estate. If, for example, the estate amounts to $20,000 and the will specifies a funeral that is likely to cost $10,000, no court will fault the widow for disregarding her husband's wishes, arranging a more modest funeral, and conserving as much of her husband's estate as she feels is necessary for her own continued support.

IDENTIFICATION OF ASSETS

As we noted in chapter 1, a properly drawn will should refer to assets in general terms rather than make a complete itemization, which would require an amendment each time the assets change. In the absence of a letter of instruction, however, the will may provide you with clues as to the existence of certain assets—as, for example, in the sentence "I give my one hundred shares of AT&T common stock to my nephew, James Brown." This should alert you to look for the stock certificate and, if you fail to find it, to get in touch with the deceased's stockbroker or with AT&T to find out whether the deceased still owned the stock at the time of death.

STEPS INVOLVING
THE PROBATE COURT

Although in the minds of most people the primary function of the probate court is the administration of the deceased's probate estate, an equally important function is the protection of the person and property of minor children orphaned by the death. If the deceased was a sole surviving parent of minor children or if both parents of minor children died simultaneously, your first—and perhaps only—contact with the probate court may be in connection with the appointment of a guardian to protect and assume custody of any minor, and a conservator to manage the minor's inheritance, or both. The probate court having jurisdiction over minor children is located in the courthouse of the county in which the children reside and is listed in the phone book under the name of the county.

GUARDIANS OF THE PERSONS OF MINOR CHILDREN

Unmarried minor children—in most states individuals under eighteen years of age—not only need to be provided with food, clothing, shelter, health care, discipline, supervision, and guidance, but, in addition, they are legally incapable of enrolling in school, consenting to medical or dental treatment, marrying, enlisting in the armed services, and engaging in a number of other activities without the consent of a parent or legal guardian. Obviously, then, the appointment of a guardian for orphaned minors is a matter of real urgency.

If the will has nominated a guardian for a minor, and if the guardian consents to undertake the responsibilities, the court will almost invariably approve the appointment. Some states permit the nomination to be made in a writing separate from the will—but in most cases parents use a will. Once the nomination is approved by the court and the guardian notifies the court in writing that he or she is willing to accept the appointment, the court issues *letters of guardianship* certifying that the guardian is entitled to act, in all respects, in place of the minor child's deceased parent or parents.

In some situations there may be conflict or confusion over the appointment of a guardian, but most of these are resolved by law. If, for example, the minor's natural father and mother name different guardians in their respective wills, the guardian named in the will of the parent last to die takes precedence. If parents are divorced and the mother has custody of the children, the guardian nominated in her will is not likely to be appointed as long as the children's natural father is willing to serve and is not found unsuitable to take custody of the child. And if the natural father dies after his divorced wife, his nomination of guardian will take precedence over hers, even though she has custody of the children.

In all such situations, however, the court is, by law, required to be concerned primarily with "the best interests of the child," and hence any interested party—grandparents, aunts, uncles—can challenge the appointment of any person they regard as manifestly unsuitable or unfit. In all states, in fact, a minor fourteen years of age or older may challenge the appointment of his or her guardian either before or after the appointment is made by the court. The objections must be submitted to the court in writing, and the child may nominate another person as his or her guardian, but the final decision is made by the court.

If the guardian nominated in a will or other writing is unable or unwilling to serve or if the minor's parents died without nominating one, the court is authorized to appoint anyone it chooses. This is usually done after a hearing, at which all interested parties may attend. Again, the court's overriding concern is "the best interests of the child," and priority will be given to a nomination by a minor fourteen years of age or older if the minor's nominee seems suitable to the probate judge.

Guardianship of a child is a responsibility that should not be undertaken lightly. To begin with, it is a long-term involvement that does not terminate until the child marries, reaches the age of majority, or is adopted by others. Second, any money bequeathed by the parents or others to the child must be used exclusively for the child's benefit and must be accounted for, and any excess must be carefully preserved for the child's future needs. On the other hand, although the guardian cannot be held *legally* responsible for the expenses involved in rearing a child, there is a *moral* responsibility that may prove burdensome to the guardian if the deceased parents did not leave enough money to cover the child's expenses—a common situation. The guardian can, of course, resign from the job by petitioning the court, but this is practicable only if another capable adult is available and willing to assume the guardianship.

PROTECTING THE PROPERTY OF MINOR CHILDREN

Because minor children are by law incapable of owning, managing, or selling any kind of property, some provision must be made for the management of any assets they inherit.

If the deceased's estate planning was thoughtful and the value of the child's inheritance is substantial, the deceased probably established a trust, to be managed by a trustee for the benefit of the minor children. If the trust was created and funded before the death, whatever assets it owned are immediately available to the trustee without any need for administration by the probate court. If, on the other hand, the trust was created in the deceased's will and (as opposed to a living trust created separate from a will) thus did not become effective until the death, any probate assets destined for the trust other than life insurance will most likely need to undergo probate administration. In either case, there is little that you as a survivor can do to alter the trust arrangement established by the deceased.

In the majority of cases, however, no trust of any kind is established by the deceased for minor children, and in such cases the procedure to be followed depends largely on the value of the deceased's assets and the laws of your state. In some states, if the value is less than a specified maximum (for example, $5,000), the executor may turn the management of the child's inheritance over to the child's legal guardian (or to the child's parents if, for example, the bequest was made by someone other than the parents). If, on the other hand, the child's inheritance exceeds the state limit, the probate court will appoint a conservator (also called a guardian in some states) of the child's estate, to receive, hold, and manage the inheritance until the child reaches the age of majority.

If the will has nominated a conservator for the child's assets, the court will usually appoint the nominee. In the absence of such a nomination, or if there is no will, the court may appoint either an individual or a financial institution.

There is no legal reason, of course, why the person appointed as guardian of the child's person should not petition the court for appointment as conservator of the child's estate as well, because unless the assets are complex and substantial, no great financial acumen is required. In fact, in most states the role of the conservator is highly restricted: he is charged solely with responsibility for protecting the assets and for ensuring that they are used exclusively for the support of the minor. Selling the assets in order to reinvest the money for higher yield usually requires the permission of the probate court, and in some states even the court is restricted to authorizing only a narrow range of ultraconservative investments.

Given these restrictions, a conservator who is highly sophisticated in financial matters is more likely to suffer personal frustration than he is to increase the value of the assets for which he is responsible. The conservator may also be frustrated by the fact that his responsibility ends when the child attains majority, age 18 in most states. At that time, the child's assets, whatever their value, are turned over to the child, whether or not he or she is mature enough to use them wisely.

Appointment of the Executor

Whether or not it nominates a guardian or a conservator for minors, every properly drawn will nominates an executor, but whether this appointment should be confirmed by the probate court immediately requires careful judgment. To begin with, if the deceased followed some of the suggestions offered in chapter 2, there may be no probate assets and hence no need for an executor. Even if probate assets exist, they may, if they do not exceed a specified amount, be transferable by simplified "small estate" probate procedures that avoid or significantly minimize probate-court administration.

In many states, however, these simplified transfer procedures are not available if a petition for the appointment of an executor, is pending or has been granted (see tables 16.1 and 16.2). If you are premature in petitioning the court to appoint an executor, you may inadvertently disqualify the survivors from taking full advantage of the "small estate" transfer procedures, which are invariably simpler, quicker, and less expensive.

On the other hand, there are many circumstances that require the appointment of an executor at the earliest possible moment. If the deceased left a business that is still operating, he may have designated in his will someone who is competent either to manage or to liquidate it. If the deceased left real estate, an investment portfolio, or even a savings account with a balance of more than $5,000 titled in his own name, you can be quite certain that an executor will need to be appointed to manage such assets and to distribute them according to the terms of the will.

If the appointment of an executor seems inevitable at the outset, you may as well proceed with the court formalities immediately, because until he is appointed, none of the assets can be managed or disposed of. Furthermore, the appointment of an executor does not in itself commit the estate to proceed with formal probate administration.

On the other hand, the appointment may involve the estate in expenses that may ultimately prove unnecessary if an inventory of the assets reveals that nothing requires probate or that the probate assets do not exceed the maximum value allowed by your state's "small estate" transfer procedures. In most cases, then, the sensible plan may be to postpone the appointment of an executor until your inventory of the assets, as explained in chapter 16, determines whether the appointment is necessary.

PROBATE ADMINISTRATION OF THE ESTATE

Thus far, we have dealt with the preliminary functions of the probate court—essentially the protection of minor children and their inheritances, and possibly the appointment of an executor. In the eyes of many people, the more important function of the court is to oversee the distribution of the deceased's probate assets—either to the beneficiaries named in the will or to the heirs specified by state law in the absence of a will.

In reality, however, only a small percentage of decedent's estates require full administration by the probate court. Moreover, the need for probate is not necessarily related to the size of the deceased's estate. Indeed, very large estates are most likely to be planned so that probate administration is successfully avoided. If however, the deceased died without leaving a will, the probate court may become involved, even if the assets amounted to only a few thousand dollars. But if the deceased left a will and assets valued at millions of dollars, you cannot be sure that probate-court administration will be necessary until you have separated the probate from the nonprobate assets. This procedure is explained in the next chapter.

✑ 15 ✑

SORTING OUT
THE ASSETS

After almost every death remains some unfinished business that becomes the responsibility of the survivors. Any property owned by the deceased, for example, must be identified, perhaps appraised, and protected until it can be disposed of. Often there are moneys coming to the deceased: salary or pension checks, for example, or stock dividends and tax refunds. Usually there are bills or other obligations that the deceased incurred but did not pay. In addition, there may be insurance proceeds to collect, tax returns to file, death benefits to claim, and other financial matters to be attended to.

Your first task as a survivor, then, is to make a complete inventory of the deceased's assets and liabilities as promptly as possible. This inventory will serve two purposes. First, it will give you and the other survivors a realistic picture of what you can expect in the way of inheritance. Second, it will tell you whether the deceased's estate will require lengthy (and often expensive) administration by the probate court or whether it can be distributed to the survivors through much simpler "small estate" transfer procedures or without any probate action at all.

If the estate is large and complex, the deceased is likely to have nominated in his will a professionally qualified executor—a bank, trust company, or trusted friend or family member—to handle the inventory and settlement processes. If this is the case, your personal responsibilities may be few, but this chapter can help you ensure that the executor does the job competently and overlooks nothing.

In the vast majority of cases, however, responsibility for handling the estate falls into the hands of a surviving spouse, a lifetime partner, or an adult child who has never before had such an experience. For such survivors, this chapter is intended as a fairly specific "how to do it" guide.

If you find yourself in this position, there are two reasons why you may be tempted to skip or merely skim this chapter. On the one hand, you may have participated so actively in the deceased's financial affairs that you feel you know everything you need to and that the procedures described in this chapter are "obvious." Experience shows, however, that such survivors often make serious mistakes, because handling the affairs of someone who has died is different in many respects from participating in them while he or she was alive.

On the other hand, you may shun this chapter for the opposite reason—because you know nothing at all about the deceased's financial affairs other than that the estate amounts to little or nothing. In such a situation, you are likely to overlook available death benefits that are all the more important if, in fact, the estate is small or insolvent and if the survivors need every cent that can be recovered.

The settlement of a deceased's estate, even a modest one, can involve so many seemingly urgent matters that you may either "freeze up" and do nothing because you don't know what to do first or, feeling the pressure of time, you may make hasty and unwise decisions. Actually, a priority sequence is fairly simple to establish: your first task is to get into the hands of the survivors whatever money and other possessions they need immediately in order to continue their normal lives; second, you need to attend to those of the deceased's assets that may depreciate (or fail to appreciate) in value until their ownership has been transferred. All other matters can be safely postponed, and some of them may take weeks or months to conclude despite your best efforts. In fact, you are likely to conclude, after reading this chapter, that settling a deceased's estate requires patience and persistence rather than financial sophistication and experience.

WILL THE ESTATE REQUIRE PROBATE ADMINISTRATION?

As we have noted, sorting out the assets will help you determinate whether or not the estate will require administration by the probate court. This is important to know because your responsibilities as a survivor will be largely governed by the answer to this question, but the answer will depend both on the nature of the assets and on your understanding of why, and under what circumstances, probate administration is necessary.

The basic purpose of the probate process is to ensure that all assets belonging to the deceased are distributed properly—that the persons named in the will (or the heirs designated by law if there is no will) receive what they are entitled to, that all taxes are paid, and that the deceased's creditors collect their lawful debts. The key phrase in this definition is "belonging to the deceased," because this means that any property owned jointly by the deceased and another person (who survived the deceased), or any assets held in by a living trust established by the deceased (see p. 44), or life insurance and financial accounts having designated beneficiaries, is *not* part of the probate estate. Thus, for example, stock certificates or bank accounts in the sole name of the deceased at the time of death are subject to probate administration, but those jointly owned with a surviving spouse simply pass to the survivor without any form of probate-court administration. Life insurance proceeds are not probate assets unless the deceased's estate or executor has been designated as beneficiary; otherwise they pass directly to whichever survivors are named on the policy as beneficiaries, as do the proceeds of pension plans and retirement accounts, including IRA, SEP, Keogh, and 401k accounts. Pay-on-death bank accounts and transfer-on-death securities accounts pass directly to the designated beneficiaries, without probate administration.

The same principle holds true for debts: charge accounts, loans, or other debts in the deceased's name alone are subject to probate, and this means that the deceased's creditors can collect what is owed them only from the estate. But debts on which another person has cosigned remain the responsibility of the surviving cosigner as well as the estate.

As you can see, the need for probate administration is not necessarily related to the value of the assets that the deceased left for the survivors. If the deceased followed the advice offered in chapter 2, he may have reduced the value of his *probate* assets to a few hundred dollars or to nothing at all, even though he left to the survivors assets worth millions. On the other hand, some people leave assets of very modest value that, because of their form of ownership, require formal administration by the probate court.

Unless you have participated actively in the affairs of the deceased, you may not know at the outset whether or not the estate includes probate assets or what the current value of these assets amounts to. By the time you have concluded your inventory, however, you will know which of the following four situations you face and precisely what you have to do:

1. *You may discover that there are no assets whatever that require probate*—because all of the deceased's assets were owned jointly, were held in a living trust, or consisted of life insurance or financial accounts that designate beneficiaries. In this situation the will does not need to be probated because, in fact, there *is* no probate estate; the deceased left nothing that belonged exclusively to him and did not automatically pass to survivors by operation of law. Hence, your only responsibility is to be of whatever help you can in seeing that jointly owned or trust-owned assets and any life insurance proceeds and financial accounts actually pass to the appropriate survivors. You may, of course, discover a long-forgotten bank account in the deceased's name alone with a balance of perhaps only $50, but you may decide that it is easier to abandon this account and let it ultimately pass to the state treasury than to go through the formalities of probate-court administration. Before abandoning such an account or, for that matter, any other asset, however, you should read p. 299 to determine whether it can be transferred to the survivors by utilizing one of the "small estate" transfer procedures that obviate full probate administration.
2. *You may need to petition the probate court to appoint you as executor.* This may be necessary if you discover assets owned exclusively by the deceased that must be sold or transferred to another person. As executor, you will be authorized by the court to manage or liquidate the deceased's property, gain access to his bank safe-deposit box, and conduct most of the transactions that the deceased could have conducted had he not died.

   Petitioning the court for appointment as executor is in itself neither expensive nor time-consuming (see p. 309), and it does not commit you to full probate administration of the estate. You should consider it, therefore, just as soon as you discover any assets that require the action of an executor—a solely owned piece of rental property, for example—because if you find one such asset, you are likely to find more as you continue your inventory.

3. *You may be able to take advantage of two swift and simple procedures known as transfer by affidavit or "small estate" probate administration.* Because the probate assets and liabilities that most people leave when they die are relatively low in value and simple in nature, all states have adopted various simplified transfer procedures that are inexpensive, informal, and relatively speedy. The legally specified maximums vary from one state to another, from a low of $3,000 to a high of $140,000, usually exclusive of the value of any motor vehicles (see p. 300). Your county probate court or a lawyer skilled in estate law can provide you with the details.

4. *The estate may have to undergo full probate-administration* if the value of the probate assets exceeds the state maximum for transfer by affidavit or "small estate" transfer procedures. Probate court administration of an estate is described in detail in chapter 16, but because it is lengthy as well as expensive, it should be initiated just as soon as your inventory proves it to be necessary. As we point out on p. 309, serving as the deceased's executor throughout the full probate process is not insuperably difficult, but since you will inevitably need the help of an estate lawyer, getting in touch with one in the early stage of your inventory gives you the advantage of his advice and help in the later stages, even before the formal probate process begins.

It is important that the lawyer you select be experienced in estate settlement law. If you cannot find one by word of mouth through trustworthy friends, you might ask the clerk of your probate court, your banker, or the lawyer-referral service of your local or state bar association for the names of several lawyers who specialize in estate planning and settlement.

IDENTIFYING AND LOCATING THE ASSETS

The difficulty you experience in identifying and making an inventory of the assets will depend, of course, on your relationship with the deceased. If you are an adult child who has lived at a distance from a deceased parent, you are very likely to be less familiar with his or her financial affairs than if you are a widow or widower who took a strong interest in your deceased spouse's every transaction. No matter what your situation, however, you would do well to read the next few pages carefully, because experience shows that even those survivors who participated actively in the deceased's affairs tend to overlook some assets, benefits, or opportunities to increase one or the other.

THE LETTER OF INSTRUCTION

If the deceased left a letter of instruction for his survivors (see chapter 10), your task will be vastly simplified. The letter, if it is reasonably up to date, will specify in full detail the nature, location, and current value of most, if not all, of the deceased's assets and liabilities. In addition, the letter will probably specify the whereabouts of a will, trust, or other estate planning papers. This is why locating the letter of instruction promptly is a matter of the highest priority.

Your search, however, should not become a frantic and time-consuming process, because most people who prepare a letter of instruction tell their survivors about its existence and whereabouts, and may have distributed copies. Actually, the letter is a relatively recent planning tool. As a consequence, many people die without having prepared one. If you don't find one after searching the deceased's safe-deposit box, his desk drawers, or any other place where personal papers are kept, and contacting the deceased's lawyer, you can safely assume that one doesn't exist.

CHECKING ACCOUNTS

In the absence of a letter of instruction, your most useful "roadmap" of the deceased's financial affairs is likely to be his checkbook, his bank statements, his file of canceled checks, and his computer files, if any. A careful review of every check written during the several months immediately preceding death should give you reasonably reliable information on the following:

Insurance policies—checks for premium payments will identify the insurance company and possibly each current life, accident, or health policy.

Land contracts and mortgages—payment checks can help you identify the properties subject to these liens.

Investment accounts—checks will identify brokerage accounts, money market or mutual funds, recent specific securities purchases, and IRA, SEP, Keogh, 401k, and other retirement accounts.

Charge accounts and loans—checks should help you determine the current level of indebtedness.

Federal, state, and local income taxes—checks will indicate payments and, hence, accounts still payable.

Property taxes—payments can identify the deceased's real estate.

Utility payments—bills paid can identify owned property not revealed by tax or mortgage payments.

Hospital, medical, and nursing expenses—payments should be checked against recent health-care bills and against health-care insurance policies for possible reimbursement.

Payments for goods and services not actually used—airline tickets, for example, which can be refunded in full if they were not used.

License fees for cars and other vehicles—checks can identify vehicles owned by the deceased.

Charitable contributions—if you will be responsible for filing an income-tax return on behalf of the deceased.

Bank safe-deposit box or post-office box rental—so that you can locate the boxes.

Similarly, a careful review of each deposit noted in the checkbook or ledger may help you identify such sources of assets or future income as:

Rents on income property

Stock dividends and bond interest payments

Payments on mortgages, land contracts, or promissory notes held by the deceased

Royalties on patents, mineral rights, or books

Insurance dividends—a clue to paid-up policies

Tax refunds

Social Security, Veterans Administration, and pension benefits

Fees for consultation or other services
Deposits for electricity, telephone, and other services

This review is not likely to unearth every single asset. The deceased may have had some stock dividends that were paid directly into a savings account or a money market fund. Similarly, he may have made some regular payments by means of money market fund checks. And paid-up life insurance policies that do not pay dividends will not appear in the bank record. Nevertheless, tedious though it may be, your examination of the deceased's banking activities will save you a great deal of time and trouble in the later stages, especially if you take responsibility for filing the deceased's last federal and state income-tax returns.

THE DECEASED'S MAIL

A second source of information about assets and liabilities is the mail that will continue to arrive for the deceased, because, in addition to advertising matter and social correspondence, it is likely to contain dividend and pension checks, bank and brokerage statements, payments on debts owed to the deceased, utility bills, and bills or notices about insurance premiums, charge accounts, and other liabilities.

The postal regulations governing delivery of the deceased's mail are reasonably clear. When the local post office hears of the death of a mail recipient (either through notification by a survivor or, informally, through the letter carrier, who may notice mail accumulating at the address), it will hold the mail for fifteen days and then return it to the sender. Most of the deceased's mail can be claimed at the post office or readdressed through the usual change-of-address form either by an adult family member or an heir who can provide the postmaster with satisfactory identification and a copy of the death certificate or by a formally appointed executor, who must show the postmaster his letters of authority (see p. 310).

But not all the deceased's mail will be available to you through these procedures. Most U.S. Treasury checks—for Social Security or Veterans Administration benefits, for example, but not income-tax refunds—must be returned by the postmaster to the sending agency. Other government checks—state, county, or municipal—must be handled in accordance with instructions printed on their envelopes, as must mail containing driver's licenses, credit cards, and other documents intended for the exclusive use of the deceased.

If the deceased rented a post-office box, a survivor who has the key or the combination can continue to collect all mail but is legally obligated to return to sender any U.S. Treasury checks and other materials mentioned in the preceding paragraph. Usually, however, the survivor will find it more convenient to sign and file a change-of-address form and thus avoid periodic visits to the post office to monitor the box.

Normally the mail-collection procedure works smoothly, but occasionally problems arise: the postmaster may, for example, receive two different change-of-address forms, each signed by a different survivor, either because the survivors are in conflict or because they did not communicate adequately with one another. In such circumstances the postmaster will honor the change form signed by the executor; otherwise the deceased's spouse will have priority. If family conflict persists, the postmaster is authorized to deliver the mail to a third party agreed upon by the family members or to refer the dispute to the U.S. Postal Service regional counsel, whose decision as to who may receive the deceased's mail is final.

If you become responsible for the deceased's mail, you should immediately sort out all mail addressed to joint owners (bank statements, dividend checks, bills, etc.) and send it on to the surviving joint owner, because none of it constitutes part of the deceased's assets or liabilities. The rest of the mail should be separated into five categories:

1. Assets—checks and other items payable to the deceased alone
2. Liabilities—credit card and charge-account statements, utility bills, premium notices, tax bills, and other notices of payments due
3. Social correspondence
4. Magazine subscriptions
5. Advertising and other "junk mail."

The handling of assets and liabilities will be dealt with later in this chapter and in the chapter that follows. Social correspondence can be answered personally by you or another survivor or by means of a simple printed announcement of death. Magazine subscriptions, if they are of no interest to the survivors, may be transferred to a friend or a local library or, if relatively recent, can be canceled along with a request for a refund for future issues. Advertising mail can, of course, be discarded when received.

Although the volume of mail addressed to the deceased is likely to diminish rapidly, it should be monitored conscientiously for at least six months and preferably for a year. Some banks, money market funds, IRA, Keogh, and 401k account managers, and other investment facilities issue statements only annually; most bond interest is payable only semiannually; and many certificates of deposit have terms of one year or more. Similarly, some insurance premiums are payable semiannually or annually. Unless you watch the mail over a long period of time, you may overlook both assets and liabilities.

There is no need, however, to delay settling the deceased's estate in the hope that such assets may turn up later. It is always possible to reopen the probate estate—months or years after it was closed—for the purpose of settling and distributing newly discovered assets.

THE BANK SAFE-DEPOSIT BOX

Like the deceased's mail, his bank safe-deposit box may contain actual assets (such as cash, collectibles, jewelry, or unregistered bonds) or documentary evidence of assets (such as insurance policies, property deeds and land contracts, stock certificates, bills of sale, receipts, vehicle titles and registrations, savings passbooks, money market certificates, promissory notes, mortgages, and the like). In addition, the box may contain a will, a trust agreement, a letter of instruction, a property inventory or other documents identifying the whereabouts and ownership of certain assets. It may also contain a military service record.

Unless you are a surviving joint lessee of the box, you may not be aware that the deceased rented one, but it is a mistake to assume that he didn't. If your review of the checking account did not turn up any evidence of box-rental payments, look among the deceased's personal belongings for a flat, multinotched key, often enclosed in a small envelope, or inquire at the banks at which the deceased maintained accounts or conducted business.

Access to the box and its contents may present problems. Unless you have been appointed executor or unless you can enlist the cooperation of a surviving co-lessee, the bank will not permit you to open the box. Even if you are a surviving co-lessee, the bank, on hearing of the death, will often "seal" the box and allow you to open it only in the presence of a representative of the state treasurer, who will inventory its contents for tax purposes.

In those states that require it, requesting a state treasurer representative to make the inventory is quite simple, and any bank officer should be able to arrange it without delay or tell you how to do it. Although its primary purpose is to protect the state against possible tax evasion, it can also protect you in case disputes arise among the interested parties as to what was or was not in the box at the moment it was opened. Even if you are a surviving co-lessee or the deceased's executor, you should not open the box unaccompanied, because this leaves you vulnerable to possible accusations with respect to its contents. If several beneficiaries are available, have them go with you and sign or initial a dated inventory of the box's contents.

Joint rental of a safe-deposit box does not in itself constitute conclusive evidence that its contents are owned jointly. Unless there is compelling evidence to the contrary, the contents may be presumed to be the sole property of the deceased and hence probatable as part of the deceased's estate. Stock certificates and bonds registered in joint ownership become, of course, the property of the surviving joint owner, but unregistered bonds and untitled assets (cash, for example) and such items as coin collections, precious stones or metals, and other valuables are considered the sole property of the deceased unless there is documentary evidence to prove joint or custodial ownership. Women's jewelry found in a box leased jointly by husband and wife will be presumed to belong to the wife, but the ownership of such jewelry found in a box leased jointly by two brothers will depend upon such evidence as receipts, bills of sale, canceled checks, or written statements of ownership.

Once the contents of the box have been inventoried by the state treasurer's representative, those assets that are jointly owned should be distributed to the surviving joint owner. Those that represent probate assets must be protected against theft, loss, or damage until they are transferred to the entitled beneficiaries by one of the procedures described in the next chapter. One way to do this is to store them in a safe-deposit box leased in your own name so that you will have access to the contents at any time.

PROTECTING THE ASSETS

Your review of the deceased's checking account, your monitoring of his mail, and your inventory of his bank safe-deposit box should give you not only a fairly clear picture of the assets and liabilities but also an answer to the question of whether the deceased's assets will require probate court administration. But whether or not the estate must eventually pass through probate, you are likely to have some immediate responsibilities. You may have to consolidate—and in some cases manage—the assets and protect them until they are disposed of. And you may have to decide which of the liabilities must be settled immediately and which can be postponed or ignored. To help you do this effectively, we will deal, in the pages that follow, with those assets and liabilities that comprise the typical deceased's estate.

HOUSE AND CONTENTS

In many, if not most cases, the house and its contents constitute the largest part of the deceased's estate and, therefore, are extremely important to the survivors.

If the house was owned jointly (usually with a surviving spouse), its ownership passes automatically to the surviving joint owner without any need for probate administration. The surviving joint owner need only record a certified copy of the death certificate with the county register of deeds to establish, as a matter of public record, that he or she is now the sole owner and is therefore exclusively entitled to occupy, rent, mortgage, sell, or otherwise control the property.

This new sole ownership by the survivor, however, makes the house part of the survivor's probate estate when he or she eventually dies. You may want to advise the surviving owner, therefore, to make a new will and to consider some of the strategies for probate avoidance described in chapter 2.

If the deceased's home was titled in the name of the trustee of a living trust (see p. 47), the procedure is just as simple: the trustee or successor trustee named in the trust will, depending on the terms of the trust, either hold the house in trust, sell it, or deed it to the beneficiaries designated in the trust, and record the new deed with the county register of deeds—again without the need for any administration by the probate court.

If, however, the house (or other real estate) was owned solely by the deceased, it is a probate asset, and it will eventually have to be disposed of by a court-appointed executor under the supervision of the probate court. Meanwhile, it is critically important that both the house and its contents be protected against any kind of loss or damage. This means that you should make mortgage payments if failure to make them may result in foreclosure; you should pay utility bills if termination of service might damage the house or its contents; and you should pay premiums to maintain insurance protection against fire, burglary, vandalism, and personal liability.

If you have been designated as executor, you are authorized to pay these expenses out of the estate assets (see p. 317). But even if you make these payments out of your own pocket before the probate court has formally appointed a executor, you are entitled to be reimbursed from the estate's assets.

The general procedures described above apply also to second homes, summer cottages, condos, co-op apartments, vacant land, and all other real property. If they are not owned jointly or by the trustee of a living trust, they should be carefully protected until they are disposed of by the transfer procedures described in the next chapter.

The fact that a house or condo was owned jointly does not mean, strictly speaking, that its contents were also owned jointly. In practice, however, joint ownership of the contents is often presumed, and the home's contents pass to the surviving joint owner, except for items specifically willed to other people—a stamp collection, for example, or a piece of antique furniture. Such items may be effectively transferred by will, however, only if they can be proved (by receipt, bill of sale, or assignment) to have been solely owned by the deceased. If, for example, the deceased bequeathed a prized shotgun to a hunting companion, his wife might refuse to let him have it on the grounds that it was jointly owned with her, having been purchased with money contributed by both spouses or by use of a credit card that was issued to both of them, or that the deceased left written evidence specifying that the shotgun was jointly owned with the spouse or another person.

If an asset is proven to be solely owned by the deceased, it is a probate asset and will pass according to the deceased's will, or if none, according to state intestate succession laws (see table 1.1). If the asset is proven to be the subject of a gift made by the deceased during his life, the donee keeps it even if the will purports to bequeath it to someone else.

MOTOR VEHICLES

Many motor vehicles are not owned jointly—and there are good reasons why they should not be—but this does not mean that their transfer to survivors necessarily requires formal probate administration. Many states have adopted swift and simple procedures for transferring titles of the deceased's vehicles to a surviving spouse, adult child, or other next of kin (see p. 300). Only if there are no interested or eligible survivors is a motor vehicle likely to require formal probate court administration.

Pending its final disposition, however, whether by transfer to a survivor, by gift to a beneficiary, or by liquidation, the deceased's motor vehicle belongs to the deceased's estate. Hence, you have a responsibility to protect it from deterioration and from involvement in accidents, because in the event of an accident the estate, as well as the driver, may be responsible for any liability exceeding the existing liability insurance coverage. Insurance premiums should be paid when due. Storage of the vehicle can protect it against both deterioration and accident. If possible, you should decline requests by survivors to borrow the vehicle as long as it remains registered in the name of the deceased.

BANK AND BROKERAGE ACCOUNTS

Like all other jointly owned assets, bank accounts, securities, and other investments, upon the death of one co-owner, become the property of the surviving joint owner. To transfer title on a joint bank account, the surviving owner merely files with the bank a new signature card identifying him or her as the sole owner, although some banks may require a copy of the death certificate. To avoid the need for probate administration when he or she dies, however, the surviving joint owner may want to create a new joint account—perhaps with an adult child or with a trusted younger friend—or to use one of the other probate avoidance measures described in chapter 2.

Funds in the deceased's pay-on-death bank accounts are also easily collected without any need for probate administration. The person designated as beneficiary on the POD account need only present identification plus a copy of the deceased's death certificate, after which the bank will pay the account balance, if any, to the POD beneficiary.

Jointly owned brokerage accounts are handled in much the same way as joint bank accounts. If securities have been held in the broker's "street name" in a joint account, the broker need only be instructed to change the name on the account to that of the survivor as sole owner. To carry out this change, the broker will require a certified copy of the death certificate, certain other forms that he can prepare for the signature of the surviving owner, and, in some states, a waiver from the state treasurer certifying that state tax has been paid or is not payable.

If, on the other hand, the securities are registered in the names of the joint owners rather than in the broker's "street name," this same procedure will have to be done for each of the securities through the corporation's transfer agent. Any stock broker can assist in this process. If the deceased's securities are held in a transfer- on-death securities account, they are immediately transferable to the designated TOD beneficiary, likewise without any need for probate administration.

The transfer of jointly held assets is not a pressing matter, because the surviving owner enjoys full control of them and of their dividends or interest even before formal transfer takes place. Assets that are held solely in the name of the deceased, however, need prompt attention, and usually their management requires that an executor be appointed. As soon as you encounter such solely owned assets, therefore, you should read the next chapter to determine whether their transfer requires the appointment of an executor and formal probate administration. If it does, a petition for appointment should be filed promptly so that the executor can be authorized to collect, manage, and ultimately dispose of those assets.

In the case of solely owned bank accounts, both savings and checking, the executor may need to provide each bank with a copy of his letters of authority and direct that the accounts be closed and that a check for the account balances be delivered to him. With respect to IRA, SEP, Keogh, 401k and other retirement accounts *on which the deceased named a beneficiary*, nothing more need be done than to see to it that the balances are paid to the beneficiary. But first consult with your lawyer or tax adviser about tax advantages in delaying withdrawal, or rolling over the funds to the beneficiary's IRA. Such accounts, like life insurance policies, are not considered probate assets. If, however, the deceased failed to name a beneficiary, the executor should handle them in the same way as other solely owned bank accounts.

MANAGING THE ASSETS

Moneys collected by the executor should be deposited in one or more bank accounts under the name "John Jones, Executor of the Estate of Mary Smith, Deceased," but the type of account chosen involves careful consideration. Since the executor will use this money to pay the funeral bill and other obligations of the deceased and to transfer assets to the beneficiaries, a checking account will be essential. On the other hand, until the checks are written, the executor should try to protect the money against erosion from inflation by depositing it into an interest-bearing account.

Any account that is federally insured (an account in a bank or a savings and loan association) offers high security but a relatively low yield. The conscientious executor may therefore feel that he should seek a higher yield through some sort of short-term investment such as a money market fund. But because most such funds are not insured, the executor should not use them unless he is authorized to do so by the will, by the probate court, by state law, or by all the estate's beneficiaries and creditors.

Any checks payable solely to the deceased that arrive after the death can legally be deposited in an account in the deceased's name or in the executor's account. But because all such deposits become probate assets, salary checks and checks representing other employee benefits should not be deposited until it is determined whether they can be distributed to the survivors by the simplified procedures described in chapter 16.

Income tax refunds on a jointly filed return may be turned over to a surviving spouse. Refunds on the deceased's individual returns are a probate asset of his estate.

Solely owned brokerage accounts require prompt action. Any margin accounts should be liquidated and closed immediately, because a sudden drop in share prices will result either in a call for more margin (for which the estate is liable) or the sale of the shares at unfavorable prices. At the same time, the executor should cancel any open orders to the broker to buy or sell shares.

Securities owned solely by the deceased, whether in his own name or in a broker's street account, should be left in the deceased's name until you have determined whether they can be transferred to the survivors by one of the "small estate" procedures described in chapter 16. If this is not feasible, they should be disposed of promptly unless you have good reason to believe that their value is likely to appreciate in the near future. A cautious and conscientious executor who feels that stock prices are low at the moment may be tempted to hold the securities until they can fetch higher prices. Because nobody can consistently predict the behavior of the stock market, however, this tactic is risky and should be used only with the consent of all interested parties. In general, the executor is expected to manage all estate assets prudently, and it is probably safer to err on the side of conservatism.

PROMISSORY NOTES, LAND CONTRACTS, AND OTHER ACCOUNTS RECEIVABLE

Your review of the assets may disclose accounts receivable that will remain owed to the deceased for a long time into the future, often in indeterminable amounts: a ten-year promissory note or land contract, for example, royalties from a book, or leases of mineral rights that may go on indefinitely in irregular amounts.

In order to avoid keeping the estate open indefinitely for the sole purpose of receiving these payments, the executor can arrange an assignment of the accounts to the entitled beneficiaries so that all future payments are made directly to them. If there are several beneficiaries, each entitled to a share of the payments, they can designate a bank as their collection agent. The bank, in return for a fee, will collect each payment and distribute it among them, either by separate checks or by direct deposit to their accounts.

"WRONGFUL DEATH" CLAIMS

A possible source of assets sometimes overlooked by survivors is money damages that may be recoverable if the deceased's death was caused, in whole or in part, by the intentional or negligent behavior of someone else. Although such damage claims are probably most common when death results from an automobile accident, it is also possible to sue physicians, hospitals, and other health-care providers for failure to make a correct diagnosis or provide appropriate medical care. Similarly, claims can be made against building owners for structural defects or inadequate maintenance, against manufacturers and retailers of unsafe or defective products, against employers for failure to maintain a safe work environment, and against police departments for use of excessive force resulting in death.

Some commentators, citing the recent rise in medical malpractice claims, conclude that we are becoming an increasingly litigious society, but the proliferation of such claims can also be explained by the fact that more people are receiving medical treatment and are better informed about their legal rights and remedies. Other commentators argue that many justifiable wrongful death claims are never pursued simply because the survivors fail to recognize that they have a viable claim or because they feel that filing a claim is not worth the time, effort, psychological stress, and possible costs.

If the deceased's death can be linked in any way to someone's intentional or negligent behavior, you should make every effort to identify the person or persons involved and discuss promptly with a skilled personal injury lawyer the possibilities of pursuing a wrongful death claim for money damages. In considering such a claim you should bear in mind two well-established legal principles. First, the death need not occur immediately after the negligence; the recovery of money damages may be justified even if death occurred many months after the precipitating event. Second, under the laws of many states, it is not necessary that the wrongdoer's negligence be 100 percent responsible for the death. Even if the wrongdoer's behavior is found by the judge or jury to have been only 25 percent responsible, the other 75 percent having been caused by the deceased's contributory negligence, 25 percent of the claimed damages may be awarded to the deceased's estate or the survivors, depending on state law.

Examples of successful negligence suits are not hard to find, and those presented here should help you understand that the underlying negligence need not always be clearly apparent or immediately present. In cases of death by fire, building owners have been sued for maintaining unsafe premises or violating fire codes even though the victim had been smoking in bed. Owners of swimming pools have been held responsible for leaving open a gate through which a child wandered in and subsequently drowned even though the child's parents may have been negligent in their supervision of their child. And, of course, automobile manufacturers have been sued as a result of deaths attributed to faulty vehicle design or manufacture even though the victim's driving behavior may have precipitated the accident in whole or in part. It is a mistake, therefore, to assume that a wrongful death claim will necessarily be unsuccessful simply because the deceased's behavior contributed in part to his own injury and consequent death.

Two further considerations may discourage survivors from pursuing damage claims. First, there is the notion that the negligent party is not worth suing "because he obviously hasn't enough money to pay a judgment of any size." This conclusion is, of course, premature until the possibilities of insurance coverage have been investigated—especially in states with compulsory automobile liability insurance. Second, many people believe that a lawsuit is simply too expensive to initiate even if the prospect of an eventual recovery seems favorable.

Actually, the cost of pursuing a claim need not be a deterrent because most lawyers who take such cases are willing to do so on a "contingent fee" basis: if the lawyer recovers money damages, he is entitled to keep a specified portion (usually one-third of the net recovery) as his fee for services. If he loses the case and recovers nothing, he receives no fee at all.

Although the contingent fee arrangement has been called "the poor man's key to the courthouse" and although it would appear to make damage claims affordable by anyone, it is not without its downside. The processing of a damage claim typically requires the lawyer to incur out-of-pocket expenses—for purchasing transcripts and other records, for hiring expert witnesses, and ordering records and tests, for taking depositions and conducting investigations, and for the payment of court costs—and these expenses, though normally advanced by the lawyer, are ultimately chargeable to the client whether the case is won or lost. Thus, if you fail to win a lawsuit, either you or the deceased's estate (depending on who hired the lawyer) may face legal costs of several thousand dollars. If you approach a lawyer about evaluating a damage claim, therefore, be sure to discuss not only the contingent fee but also the anticipated amount of and responsibility for the out-of-pocket expenses.

Although many survivors neglect to initiate a viable claim, there are others who are all too eager to bring suit. This occurs not necessarily because they are naturally litigious but because they may be trying to find an outlet for the frustration and grief caused by death. If a close relative dies after surgery, for example, the survivors may allege faulty work by the surgeon or improper care by the hospital staff even though both may have been performed in exemplary fashion. One might think that a lawyer's negative opinion would deter such people from bringing suit, since few successful personal injury lawyers are likely to reject the pursuit of a claim that has merit; but because the motivations for bringing such suits are largely psychological, an objective opinion from the lawyer to the effect that the claim is without merit may lead only to a search for a lawyer with a different opinion.

If you believe that you have grounds for a wrongful death claim on the deceased's behalf, you should consult a lawyer promptly, since such claims must be filed within one to three years following the deceased's death and because critical evidence—for example, autopsy results, medical records, accident-scene photos, preservation of a wrecked auto or its parts—must be gathered and preserved while it is still fresh. Finding a competent personal injury lawyer may be as difficult as finding one experienced in estate planning, because this is a field crowded with lawyers seeking such often lucrative cases. The state bar association's lawyer referral service is a far more reliable source than the Yellow Pages or television and Internet commercials. Once the lawyer and you sign a contingent fee agreement, he will investigate the merits of the claim and the financial condition or insurance coverage of the alleged wrongdoer. He will then submit a written claim to the wrongdoer or his insurance company setting forth the claim's factual and legal basis and demanding money compensation for some or all of the following items of damage:

Conscious pain and suffering experienced by the deceased
Ambulance, hospital, and medical expenses
Funeral and burial expenses
Loss of income or support that the deceased would have provided to his dependents had he enjoyed his full life expectancy
Loss of the society and companionship that the deceased would have provided to his family

If the claim has merit and if the wrongdoer has sufficient assets or insurance coverage, the response to your lawyer's letter is likely to be an offer of an out-of-court settlement, for an amount somewhat less than you initially demanded. Your lawyer may or may not be able to negotiate an increase in this settlement offer, but acceptance of a settlement will provide the beneficiaries with immediate cash, avoid the delay, expense, and uncertainties of litigation, and eliminate your anxiety about a procedure with which you and the other survivors are likely to be unfamiliar.

You may explore the possibility of a damage claim without having yet been formally appointed as executor, but if you have not been appointed, the lawyer's out-of-pocket expenses may become your own responsibility rather than the estate's. If, however, you receive a settlement offer or if the case must go to trial, an executor may have to be appointed. Acceptance of a settlement check requires a release that can be signed only by someone who legally represents the estate, and the initiation of a lawsuit requires the same kind of representation. In some states, monies recovered either through a settlement offer or as the result of a lawsuit accrue to the estate and become probate assets, ultimately to be distributed to the beneficiaries designated in a will, or to the heirs designated by law. In other states, however, wrongful death proceeds are payable directly to certain survivors specified by law—typically the deceased's spouse and children.

REVIEWING THE LIABILITIES

As you continue to monitor the deceased's mail, you will almost certainly find bills, statements, premium notices, and other evidence of debts. Bills for goods and services that have been bought jointly (or through a joint charge account) remain the responsibility of the deceased's probate estate as well as the surviving joint debtor. If the estate has sufficient probate assets, the surviving co-debtor may prefer that the estate pay off the debt in due course. But if the estate's assets are insufficient and the surviving debtor wants to preserve a good credit rating and avoid continuing interest charges, the debts should be paid promptly. Bills or statements addressed to the deceased alone but which involve jointly owned property (utility, oil, and telephone bills for a jointly owned home, for example) should also be paid by the surviving joint owner, especially if he or she intends to continue to own and occupy the property.

Debts incurred by the deceased alone, however, confront the executor with a dilemma. Strictly speaking, these obligations are payable by the estate, and hence the executor should not pay them until he has determined (1) that they are legitimate and (2) that the estate has enough money to pay them, because if the estate has insufficient assets, some of the creditors need not be paid in full.

Furthermore, the "small estate" procedures in some states (see chapter 16) permit the transfer of the deceased's assets to the survivors without regard to the claims of creditors. All these considerations should lead you to postpone paying any such bills until you have a clear idea of the value of the probate assets and the type of probate administration, if any, they will require.

On the other hand, failure to pay certain kinds of bills—mortgage payments, charge accounts, taxes, or utility bills—may, as we have noted, harm the estate in one way or another. In such situations, whether or not you have been formally appointed executor, you must use your best judgment. If you are convinced that the charges are legitimate and that the bills must be paid promptly, you can pay them out of your own pocket and claim reimbursement from the deceased's probate estate. But doing this entails two risks. First, the estate may have insufficient assets to reimburse you, or the estate may have such low value that it is not required to pay any of its creditors, as we shall see in the next chapter. Second, the creditors of an estate are ranked by law in a specified order of priority (see p. 317). If you have paid a low-priority creditor, you may be held personally responsible for the high-priority creditor's unpaid claim. For these reasons, you should probably postpone the payment of any bill that is reasonably postponable—at least until you have read the next chapter.

Whether or not you decide to pay charge accounts promptly, the charge card should be either destroyed or, in the case of cards issued by banks, returned to the bank that issued it. Destroying it will prevent unauthorized use, but it will not terminate the annual fee that many banks charge for the use of the card. Returning it to the bank will avert further use charges and may produce a refund of the unused annual fee.

Because many survivors apparently feel that they are paying their respects to the deceased by settling all his outstanding debts regardless of their nature, it is important to recognize that in many cases they are under no legal obligation to do so. The Uniform Probate Code provides that under certain circumstances (see p. 306) the deceased's debts may be ignored. The intention here was to discourage survivors from depleting small estates because they felt morally obligated to prevent the deceased from "having died a debtor." Every creditor makes provision for a certain percentage of "bad debts," and there is no reason why survivors should not recognize this reality.

Of course, if the deceased left no assets whatever, there is no reason for the survivors to pay his debts, because no law requires anyone to assume the debts of another, no matter what their relationship.

COLLECTING NONPROBATE ASSETS

Once you have taken care of the chores enumerated above, you should have a fairly clear notion about the value of the deceased's probate assets and the amount of the estate's liabilities. You should also know whether any kind of probate procedure will be necessary—although you may not know what kind of probate is involved until you read the next chapter.

There are, however, several other types of assets to be collected that, although they are not part of the probate estate, nevertheless belong to the beneficiaries. Because these assets do not require probate administration, collecting them may not strike you as urgent. They may, however, amount to a considerable sum of money that is urgently needed by the survivors, and it is likely that they are earning little or no interest at the moment. Accordingly, you should not postpone collecting them any longer than is absolutely necessary.

LIFE INSURANCE

The proceeds of the deceased's life insurance policies, if the designated beneficiary is one or more living persons, a charitable institution, or any kind of existing organization, are payable directly to the named beneficiary without the need for any probate procedures. Only if the designated beneficiary is the deceased's *estate* or the *executor of the estate*, or if there is no surviving designated beneficiary, do the proceeds become part of the probate estate. Because policies with a designated beneficiary other than the "estate" need not be used to pay any of the deceased's debts, they sometimes constitute the most important asset left to the survivors, and hence the proceeds should be collected promptly.

If the deceased left a letter of instruction, it will almost certainly list and describe any current life insurance policies. If, however, you find no policies in the various places where you looked for a will—a safe-deposit box, desk drawers, etc.—don't conclude that none exist. Review the deceased's canceled checks for the preceding twelve months for a check payable to a life insurance company or agency, review the checkbook deposit record for evidence of a dividend check on a paid-up policy, and question the agent who handled the deceased's other insurance coverages. Also, be sure to ask the deceased's employer whether it has provided any life insurance coverage on the deceased's life, as this is a common fringe benefit available in both private and public employment. Lastly, check the deceased's automobile insurance policy or member association for possible death benefits.

Once you have discovered life insurance coverage, obtain from the local agent or from the insurance company a claim form, which you will have to submit to the company together with a certified copy of the death certificate. The application form need not be signed by a formally appointed executor unless the beneficiary is the deceased's estate, in which case the executor must submit a copy of his letters of authority along with the claim form.

If the insurance company requires you to surrender the original policy along with the claim form and any supporting documents, be sure to photocopy the face sheet of the policy as well as the application form and your covering letter, which should list and describe all the enclosures. If you cannot find the original policy, ask the insurance company for an affidavit form on which you can indicate that the policy has been lost. The fact that the policy is lost is not, by itself, a legal basis for denying benefits. Your letter should also request the return of any unearned premiums (because the deceased may have died only a month or two after having paid an annual premium) as well as any dividends due if the policy normally earned dividends. The entire package should be sent by registered or certified mail so that you will have a receipt in case the company later asserts that it never received your claim.

Because insurance companies occasionally are reluctant to pay life insurance proceeds, you need to be prepared to act aggressively in response to the following tactics, which have been used to delay or avoid payment:

The Claim Was Not Submitted Promptly

Some policies contain a clause specifying that the claim must be submitted within a certain time after the death—usually 90 or 180 days. Although it is doubtful that this restriction would be enforced by the courts today, you can avoid expensive litigation by submitting the claim promptly.

Fraud in the Original Application

The company may assert that the insured, in making the initial application for coverage, misrepresented or omitted parts of his medical history that might have led the company to reject him as uninsurable. This pretext is sometimes used, because virtually nobody, in filling out an insurance application, can accurately list *every* detail of his medical history. Some beneficiaries, however, are so intimidated by the mention of "fraud" that they fail to pursue the claim.

It is important to note that an insurance company that alleges fraud must assume the burden of proof: it must demonstrate that the insured's misstatements or omissions were intentional rather than the result of a memory lapse, that the misstated or omitted condition was related to the insured's death, and that the company relied and had a right to rely on the insured's misstatements in deciding to issue the policy. Generally the fraud defense cannot be successfully raised by the insurer after two years beyond the issue date of the policy.

Suicide

Most policies provide coverage for death by suicide if it occurs more than two years after the issue date of the policy. When such coverage is excluded, however, insurance companies occasionally claim that an accidental death was in fact a suicide. Again, it is important to recognize that the burden of proof lies with the insurer and that suicide is often difficult to prove. In such circumstances an autopsy may be critical in determining the cause of death. Some apparent suicides can be proven by autopsy to have been accidental. Furthermore, what appears to be a suicide may be authoritatively characterized otherwise by the attending physician or the medical examiner if the deceased was mentally ill at the time of death.

Lapse for Nonpayment of Premiums

Insurance companies sometimes reject a claim for benefits on grounds that the policy had lapsed for nonpayment of premiums. This rejection should not be accepted without a careful scrutiny of the policy. Many policies specify that if premiums are not paid, a certain amount of coverage nevertheless remains in effect or that the policy's accumulated cash value can be used to maintain some level of continued coverage. Moreover, the insurer may be legally barred from raising a lapse payment defense if it fails to prove that it gave the insured adequate notice of the lapsed payments.

If you sense any recalcitrance on the part of the insurance company or if your claim is denied for any reason, your first step is to contact your state insurance commission or similar regulatory agency and inquire if they will help. If this fails—or if your state regulatory agencies have a poor record of consumer advocacy—consult a lawyer. Often the mere threat of legal action gets results from large insurers who may be reluctant to have a jury decide a dispute between a multimillion dollar insurance company and a widow whose survival depends entirely on the modest proceeds from her deceased's husband's life insurance policy.

In such a situation, however, avoid the contingent fee arrangement for paying the lawyer. Because the lawyer is likely to get results by writing two or three letters, he is not entitled to a substantial share of the insurance proceeds for this minimal investment of time. You would be better advised to agree to pay him on an hourly fee basis. Only if the claim involves a lawsuit should you consider a contingent fee arrangement—and only provided that the lawyer agrees to a lower percentage than the customary one-third charged for handling wrongful death claims. Don't hesitate to try negotiating a fee lower than the percentage initially quoted by the lawyer.

SOCIAL SECURITY BENEFITS

If the deceased was covered by Social Security long enough to be eligible, his survivors are entitled to two kinds of benefits: a lump-sum benefit, which is intended to help defray funeral expenses, and survivors' benefits to help support his children and, in some cases, his spouse.

A one-time Social Security benefit of $255 is payable to the surviving spouse if he or she was living with the worker at the time of death, or if living apart, was eligible for Social Security benefits on the deceased's earnings record for the month of death. If there is no surviving spouse, the funeral benefit is paid to a child who was eligible for benefits on the deceased's earnings record in the month of death.

When a worker dies, certain family members may be eligible for survivors benefits based on his or her record if the worker had enough Social Security earnings credits. For many survivor cases, the number of required earnings credits is based on the worker's age at the time of death. In general, younger workers need fewer earnings credits than do older workers. However, no worker needs more than 40 earnings credits (10 years of work) to be fully insured for any Social Security benefit.

Social Security survivor's benefits can be paid to:

- A widow/widower: full benefits at full retirement age, or reduced benefits as early as age 60. A disabled widow/widower may receive benefits as early as age 50;
- A widow/widower: at any age if he or she takes care of the deceased's child under age 16 or disabled, who receives Social Security benefits;
- Unmarried children under 18, or up to age 19: if they are attending elementary or secondary school full time. A child can receive benefits at any age if he or she was disabled before age 22 and remains disabled. Under certain circumstances, benefits can also be paid to stepchildren, grandchildren, or adopted children;
- Dependent parents at 62 or older.

A former spouse of the deceased worker can receive benefits under the same circumstances as a widow/widower if the marriage lasted 10 years or more. Benefits paid to a surviving divorced spouse who is 60 or older will not affect the benefit rates for other survivors receiving benefits. In general, a widow/widower cannot receive benefits if he or she remarries before the age of 60 (50 if disabled) unless the latter marriage ends, whether by death, divorce, or annulment. However, remarriage after age 60 (50 if disabled) will not prevent payments on a former spouse's record.

The amount of the survivors benefit is based on the earnings of the deceased worker. The more he or she paid into Social Security, the higher the benefits will be. The amount a survivor receives is a percentage of the deceased worker's basic Social Security benefit. The following provides the most typical situations:

- Widow or widower full retirement age or older—100%;
- Widow or widower age 60 to 64—about 71%–91%;
- Widow or widower at any age with a child under age 16—75%;
- Children—75%.

If a survivor is receiving widow/widower's benefits, he or she can switch to his or her own retirement benefits (assuming they are eligible and their retirement rate is higher than the widow/widower's rate) as early as age 62. In many cases, a widow/widower can begin receiving one benefit at a reduced rate and then switch to the other benefit at an unreduced rate at full retirement age. However, he or she will not be paid both benefits—he or she will be paid the higher of the two benefits.

If the deceased had been receiving Social Security retirement benefits, he is not entitled to benefits for the month in which he died. Thus, if the death occurred at any time in July, the check dated August 3 (representing the payment for July) must be returned unless it is made out jointly to husband and wife, in which case the surviving spouse should consult the local Social Security office before cashing it. If Social Security checks were deposited directly in the deceased's bank account, the bank should be instructed to return any payments received after the death.

An application for benefits can be obtained (usually by telephone) from the nearest Social Security Administration office. The documents that must accompany the application include the deceased's Social Security card, certified copies of both birth and death certificates, and copies of the deceased's most recent W-2 or 1099 form and federal income tax return. For more information, visit the Social Security Administration Web site http://www.social security.gov.

VETERANS' BENEFITS

A deceased veteran's burial benefits include a grave site in any of the Veterans Administration's 122 national cemeteries that have available space, plus opening and closing of the grave, perpetual care, a government headstone or marker, a burial flag, and a Presidential Memorial Certificate, all at no cost to the family. Some veterans may also be eligible for burial allowances. Cremated remains are buried or inurned in national cemeteries in the same manner and with the same honors as casketed remains.

Burial benefits available for veterans buried in a private cemetery include a government headstone or marker, a burial flag, and a Presidential Memorial Certificate, at no cost to the family. Some veterans may also be eligible for burial allowances. There are not any benefits available to veterans' spouses and dependents buried in a private cemetery.

Burial benefits available for veterans' spouses and dependents buried in a national cemetery include burial with the veteran, perpetual care, and the spouse or dependent's name and date of birth and death will be inscribed on the veteran's headstone, at no cost to the family.

A VA burial allowance is a partial reimbursement of an eligible veteran's burial and funeral costs. When the cause of the veteran's death is not service related, the reimbursement is generally described as two payments: (1) a burial and funeral expense allowance, and (2) a plot interment allowance. You may be eligible for a VA burial allowance if you paid for a veteran's burial or funeral and you have not been reimbursed by another government agency or some other source, such as the deceased veteran's employer, and if the veteran was discharged under conditions other than dishonorable.

In addition, at least <u>one</u> of the following conditions must be met:

- the veteran died because of a service-related disability or
- the veteran was receiving VA pension or compensation at the time of death or
- the veteran was entitled to receive VA pension or compensation but decided not to reduce his or her military retirement or disability pay or
- the veteran died in a VA hospital or while in a nursing home under VA contract, or while in an approved state nursing home.

Service-Related Death

The VA will pay up to $2,000 toward burial expenses for deaths after September 11, 2001. If the veteran is buried in a VA national cemetery, some or all of the cost of moving the deceased's remains may be reimbursed.

Nonservice-Related Death

The VA will pay up to $300 toward burial and funeral expenses, and a $300 plot interment allowance for deaths after December 1, 2001. If the death occurred while the veteran was in a VA hospital or in a nursing home under VA contract, some or all of the costs of transporting the deceased's remains may be reimbursed.

The surviving spouse and minor children of veterans who received benefits for service-connected disabilities are also entitled to monthly payments from the Veterans Administration, the exact amount of which will be based on the veteran's earning record during military service or on his or her occupation at time of death. For more information or to download the VA's helpful publication, *Federal Benefits for Veterans and Dependents*, visit the Veterans Administration Web site at http://www.va.gov.

EMPLOYEE BENEFITS

If the deceased was employed (or on sick leave) at the time of death, you should get in touch with the employer to collect any wages (including vacation and sick-leave pay) that were due at the time of death. Under many state laws, the employer can pay such sums directly to the spouse or next of kin (see p. 301), and hence they are not considered probate assets.

Group life insurance, pension plans, profit-sharing plans, health insurance, accidental death insurance, and any other fringe benefits provided by the employer should also be investigated for possible payments. Many labor unions, professional associations, and fraternal societies also provide special death benefits for their members.

Another potential source of benefits, if the death occurred at, during the course of, or as a consequence of the deceased's employment, is the worker's compensation disability benefit system. This often mandatory form of worker protection, which functions on a "no fault" basis, provides a wide range of benefits to the surviving spouse and children of employees who die of work-connected injuries or occupational diseases.

One might expect employers to be cooperative in paying worker's compensation claims in full, but there are several reasons why they may not be. Those employers who are self-insured are naturally reluctant to pay claims. Those who are protected by private or public insurers may fear a rise in their premiums if they have numerous claims. And some employers fear that a worker's compensation claim may disclose working conditions that violate state or federal occupational safety codes. If an employer denies a claim or offers a settlement short of full payment, you would do well to consult a lawyer experienced in handling worker's compensation claims. In such circumstances a contingent-fee arrangement may be appropriate because the fee is sometimes regulated by the state and is usually less than the one-third fee charged in the typical personal-injury or wrongful-death claim.

Credit Union Benefits

Many credit unions offer one of two kinds of death benefits to their members: a life insurance policy whose value equals the member's account balance at the time of death or credit life insurance that pays off any loans outstanding at the time of death. Before making any payments on credit union loans, therefore, be sure to rule out the possibility that the loan balances have been paid off by this form of insurance or that the life insurance benefit has doubled the balance in the deceased's savings account.

BENEFICIARY BEWARE

Statistics indicate that women are likely to outlive their husbands by several years. When all the deceased's assets have been assembled, it is possible that the surviving spouse (most often a widow) may find herself in control of a larger sum of money than she is accustomed to dealing with. If she is inexperienced in the handling of money, she will need to think carefully about possible investments. Well-meaning relatives may suggest business ventures or other investments. Brokers' representatives, mutual fund sales-people, and others may offer financial advice that is neither prudent nor altogether disinterested. And feelings of bereavement, isolation, and helplessness may increase a surviving spouse's vulnerability to a variety of "sure things" or get-rich-quick schemes.

Although no investment offers complete immunity against the ravages of inflation or fluctuations in the economy, it is important that the surviving spouse err on the side of conservatism. If the survivor is in fact a woman, who is likely to outlive her spouse for a considerable period of time, careful conservation of her assets is essential if she does not relish the prospect of becoming dependent on others.

$\approx$ **16** $\approx$

SETTLING AND CLOSING THE ESTATE

Once you have assembled and evaluated all the assets listed in chapter 15, you are ready to settle and close the deceased's estate. Your separation of the assets into probate and nonprobate categories should give you a fairly clear notion as to what, if any, formal probate procedures are necessary, because the value of the probate assets is a major factor in determining whether they must be administered by the probate court.

Actually, the vast majority of estates are settled and closed without any intervention by the probate court. If your own situation is typical, a reading of the next few pages should relieve you of any anxieties you may have concerning the probate process.

IS PROBATE NECESSARY?

The basic purposes of probate administration, as we have noted, are to determine whether a will is valid, to protect minor children and their property, to see that taxes and creditors are paid, and to distribute the remaining probate assets to the beneficiaries named in the will or, if no will, to the heirs specified by state intestacy laws.

Obviously, if the deceased left no orphaned minor children and no probate assets—because he owned nothing or because everything he possessed was given away before death, was owned jointly, was in a trust, or consisted of life insurance or some other account or contract right that named a surviving beneficiary—there are no probate assets and hence nothing to probate. If this describes the estate confronting you, there is no need for you to read the rest of this chapter. Once you have seen to the transfer of jointly held and trust-held assets and the collection of life insurance proceeds, financial accounts, and other benefits as described in chapter 15, your responsibilities are at an end. Although some states permit creditors to file claims against a trust or its assets, creditors' claims against the deceased can be ignored, although it would be courteous (though not legally necessary) to notify creditors that the deceased left no assets with which to pay their bills.

Some form of probate court action, however, will be necessary in each of the following circumstances, although in most cases the estate can be settled by procedures that are simpler, quicker, and cheaper than full probate court administration.

If the deceased left minor orphans—a not uncommon occurrence when husband and wife die simultaneously in an accident—the probate court must be involved so as to appoint a guardian for the minor children and, if their inheritance is substantial, a conservator to manage each minor child's inheritance until the child reaches adulthood. This type of mandatory probate action is dealt with in chapter 14, and it may not necessarily involve the court in the administration of the deceased's estate. The estate itself, depending on its value, may be eligible for one of the informal small-estate transfer procedures described below.

If the deceased died in circumstances giving rise to a wrongful-death claim (see p. 281), the probate court may be required to appoint an executor to evaluate the claim, to initiate a lawsuit, to sign settlement and release papers if money damages are recovered, and to distribute the proceeds to survivors specified by state law.

If the deceased was covered by life insurance but was not survived by the policy designated beneficiary or if the beneficiary he designated was his own estate or its executor, the distribution of the life insurance proceeds may require some probate court action, the precise procedure depending on the amount involved.

If the deceased left probate assets, the probate court may need to appoint an executor to consolidate, protect, and manage the probate assets; to pay the deceased's debts; and to distribute the balance to the entitled beneficiaries. You need not, however, take this requirement too literally, because it depends on both the amount and the nature of the probate assets. For example, household furnishings and appliances, stamp collections, and other contents of a jointly owned home may technically be regarded by law as the sole property of the deceased, but in everyday practice their ownership will pass informally to the surviving joint owner of the house unless some other person raises an objection or asserts a claim. Thus, a surviving spouse will automatically assume ownership of the deceased's personal effects unless adult children or some other interested person asserts a claim to some of them—in which case the conflict may have to be resolved by the probate court.

More important, if the value of the deceased's probate assets is modest, you may still be able to avoid lengthy probate administration. In response to public criticism of the probate process as being antiquated, time-consuming, expensive, and designed to protect the job security of lawyers and judges rather than the interests of widows and orphans, nearly all states have adopted streamlined, simplified, and relatively informal procedures for the settlement of so-called *small estates*. Many of these procedures do not require a lawyer, and most of them can be completed in a matter of days, whereas full probate court administration takes at least several months and may drag on for years.

SMALL ESTATE AND OTHER INFORMAL TRANSFER PROCEDURES

Once you identify the deceased's probate assets, your first step is to find out—by consulting tables 16.1 and 16.2 and inquiring of the local probate court, a local law library, a reliable Web site, or a lawyer skilled in probate law—precisely what the requirements are for small estate transfers in the deceased's state of residence. If, instead, you simply approach a lawyer and tell him to "probate the estate," he may, knowingly or unknowingly, involve you in the full process of formal probate court administration at a substantial cost to the survivors in both time and money.

As tables 16.1 and 16.2 indicate, the eligibility of an estate for settlement through one of the small estate transfer procedures varies from one state to another, but generally it hinges on (1) the value of the assets, (2) the nature of the assets, (3) the relationship of the survivors to the deceased, and (4) whether or not the funeral bill has been paid. The small estate transfer procedures described below are sufficiently typical, however, to serve as guidelines, although the precise requirements and procedures in your state may differ in some respects from the general model.

Motor Vehicles

If the deceased's assets included motor vehicles (not only passenger automobiles but also trucks, motor homes, recreational vehicles, and motorcycles), they may have been registered in his name alone. If their total value does not exceed a specified amount—usually between $25,000 and $75,000—ownership of these vehicles can be transferred to a surviving spouse or next of kin without any intervention by the probate court or help from a lawyer.

The local branch of your state motor vehicle bureau, or its Web site, can inform you whether the simplified transfer procedure is available and what it involves. Usually all the surviving spouse or next of kin need do is present the vehicle title (which in some states is the current registration certificate) and a certified copy of the owner's death certificate. Once the applicant has signed an affidavit of heirship (provided by the motor vehicle bureau), title can be transferred into his or her name on payment of a nominal title transfer fee. The applicant's estimate of the vehicle's current value is not likely to be questioned, but reliable figures are available in several used-car pricing guides found at banks, libraries, and auto dealerships, or on one of several Web sites, including Kelley Blue Book at http://www.kbb.com.

If neither the spouse nor any eligible next of kin transfers ownership of the deceased's vehicle, it becomes a probate asset and hence may require action by the probate court. To avoid this—especially if there are no other probate assets—it might be advisable for the spouse or next of kin to have ownership of the vehicle transferred to his or her name and to sell it promptly. If there are other probate assets, this tactic will have the effect of reducing their total value. In some states, however, this transfer procedure is not available if probate administration is pending.

Of course, if the vehicle was registered jointly, its ownership passes automatically to the surviving joint owner, as is the case with any other jointly owned property. Similarly, if the vehicle's title is held in trust, it remains in the trustee's name for disposition according to the terms of the trust document. And in some states the owner may have designated on the title or registration a transfer-on-death beneficiary which, if done, avoids probate.

WAGES AND FRINGE BENEFITS

Any salary, wages, accumulated vacation and sick pay, and other fringe benefits owing to the deceased may, according to the laws of many states, be paid by the deceased's employer directly to a surviving spouse, children, or other next of kin without the need for any probate proceedings. The employer may, in order to protect his interests, require the claimant to produce a death certificate and to sign an affidavit that identifies the claimant and specifies his or her priority right to receive the deceased employee's benefits.

TABLE 16.1

Requirements for Small Estate Transfer by Affidavit Procedures, by State

State	Dollar Limitation ($)	Waiting Period Following Death	Applicable to Real Estate	Creditors Must First Be Paid
Alabama		Procedure not available		
Alaska[1]	15,000	30 days	No	No
Arizona[1]	50,000	30 days	No	No
Arkansas[1]		Procedure not available		
California	100,000	40 days	No	No
Colorado[1]	50,000	10 days	No	No
Connecticut[1]		Procedure not available		
Delaware[1]	30,000	30 days	No	Yes
District of Columbia	2 cars	No	No	Yes
Florida		Procedure not available		
Georgia		Procedure not available		
Hawaii[1]	100,000	30 days	No	No
Idaho[1]	75,000	30 days	No	No
Illinois	100,000	No	No	Yes
Indiana[1]	25,000	45 days	No	No[6]
Iowa	25,000			
Kansas	20,000			

TABLE 16.1

Requirements for Small Estate Transfer
by Affidavit Procedures, by State *(continued)*

State	Dollar Limitation ($)	Waiting Period Following Death	Applicable to Real Estate	Creditors Must First Be Paid
Kentucky		Procedure not available		
Louisiana[2]	50,000	No	No	Yes
Maine[1]	10,000	30 days	No	No
Maryland		Procedure not available		
Massachusetts		Procedure not available		
Michigan[1]	15,000	28 days	No	No
Minnesota	20,000	30 days	No	No
Mississippi	12,500	30 days	No	No
Missouri		Procedure not available		
Montana[1]	20,000	30 days	No	No
Nebraska	25,000	30 days	No	No
Nevada	20,000	30 days	No	No
New Hampshire		Procedure not available		
New Jersey[2]	10,000	No	Yes	No
New Mexico[1]	30,000	30 days	No	No
New York		Procedure not available		
North Carolina		Procedure not available		
North Dakota[1]	15,000	30 days	No	No
Ohio		Procedure not available		
Oklahoma		Procedure not available		
Oregon		Procedure not available		
Pennsylvania		Procedure not available		
Rhode Island		Procedure not available		
South Carolina[1]	10,000	30 days	No	No
South Dakota	50,000	No	No	Yes
Tennessee		Procedure not available		
Texas[3]	50,000	30 days	Yes	No
Utah[1]	25,000	30 days	No	No
Vermont		Procedure not available		

TABLE 16.1

Requirements for Small Estate Transfer
by Affidavit Procedures, by State (continued)

State	Dollar Limitation ($)	Waiting Period Following Death	Applicable to Real Estate	Creditors Must First Be Paid
Virginia[1]	15,000	60 days	No	No
Washington[1]	60,000	40 days	No	Yes
West Virginia		Procedure not available		
Wisconsin	20,000	No	No	No
Wyoming[1]	150,000	30 days	No	Yes

[1] Not available if petition for appointment of personal representative has been granted or is pending

[2] Available only if deceased left no will

[3] Available only for bank account funds.

TABLE 16.2

Requirements for Small Estate
Summary Probate Procedures, by State

State	Dollar Limitation ($)	Waiting Period Following Death	Applicable to Real Estate	Creditors Must First Be Paid
Alabama	3,000	No	No	Yes
Alaska	Formula[2]	No	Yes	No
Arizona	50,000	No	Yes	No
Arkansas	50,000	No	No	No
California	100,000	No	Yes	No
Colorado	Formula[2]	No	Yes	No
Connecticut	20,000	No	Yes	No
Delaware		Procedure not available		
District of Columbia	40,000	No	Yes	No
Florida	75,000	No	Yes	Yes
Georgia		Procedure not available		
Hawaii		Procedure not available		
Idaho	Formula[2]	No	Yes	No

TABLE 16.2
Requirements for Small Estate
Summary Probate Procedures, by State *(continued)*

State	Dollar Limitation ($)	Waiting Period Following Death	Applicable to Real Estate	Creditors Must First Be Paid
Illinois[4]	100,000[3]	No	Yes	Yes
Indiana	25,000	No	Yes	No
Iowa[5,7]	50,000	No	Yes	Yes
Kansas	Formula[2]	6 mos.	Yes	Yes
Kentucky[4 or 6]	15,000	No	Yes	Yes
Louisiana	Procedure not available			
Maine	Formula[2]	No	Yes	No
Maryland	50,000	No	No	No
Massachusetts	15,000	30 days	No	No
Michigan	Formula[2]	No	Yes	No
Minnesota[1,7]	30,000	No	Yes	No
Mississippi	Procedure not available			
Missouri	40,000	30 days	Yes	No
Montana	Formula[2]	No	Yes	No
Nebraska	Formula[2]	No	Yes	No
Nevada	200,000	60 days	Yes	Yes
New Hampshire	10,000	No	Yes	Yes
New Jersey	Procedure not available			
New Mexico	Formula[2]	No	Yes	Yes
New York[7]	20,000	No	Yes	No
North Carolina	20,000	30 days	No	No
North Dakota	Formula[2]	No	Yes	No
Ohio	100,000	No	Yes	Yes
Oklahoma	60,000	No	Yes	Yes
Oregon	140,000	No	Yes	Yes
Pennsylvania	25,000	No	No	No
Rhode Island	15,000	No	No	Yes
South Carolina[7]	10,000	No	Yes	No

TABLE 16.2
Requirements for Small Estate
Summary Probate Procedures, by State *(continued)*

State	Dollar Limitation ($)	Waiting Period Following Death	Applicable to Real Estate	Creditors Must First Be Paid
South Dakota		Procedure not available		Yes
Tennessee	25,000	45 days	Yes	Yes
Texas	Formula[2]	No	Yes	Yes
Utah	Formula[2]	No	Yes	No
Vermont	10,000	No	No	Yes
Virginia		Procedure not available		
Washington		Procedure not available		
West Virginia	100,000	No	Yes	No
Wisconsin[5]	50,000	No	Yes	Yes
Wyoming	150,000	No	Yes	Yes

[1] Not available if petition for appointment of executor has been granted or is pending

[2] Available where entire estate, less liens and encumbrances, does not exceed certain statutory allowances plus expenses or last illness, funeral, and administration . . . all of which may approximate $25,000 in some cases

[3] Includes deceased's probate and nonprobate assets

[4] Available only if all beneficiaries consent in writing

[5] Available only if deceased is survived by a spouse, children, or a parent

[6] Available only if deceased is survived by a spouse

[7] Available only if deceased left no will

[8] Exclusive of statutory family allowances or exempt property.

The personnel or human resources departments of most large companies are quite familiar with this procedure, but small employers may not be. If you encounter problems, ask your local probate court or your state's department of labor for information. You should be able to collect the money without hiring a lawyer. If you feel that the employer is withholding payment or delaying it unreasonably, however, you might consider seeking help from your state department of labor, filing suit in your local small-claims court or, if the amount is substantial, retaining a lawyer.

TRANSFER BY AFFIDAVIT

For the transfer and settlement of "small estates"—usually defined as personal property not exceeding a specified maximum ($10,000 to $150,000)—many states offer an affidavit transfer procedure that eliminates the need for an executor, probate court action, or notification of the deceased's creditors. The transfer affidavit, usually a printed form available from the financial institution holding the deceased's money, securities, or other assets, must recite that (1) the claimant is legally entitled to inherit the deceased's assets, (2) the value of the deceased's estate, less liens, does not exceed the maximum specified by state law, (3) that a minimum number of days (usually 30 to 45) have elapsed since the death, and (4) no petition for the appointment of an executor is pending or has been granted by the probate court.

Under the Uniform Probate Code (adopted by fifteen states as of this writing), anyone indebted to or holding personal property of the deceased is required, upon receipt of the transfer affidavit, to pay the debt or deliver the property to the person who claims to be an entitled beneficiary of the deceased. In simpler language, this means that the affidavit procedure can be used to collect and transfer the deceased's solely owned bank accounts, money market accounts, promissory notes, stocks, bonds, and mutual funds, and the contents of bank safe-deposit boxes—provided their total value falls within the bank state-specified monetary limit. Under this procedure, the deceased's creditors need not be paid, or even notified.

Other states, even though they have not adopted the Uniform Probate Code, provide similar procedures for the swift and informal transfer of "small estates" by affidavit. You may or may not need the help of a lawyer to take advantage of this abbreviated settlement procedure. Before obligating yourself to legal expenses, find out what you can about your own state's small estate affidavit transfer procedures by reviewing table 16.1, contacting the local probate court, doing some research in a library, or visiting your state court system's Web site.

SUMMARY PROBATE ADMINISTRATION

If the deceased's probate assets exceed the maximum values specified by state law or do not consist of assets eligible for transfer by affidavit, or if the assets include real estate, most states offer an abbreviated form of probate procedure, sometimes called "summary" or "small estate" probate administration. This procedure is usually available if (1) assets do not exceed a specified value ranging from $3,000 to $150,000, (2) no interested party (such as a creditor) objects to it, and (3) the will does not direct otherwise.

In California, for example, you may petition the probate court to issue an order specifying the survivors' right to acquire the deceased's property without the need for full probate administration. The petition must include an inventory and appraisal by a probate referee of the deceased's probatable real and personal property, showing its gross value. The petition is scheduled for a hearing, and notice must be given to all interested parties. If the petition is granted the probate court will issue an order specifying who acquires the title to the property. A certified copy of this order is then delivered to the person or entity holding personal property and is recorded in the county in which any real property is located.

The Uniform Probate Code, currently adopted by 15 states, also provides for summary probate administration if the survivors include a spouse or minor children. As the nominated executor, you may file an application for informal appointment and thereby obtain letters of authority. If, after you have filed an inventory and appraisal, it appears that the value of the deceased's probate assets do not exceed the aggregate value of (1) the statutory "family protection allowances" (approximately $25,000 but varying among states), (2) funeral expenses, (3) necessary expenses for the deceased's final health care, and (4) costs of administration, you may immediately distribute the estate to the surviving spouse and minor children without giving notice to the deceased's creditors and an opportunity for presentation of their claims.

After the deceased's assets have been distributed, you can immediately close the estate by filing a sworn statement that to the best of your knowledge the value of the estate did not exceed the sum of items 1 through 4 above, that the distribution of assets is complete, and that a copy of the final statement was sent to all beneficiaries and to known unpaid creditors. Under this procedure, creditors need not be paid.

FORMAL PROBATE ADMINISTRATION

If the value of the deceased's probate assets exceeds the maximum for your state's "small estate" transfer procedures or if a lawsuit for wrongful death benefits seems likely, the estate must undergo formal probate court administration. Depending on the amount and complexity of the probate assets, claim disputes, will contests, arguments among beneficiaries, and whether there is delay in obtaining tax clearances, this process can take from six months to several years. And it can be rather expensive, because the executor, sometimes called a personal representative, is entitled to be paid for his services, plus attorney fees and court costs must be paid by the estate before it can be closed. Although formal probate administration might have been avoided had the deceased adopted some of the probate avoidance strategies suggested in chapter 2, it is, unfortunately, inevitable at this juncture.

The basic purposes of probate administration help to explain why the process can be lengthy and costly. The court must appoint an executor to identify, collect, manage, and settle the probate estate; it must determine the validity of any purported will; it must identify and notify the beneficiaries named in the will as well as the heirs designated by state law; it must notify the deceased's creditors and determine the legitimacy of their claims; and it must ensure that the remaining assets, after the payment of debts, taxes, and administration expenses, are properly distributed to the will-designated beneficiaries or, if no will, to the state-specified heirs at law.

INITIATION OF PROBATE PROCEEDINGS

Even if the deceased's will has been filed with the local probate court, probate proceedings do not begin automatically upon his death. To initiate probate administration, some "interested party" must petition the court to appoint an executor and commence proceedings. If the probate assets are substantial, there will be no dearth of interested parties: beneficiaries or heirs eager to get possession of the deceased's assets or even creditors to whom the deceased owed large sums. Because the deceased's probate assets can be transferred only by an executor, his formal appointment by the court is the first order of business.

If you have been named in the will as the executor or if, in the absence of a will, you seem to be the logical choice, you may feel daunted by the responsibilities that confront you. Bear in mind, however, that as executor you have the right to hire lawyers, accountants, and other professionals to help you and that their fees

are chargeable against the estate. In addition, unless the will specifies otherwise, you are entitled to reasonable compensation for your
work and reimbursement for your expenses.

You can, of course, decline to serve, in which case the probate
court will appoint someone else, usually observing the following
priority sequence:

Priority Rank	Description of Candidates
1.	Persons named in will as executor and successor executor.
2.	Surviving spouse who is a will-designated beneficiary (or spouse's nominee).
3.	Other will-designated beneficiaries (or their nominee).
4.	Surviving spouse (or his/her nominee).
5.	Other heirs at law by degree of kinship (or their nominee).
6.	Any creditor 45 days after death.

If none of these people is willing to petition for the appointment,
the court may request that anyone file a petition, and in such circumstances the court may appoint a bank, a lawyer (sometimes a
political friend), or some other stranger.

Your decision to undertake the responsibility, then, may depend
on your own status as a beneficiary and your relationship to other
beneficiaries. If you are concerned with conserving the assets, you
are likely, despite your "amateur" standing, to do a more conscientious job than a bank or a professional who takes on the task solely
for financial gain. If you decide to serve, your first step is to have
your lawyer prepare and file a petition requesting your formal
appointment as executor and the commencement of probate proceedings. If your petition is approved, the probate court will formal-
ize your appointment and issue you the necessary *letters of authority*
(see figure 16.1), sometimes called letters testamentary—often
immediately.

THE EXECUTOR

Once appointed by the court, the executor has much the same
powers over the assets as the deceased had during his lifetime.
Armed with the letters of authority, the executor can sell property
owned by the estate, continue to manage an existing business, make

Figure 16.1

LETTERS OF AUTHORITY

STATE OF MICHIGAN PROBATE COURT COUNTY OF	LETTERS OF AUTHORITY FOR PERSONAL REPRESENTATIVE	FILE NO.

Estate of _____

TO: | *Name, address, and telephone no.* |

You have been appointed and qualified as personal representative of the estate on _____ . You are authorized to do and perform all
Date
acts authorized by law except as to the following:

❑ Real estate or ownership interests in a business entity excluded from your
responsibilities in your acceptance of appointment

❑ Restrictions:

❑ These letters expire: _____
Date

_____   _____
Date   *Judge (formal proceedings)/Register (informal proceedings)*   *Bar no.*

SEE OTHER SIDE FOR NOTICE OF DUTIES.

_____
Attorney name (type or print)   *Bar no.*

_____
Address

_____
City, state, zip   *Telephone no.*

I certify that I have compared this copy with the original on file and that it is a correct copy of the original and that these letters are in full force and effect as of the date on the letters.

_____   _____
Date   *Deputy register*

Do not write below this line - For court use only

investments with estate capital, mortgage estate property, and do anything else that is necessary to preserve or increase the value of the estate. In brief, he may be regarded, for all intents and purposes, as the ghost or the alter ego of the deceased, empowered to manage all of the deceased's financial affairs that were interrupted by death.

The executor's activities are, however, subject to three limitations. First, unlike the deceased, who could do absolutely whatever he wished with his property, the executor must always act "prudently" so as not to jeopardize the value of the estate—through speculative investments, for example. Second, he must do everything he can to settle the estate—pay its debts and distribute the residue to the beneficiaries or heirs—as promptly as possible. Third, he must do nothing with respect to the estate that works to his personal advantage—for example, buying for himself at an unreasonably low price a business, securities, or other probate asset belonging to the estate.

The deceased's will may stipulate that the nominated executor is to serve without bond. But if this is not specified, the estate is chargeable for the executor's bond premium. In some states, the executor's compensation is specified as a percentage of the value of the estate; in other states the fee must be "reasonable compensation," typically subject to review by the probate court. Even when it is not regulated, however, compensation is expected to be "reasonable" and is subject to challenge in the probate court by any beneficiary, heir, or creditor. For a state-by-state listing of fees chargeable by an executor, see table 16.3.

TABLE 16.3
EXECUTORS' FEES, BY STATE

State	Fee
Alabama	Just and fair amount up to 2.5% of receipts and disbursements.
Alaska	Reasonable compensation.
Arizona	Reasonable compensation.[1]
Arkansas	Up to 10% of first $1,000 of personal property; 5% of next $4,000; 3% of balance plus reasonable additional fee for services involving real estate.
California	Up to 4% of first $15,000; 3% of next $85,000; 2% of next $900,000; 1% of next $9,000,000; 0.5% of next $15,000,000; plus reasonable fee for the balance.

TABLE 16.3
EXECUTORS' FEES, BY STATE (continued)

State	Fee
Colorado	Reasonable compensation.[1]
Connecticut	Reasonable compensation.
Delaware	Combined executor's and attorney's fees up to $250 plus 11.3% of amount over $2,000 for estates under $5,000; $565 plus 6.8% of amount over $5,000 for estates under $10,000; $905 plus 5.6% of amount over $10,000 for estates under $20,000; $1,465 plus 5.1% of amount over $20,000 for estates under $30,000; $1,975 plus 4.5% of amount over $30,000 for estates under $40,000; $2,425 plus 3.9% of amount over $40,000 for estates under $60,000; $3,205 plus 3.7% of amount over $60,000 for estates under $80,000. For fees on larger estates, see court rules.[2]
District of Columbia	Reasonable compensation.
Florida	3% of the first $100,000; 2.5% of the next $5 million; 2.0% of the next $10 million; and 1.5% of the balance.
Georgia	2.5% of money received and paid out plus additional fee for extraordinary services.
Hawaii	Reasonable compensation.[1]
Idaho	Reasonable compensation.[1]
Illinois	Reasonable compensation.
Indiana	Reasonable compensation.[1]
Iowa	Reasonable compensation not to exceed 6% of first $1,000; 4% of next $4,000; 2% over $5,000.
Kansas	Reasonable compensation.[1]
Kentucky	Up to 5% of personal property plus 5% of income collected.[2]
Louisiana	2% of value of estate.
Maine	Reasonable compensation.
Maryland	Up to 9% of first $20,000; $2,000 plus 3.6% of amount over $20,000; limit of 9% of real estate sold by executor[2].
Massachusetts	Such compensation as court may allow.
Michigan	Reasonable compensation.

TABLE 16.3
EXECUTORS' FEES, BY STATE (continued)

State	Fee
Minnesota	Reasonable compensation.
Mississippi	Such compensation as court may allow.
Missouri	Up to 5% of first $5,000; 4% of next $20,000; 3% of next $75,000; 2.75% of next $300,000; 2.5% of next $600,000; 2% of amount over $1 million.[2]
Montana	Reasonable compensation.
Nebraska	Reasonable compensation.
Nevada	4% of first $15,000; 3% of next $85,000; 2% on excess over $100,000.[2]
New Hampshire	Reasonable compensation.
New Jersey	5% of first $200,000; 3.5% of excess up to $1 million; 2% on balance.[2]
New Mexico	Reasonable compensation.[1]
New York	5% of first $100,000 of assets received and paid out; 4% of next $200,000; 3% of next $700,000; 2.5% of next $4 million; 2% of amounts over $5 million.
North Carolina	Up to 5% of receipts and expenditures. On estates of less than $2,000, court clerk sets fee.
North Dakota	Reasonable compensation.
Ohio	4% of first $100,000; 3% of next $300,000; 2% of balance, determined with reference to personal property, income received, and proceeds of real estate.[2]
Oklahoma	5% of first $1,000; 4% of next $5,000; 2.5% of excess over $6,000.[1,2]
Oregon	7% of first $1,000; 4% of next $9,000; 3% of next $40,000; 2% on amount over $50,000; plus 1% of property subject to state inheritance or federal estate tax.[1,2]
Pennsylvania	Reasonable compensation.
Rhode Island	Reasonable compensation within court's discretion.
South Carolina	Up to 5% of personal property plus 5% of proceeds of sold real estate plus 5% of income earned by the estate.[2]
South Dakota	Reasonable compensation.[1]

TABLE 16.3
EXECUTORS' FEES, BY STATE (continued)

State	Fee
Tennessee	Reasonable compensation.
Texas	5% of incoming cash and 5% of outgoing cash.
Utah	Reasonable compensation.[1]
Vermont	$4 per day while performing duties of office.[2]
Virginia	Reasonable compensation.
Washington	Reasonable compensation.[1]
West Virginia	Reasonable compensation (usually 5% of receipts).
Wisconsin	2% of estate, less mortgage and liens, plus higher fee if approved by decedent or beneficiaries who receive majority of estate.
Wyoming	10% of first $1,000; 5% of next $4,000; 3% of next $15,000; 2% of amount over $20,000.[2]

1 Executor may renounce fee limits in will and collect higher fee allowed by law unless compensation is set by contract

2 Court may award higher fee.

The purpose of the bond is to protect all interested parties against fraud, embezzlement, or negligence by the executor in his management and disposal of the estate's assets. Like the executor's compensation, the annual premium for the bond is based on the total value of the probate assets plus any income they are expected to produce. The annual bond premium costs are typically ten percent of the bond's face value.

Although the will may specify that the executor is to serve without bond, the probate judge may override this aspect of the will and require bonding if he believes it necessary for the protection of the beneficiaries and the creditors. On the other hand, if the will does not address bonding and if the executor is the sole heir or beneficiary, the judge may waive the bonding requirement.

Bonding is easy to arrange through almost any insurance agent, but despite the pressure of time, some shopping around is advisable—as it is in the purchase of any other kind of insurance. If the value of the estate's assets is substantial, the executor can sometimes negotiate a discount on the premium from an insurance agent who is particularly eager to sell this coverage.

Bonding premiums are payable annually until the probate process is completed. Because they are renewed automatically, the executor should cancel his bond as soon as the estate is closed by sending the insurance company a copy of the probate court's final "Order Closing Estate and Discharging Executor" (see p. 319) and request a refund of any unearned premium.

"Proving" the Will

The initial petition for appointment as executor typically includes a request that the court approve the will or, if there is no will, to determine which of the heirs at law listed in the petition are entitled, according to state law, to share in the deceased's estate. In response, the court schedules a hearing and sends a notification of its time and place to all parties who may have an interest in the estate: creditors, beneficiaries named in any will, and heirs at law who, under state law, are entitled to inherit if there is no valid will.

At this hearing, the will may be contested by any interested party who contends that the deceased signed it in a state of diminished capacity or was unduly influenced or under duress, that he made errors in executing the will, or that he subsequently amended or revoked it. If any of these claims are proved, the court will not "admit" the will to probate, with the result that the deceased is regarded as having died intestate, unless there exists an earlier will that is valid.

If, on the other hand, the will is not successfully contested, the court will admit it to probate or, if there was no will, formally identify the heirs at law entitled to share the estate.

Notification of Interested Parties

Once formally appointed, the executor must send to each interested party (creditors, beneficiaries, and heirs) written notification of his appointment, including his name and address and the location of the probate court where the will and all other documents relating to the estate are filed. The basic purpose of this notice is to inform all interested persons about the appointment and to offer them an opportunity to challenge it if grounds for a challenge exist. In

Figure 16.2

NOTICE TO CREDITORS

STATE OF MICHIGAN PROBATE COURT COUNTY OF	LETTERS OF AUTHORITY FOR PERSONAL REPRESENTATIVE	FILE NO.

Estate of _____ Date of birth:

TO ALL CREDITORS:·

NOTICE TO CREDITORS: The decedent,_____, who lived at

_____, Michigan died
      Street address   *City*

_____.
    Date

Creditors of the decedent are notified that all claims against the estate will be forever barred unless presented to _____, named personal representative or proposed personal representative, or to both the probate court at _____
              Address   *City*
and the named/proposed personal representative within 4 months after the date of publication of this notice.

                                 _____
                                    Date

_____   _____
    Attorney name (type or print)   *Bar no.*

_____
  Personal representative name (type or print)

_____   _____
      Address   *Address*

_____   _____
City, state, zip   *Telephone no.*   *City, state, zip*   *Telephone no.*

PUBLISH ABOVE INFORMATION ONLY

Publish _____ time(s) in_____ in _____County
                 Name of publication

Furnish _____ copies to _____

Furnish affidavit of publication to the probate court with copy to _____

_____

Forward statement for publication charges to _____.
·NOTE TO PREPARER: If there is a known creditor whose address is unknown and cannot be ascertained after diligent inquiry, insert "including [name of creditor] whose address and whereabouts are unknown:"

Do not write below this line - For court use only

addition, however, it invites the interested parties to ascertain the value of the deceased's probate estate by reviewing an inventory, which the executor must file with the probate court, listing the current value of each of the estate's assets as well as any mortgages or liens against them. By consulting this inventory, beneficiaries or heirs at law can estimate what they may expect to receive, and creditors can determine whether they are likely to collect their debts.

DEALING WITH CREDITORS

Upon his appointment, the executor must send written notice to each of the deceased's known creditors inviting them to submit in writing all claims against the estate within a specified time. In addition, he must publish a copy of this notice in a newspaper distributed within the county in which the deceased lived so as to inform possible creditors of whom he is unaware (see figure 16.2). Both the number of times the notice must be published and the period of time during which they must appear are governed by state law, as is the deadline for the submission of claims. Typically, the creditor must submit its claim to the executor and file a copy with the probate court. In all states, claims submitted after the deadline are barred.

Although the executor may pay legitimate claims in the order in which he receives them, he should be cautious about doing this if the possibility exists that the estate's assets will not be sufficient to cover all claims. In such circumstances, claims must be paid according to a priority sequence established by state law, which is typically as follows:

1. Costs of administering the estate, including the executor's and lawyers' fees, court costs, and bond premiums
2. Reasonable funeral expenses, plus medical and hospital bills incurred by the deceased immediately before death
3. Taxes and those debts that state law specifies as having priority
4. All other legitimate debts

In this priority system, high-priority claims are paid in full, and if no assets remain, low-priority creditors get nothing.

For example, if after paying all debts in priorities 1, 2, and 3, the estate remains with $500 in assets and $1,000 in debts, each class-4 creditor will receive 50 percent of his claim.

INCOME TAXES

The executor is responsible for preparing and filing the deceased's final federal, state, and local income tax returns, as well as tax returns on behalf of the estate itself.

If the deceased left a surviving spouse and it was their custom to file a joint return, the final return may also be joint even if the death occurred during the first few days of the tax year. On the other hand, there is no obligation to file a joint return if the surviving spouse finds it advantageous to file an individual return.

If the estate itself has received taxable income during any year—from the operation of a business, for example, or from yields on investments or interest on bank funds—the executor must file returns on its behalf.

FEDERAL ESTATE TAX

The federal estate tax is an excise tax levied against all assets (both probate and nonprobate) in which the deceased had an interest at the time of death, and it must be paid by the executor within nine months following the death. The tax rates, deductions, and credits, however, have been so liberalized in recent years that only 2 percent of all estates are liable for estate tax. See chapter 6. Because the chances are very high that the estate with which you are dealing will not be subject to this tax, we will not attempt here to provide you with complete instructions for calculating the tax and filing the return. This is a task you should not undertake unassisted unless you are an experienced tax lawyer or accountant. IRS Publication 559, which offers helpful tax information for executors and survivors, can be accessed at the IRS Web site: http://www.irs.gov/pub/irs-pdf/p559.pdf.

STATE ESTATE AND INHERITANCE TAXES

Some states may impose either of two kinds of death taxes: an estate tax, which is payable by the estate itself, or an inheritance tax, which is payable by the beneficiary receiving an inheritance. See chapter 6.

Although state inheritance taxes are payable by the beneficiary, the deceased's will may specify that the tax be paid by the estate on behalf of the beneficiary. (See table 6.2.) In any event, however, it is the executor's responsibility to make sure that the tax is paid, because the probate court will normally require that he file a tax clearance letter, issued by the state treasurer's office, before the court will sign an order discharging the executor and closing the estate.

DISTRIBUTING THE REMAINING ESTATE

Once all debts, taxes, and other liabilities of the estate have been discharged, the executor is ready to submit to the court a final accounting of his actions and to distribute the remaining probate assets to the beneficiaries named in the will or if no will to the heirs specified by state law.

Certain changes in the distribution specified either by the will or by state law can be made provided that all beneficiaries or heirs give their written consent. For example, a parent who is a beneficiary can ask that his share be distributed equally to his two children, even though they were not mentioned in the will, or an heir who is affluent may ask that his share be added to that of his less affluent sister.

If one or more of the beneficiaries is a minor and the value of his share is not large, the distribution can be made to his parent or guardian. If, however, the amount is substantial—over $5,000—it must usually be paid to the conservator of the minor's estate, who is appointed by the probate court if one has not been designated in the will (see p. 261).

As soon as he has completed all the details of the distribution, the executor prepares for signature by the probate judge an order allowing the final account and assigning residue. Once it is signed, the order serves as a formal record indicating when, how, and to whom the estate's assets were distributed.

CLOSING THE ESTATE

After the distribution has been completed, the executor files with the probate court a closing statement certifying that he has discharged all his responsibilities—that he has notified all creditors, paid all debts, distributed the residue of the estate in accordance with the terms of the will or with state law, and mailed a copy of the closing statement to all interested parties.

Upon approval of the closing statement, the probate court issues to the executor an order discharging him from his position and relieving him of all further responsibilities. At this point the probate estate is closed.

APPENDIX
SOURCES OF
FURTHER INFORMATION

Estate Planning
American Association of Retired Persons
http://www.aarp.org/estate_planning/
Provides an estate planning guide on estate taxes, how to be a power of attorney agent, advance medical directives, living trusts, wills, probate, and links to many self-help guides

American Bar Association
http://www.abanet.org/rppt/public/home.html
Provides estate planning answers regarding wills, nonprobate assets, trusts, powers of attorney, living wills, probate, planning for retirement benefits, and guidelines for executors

CCH Financial Planning Toolkit
http://www.finance.cch.com
Provides information for managing your personal finances including estate planning, wills, trusts, death taxes, tax planning, and probate

Cornell Law School
http://www.law.cornell.edu/topics/estate_planning.html
Legal information institute on estate planning. Provides estate planning overview with links to many sites

National Association of Financial and Estate Planning
http://www.nafep.com
Offers a public information section that provides information on financial and estate planning. Also offers online brochures on many topics, including various types of trusts

University of Minnesota Extension Service
http://www.yellowpieplate.umn.edu/07-lm.html
Extension services project on "Who Gets Grandma's Yellow Pie Plate."
Provides unbiased, research-based education as an outreach arm of the
University of Minnesota to help families make more informed decisions
on who gets what in terms of inheritance, including personal property
that may not have much financial worth, but often has a great deal of
sentimental or emotional value

LIFE INSURANCE

CCH Financial Planning Kit
http://www.finance.cch.com
Provides information for managing your personal finances including life
insurance, how much do you need, term vs. cash value policies, compara-
tive tables, and annuities

Insurance Information Institute
http://www.iii.org
The stated mission of the Institute is to "improve public understanding of
insurance—what it does and how it works." Provides consumer informa-
tion including help in buying life insurance, how much to buy, which type
of product to buy, and which company to choose

Life Insurance Settlement Association
http://www.lisaassociation.org
The stated mission of the Association is to promote the develop-
ment, integrity, and reputation of the life insurance settlement
industry. Provides consumer information on selling a life insur-
ance policy, including state and federal viatical and life settlement .
resources

MIB Group, Inc.
http://www.policylocator.com
Offers a lost insurance policy locator service to help survivors locate lost
life insurance policies owned by a deceased spouse or family member.
The deceased's name is searched against a policy locator database, for
a fee of $75 per search

DEATH AND TAXES

CCH Financial Planning Toolkit
http://www.finance.cch.com
Provides information for managing your personal finances including federal estate taxes, strategies for avoiding estate tax, and state estate and inheritance taxes (including state-by-state charts demonstrating rates and exemptions)

Internal Revenue Service
http://www.irs.gov
IRS, a part of the US Department of Treasury, is the nation's tax collection agency and administers the Internal Revenue Code. Provides tax forms, publications, and answers to many tax questions. IRS Publication No. 559, "Survivors, Executors, and Administrators," provides detailed information on a decedent's income, gift, and estate taxes

LIVING WILLS AND MEDICAL POWERS OF ATTORNEY

American Bar Association
http://www.abanet.org/aging/toolkit
Commission on Law and Aging. Provides online publication "Consumers Toolkit for Health Care Advance Planning," that contains self-help worksheets, suggestions, and resources. Although the "Toolkit" does not create an advance directive, it "helps you do the much harder job of discovering, clarifying, and communicating what is important to you in the face of a serious illness."

Caring Connections
http://www.caringinfo.org
A program of the National Hospice and Palliative Care Organization (NHPCO), is a national consumer initiative to improve care at the end of life. Provides free resources including end-of-life information, brochures, and state-specific living wills and medical powers of attorney

ORGAN, TISSUE, AND BODY DONATIONS

The Living Bank
http://www.livingbank.org
An independent, non-profit, public interest foundation that claims to be the oldest and largest organ donor education organization in the United

States. and the only national organ donor registry that keeps computerized records of organ donor data for future retrieval in an emergency

National Kidney Foundation
http://www.kidney.org
A major voluntary health organization that seeks to prevent kidney and urinary tract disease, and increase the availability of all organs for transplantation. Provides information on organ and tissue donations, including free donor cards

Organdonor.gov
http://www.organdonor.gov
The official U.S. government Web site for organ and tissue donation and transplantation is maintained by the Health Resources and Services Administration (HRSA), an agency of the U.S. Department of Health and Human Services. Provides information, data, publications, links, and online organ and tissue donor cards

United Network of Organ Sharing
http://www.unos.org
UNOS oversees a national database of transplant information, matches donors to recipients, monitors organ matches, provides support services, and assistance to patients, family, and friends, and sets professional standards. Provides information on how to become a donor and provides free donor cards

FUNERAL, BURIAL, AND CREMATION

AARP Fulfillment
http://www.aarp.org
The American Association of Retired Persons is a nonprofit organization dedicated to helping older Americans. Its publications "Funeral Goods and Services" and "Preplanning Your Funeral" are available online, together with other funeral-related information

Cremation Association of North America
http://www.cremationassociation.org
CANA is an association of crematories, cemeteries, and funeral homes that offer cremation. Provides several free online publications dealing with cremation

Federal Trade Commission

http://www.ftc.gov

Provides funeral information, including online publication "Funerals: A Consumer Guide." (Access tip: Open Web site, select "Consumer Information," select "Products and Services," and then scroll alphabetically to publication title.)

Funeral Consumers Alliance

http://www.funerals.org/

FCA, a nonprofit educational organization that supports increased funeral consumer protection, is affiliated with the Funeral and Memorial Society of America (FAMSA). Provides information on caring for the dead, preplanning and pre-arranging funerals, plus an online bookstore, and a free library for online legal questions

Internet Cremation Society

http://www.cremation.org

A collection of online cremation resources, the ICS claims to be the only cremation portal on the Internet. Provides listings and links to cremation societies and cremation service providers in the United States and Canada. ICS further claims that "The main thrust of our site is still to help consumer research and select a low-cost cremation provider."

GOVERNMENT BENEFITS

Firstgov.gov

http://www.firstgov.gov

The U.S. Government's official Web portal, a gateway to all government information, is a rich treasure of online information, services, and resources available from local, state and federal government agency Web sites

Social Security Administration

http://www.ssa.gov

The official Web site of the U.S. Social Security Administration. SSA pays retirement, disability, and survivors' benefits to workers and their families, and administers the Supplemental Security Income (SSI) program. Web site provides many online publications

Veterans Administration
http://www.va.gov

Official website of the U.S. Department of Veterans Affairs. Provides extensive information on VA benefits including life insurance, survivor's benefits, burial and memorial benefits, VA cemeteries, headstones and markers, presidential memorial certificates, and a nationwide grave site locator

SETTLING AND CLOSING ESTATES

Internal Revenue Service
http://www.irs.gov

IRS, a part of the US Department of Treasury, is the nation's tax collection agency and administers the Internal Revenue Code. Provides tax forms, publications, and answers to many tax questions. IRS Publication No. 559, "Survivors, Executors, and Administrators" includes detailed information regarding a decedent's income, gift, and estate taxes

FINDING AN ESTATE PLANNING LAWYER

American College of Trust and Estate Counsel
http://www.actec.org

ACTEC is a nonprofit association of lawyers skilled in estate planning and estate settlement. Provides consumer information on estate planning and also lists its member lawyers by state and country. Web site also offers links to local resources, many of which are helpful to consumers

National Academy of Elder Law Attorneys
http://www.naela.org

The NAELA is a nonprofit association that supports attorneys, bar organizations, and others who work with older clients and their families. NAELA members assist clients with Medicaid, Social Security, and other governmental benefits, estate planning, guardianship, and long-term care planning. Provides tips on finding an attorney skilled in "elder law" and provides an online locator to assist consumers in finding an elder law attorney

GLOSSARY

AB trust Trust established by married couples to receive and manage property in order to exclude it from (or bypass) the estate of the surviving spouse, who receives income but not principal from the trust. Also called a *bypass trust*, *credit shelter trust*, a *family trust*, or a *non-marital trust*.

abatement Reduction of one or more will bequests when an estate's assets are insufficient to pay all taxes, expenses, and bequests in full.

accounting Financial report to the court, creditors, and beneficiaries showing all assets and income received, and expenses incurred following appointment of the executor.

acknowledgment Statement in the presence of a notary public that a document bearing one's signature was indeed signed by that person.

ademption When an asset described in a will is later sold or otherwise disposed of before death, thus precluding the named beneficiary from inheriting the asset.

administration Management and settlement of a decedent's estate, including collecting assets, paying taxes and debts, and distributing the balance to the entitled beneficiaries.

administration expenses Expenses incurred in administering an estate, including court costs, attorney fees, and executor fees.

administrator Person appointed by the court to settle the estate of one who dies without a will, or one who left a will but no named executor.

adult Person who is age 18 or older.

advancement Money or other asset given by a parent to a child or other heir during the parent's life and intended as an advance or pre-payment against the heir's share under the parent's will.

affiant   Person who signs an affidavit.

affidavit   Written statement of facts, made under oath, and signed in presence of a notary public.

after-born child   Child born after the signing of a parent's will.

agent   Person legally authorized to act on behalf of another.

alternate beneficiary   Beneficiary who inherits only if the primary beneficiary has died or disclaims the inheritance.

alternate valuation date   The date six months after one's death. For tax purposes the decedent's representative has the option of valuing the estate's assets as of the date of death or as of the *alternate valuation date.*

anatomical gift   Gift of one or more of a person's organs during life or upon death.

ancillary probate   Probate proceeding commenced in a state different from the state where the decedent resided, if the decedent owned real estate in the other state.

annual gift tax exclusion   For federal gift-tax purposes, an annual exclusion of $12,000 (indexed annually for inflation) is available to the donor.

attestation clause   Statement at the end of a will reciting that the witnesses saw the testator sign the will in their presence, and that they then signed in his presence and in each other's presence.

attorney at law   Person legally qualified and authorized to represent clients in legal matters.

attorney in fact   Person who acts as agent with written authorization from another person to transact business on his or her behalf.

autopsy   Medical examination of a decedent's body to ascertain the cause of death.

basis for tax purposes   The valuation of one's property in determining taxable gain or loss on sale.

beneficiary   Person or organization entitled to receive assests under a will, trust, life insurance policy, financial account, or other arrangement.

bequeath   To give personal property, by will, to another. Distinguishable from *devise*, which means to give real property, by will, to another.

bequest   Gift of personal property, by will, to another.

bond   Monetary guarantee (similar to insurance) that should an executor or trustee wrongfully deprive a beneficiary or creditor of his property, the bonding company will replace it, up to the limits of the bond.

bypass trust   Trust established by married couples to receive and hold property in order to exclude it from (or bypass) the estate of the surviving spouse, who receives income but not principal from the trust. Also called an *AB* trust, a *credit shelter trust*, a *family trust*, or a *non-marital trust*.

charitable remainder trust   Trust designed so the grantor, during his life, retains income from the trust assets and upon his death, the trust's remaining principal passes to a qualified charity.

charitable trust   Trust designed to make a gift for the benefit of a qualified charity while also achieving income and estate tax savings for the grantor.

codicil   Amendment to a prior will, but signed with the same formalities as a will.

co-executor   Person who serves as executor simultaneously with one or more other executors.

common disaster   Where two or more persons, including the testator and a beneficiary, die in the same accident leaving no evidence who died first.

community property   Property acquired during marriage in which both spouses own an undivided one-half interest. Not more than half of the property can be disposed of by will. Currently, there are eight community property states: Arizona, California, Idaho, Louisiana, Nevada, New Mexico, Texas, and Washington.

conditional gift   Gift that takes effect only under specified conditions. For example, "I give $10,000 to my nephew, Mike, if, by the time of my death, Mike has received his undergraduate degree."

conservator   Person or bank appointed by the court to protect and manage property of a minor or incompetent person. In some states, this person is called a *guardian*.

contingent beneficiary   Beneficiary who inherits only if the primary beneficiary has died or disclaims the inheritance.

convenience account   Financial account, typically a bank savings or checking account, opened in joint names but only for convenience of one joint owner and not with intent that the noncontributing owner receive the account balance on death of the contributing owner.

creditor Person or company to whom a debt is owed by another person called a *debtor*.

custodian Person authorized to hold and manage property given to or inherited by a minor, under the Uniform Transfers to Minors Act or the Uniform Gifts to Minors Act.

death tax Tax imposed on the transfer of property at death. The federal *estate tax* is sometimes called a death tax. State death taxes, if any, are called *estate tax* or *inheritance tax*.

debtor Person who owes a debt to another person or company called a *creditor*.

decedent Person who has died.

decree Order signed by a court.

deed Legal document by which a person transfers title to real property (real estate) to another person or entity.

descendant Person who descends from another. Lineal descendants include children and grandchildren.

devise Gift of real property, by will, to another.

disclaimer To decline to accept a gift under a will, an estate, or a trust, thus causing it to pass to an alternate beneficiary, or to lapse.

discretionary trust Trust designed to permit its trustee to decide, in its discretion, when and how much to distribute to the trust's beneficiaries.

disinherit The act by which the owner of property deprives a person who would otherwise be his heir, of the right to inherit.

distribution The act by which an executor or trustee delivers the estate's assets to the entitled beneficiaries.

domicile State in which a person has established a permanent residence, even though he may not spend all or even most of his time in that state.

donee Person or organization that receives a gift.

donor Person who makes or gives a gift.

dower and curtesy Right of a surviving spouse to receive a portion of the deceased spouse's property (usually one-third to one-half), if the surviving spouse is not left at least that share by will. *Dower* is the widow's right, and *curtesy* is the widower's right.

durable power of attorney   Power of attorney that remains in effect even after the person who signed it becomes incapacitated. There exist two types of durable powers of attorney: *financial* and *medical*.

escheat   Legal process under which the probate assets of a person who dies leaving no will and no surviving heirs, passes to the state.

estate   All property, real and personal, that a person owns.

estate planning   Preparing for the management of one's estate to provide for disability and for its transfer at death to designated beneficiaries.

estate tax   Tax imposed on the right of a person to transfer property at death.

executor   Person named in one's will to manage an estate, collect probate assets, pay legitimate claims, and distribute the balance as specified in the will. In some states, this person is called a *personal representative*.

family allowance   Amount of a decedent's property to which family members, usually the spouse and minor children, are entitled to receive shortly after death.

fiduciary   Person occupying a position of trust who is responsible for the custody and management of property belonging to others. An executor, administrator, trustee, custodian, guardian, and conservator are fiduciaries.

forced share   Portion of the estate of a deceased spouse that must, under state law, be inherited by the surviving spouse.

funding a trust   The act of transferring ownership of property to a trust, in the name of its trustee, so that the property becomes subject to the trust's provisions.

generation-skipping tax   Federal tax imposed on transfers of assets that "skip" a generation, typically transfers to grandchildren. Presently the first $2 million of transfers are exempt from the GST tax, increasing to $3.5 million in 2009.

generation-skipping trust   Trust designed to provide benefits for two or more successive generations beyond that of the grantor, while avoiding federal estate tax from generation to generation, and also avoiding the federal generation-skipping tax.

gift   The transfer of property from one person to another for nothing in return or for substantially less than its actual market value.

gift tax   Federal tax imposed on lifetime gifts, usually charged to the donor of the gift. Some states also impose a gift tax.

gift tax exclusion   The amount of a gift not subject to gift tax. The federal gift tax exclusion for 2007 excludes annual gifts of up to $12,000. Any gift of more than $12,000 per year requires the filing of a gift tax return and may be subject to gift tax.

grantor   Person who establishes a trust, also sometimes called a *settlor* or *trustor*.

grantor trust   Living trust in which the grantor maintains enough control over trust assets so that the trust's income is taxed to the grantor, not to the trust or its beneficiaries.

gross estate   For federal estate tax purposes, the total value of all property in which the decedent had an interest, without regard to any debts or liens against the property or the costs of administering the estate.

guardian ad litem   Legal representative, usually an attorney, appointed by the court to represent the interest of a minor or incompetent person in a particular matter before the court.

guardian of person   Person appointed by the court to care for the person of a minor or incompetent person.

guardian of property   Person appointed by the court to manage the property of a minor child or an incompetent adult.

heir   Person designated by state law to inherit the probate assets of one who dies intestate, that is, without leaving a valid will.

holographic will   An unwitnessed will that is completely handwritten, signed, and dated by the testator. Although legal in many states, its use is not recommended except as a last resort.

income beneficiary   Beneficiary of a trust who receives only income from the trust assets and not the assets themselves.

incompetent   Person declared by a court to be unable to manage his own affairs due either to physical or mental incapacity.

inherit   To receive property from the estate of one who dies.

inheritance tax   Tax imposed by some states on the right to inherit property.

insolvent estate   Estate whose debts exceed its assets.

insurance trust   Trust funded in whole or in part with life insurance proceeds.

in-terrorem clause   Will or trust clause reciting that any beneficiary who contests the document forfeits whatever he would have inherited through the document. Also called a *no-contest* clause.

intervivos trust   Trust established and effective during the grantor's life and which often remains under the grantor's control until death. Also called a *living trust*.

intestate   The act of dying without leaving a valid will.

intestacy laws   State laws that provide for distribution of the probate assets of a person who dies without leaving a valid will.

inventory   Complete listing of an estate's assets, which must be filed with the court within a prescribed time following appointment of the estate's executor.

irrevocable trust   Trust which, after it is signed, cannot be revoked, amended, or changed in any way.

issue   All persons descending from a common ancestor, generally meaning a person's children, their children, and so on. Also called *lineal descendants*.

joint ownership   Form of ownership where two or more persons own the same property, generally in equal shares, with the understanding that upon death of any one, the survivor(s) will own the property. Also called *joint tenancy*.

joint will   A single will signed by two or more persons, usually husband and wife. Since joint wills can produce ambiguity and litigation, they are not recommended.

joint tenant   One of the co-owners involved in joint ownership of property.

lapsed gift   Will or trust-created gift that fails because the designated beneficiary is dead and no alternate beneficiary is named. Under some state *anti-lapse laws*, the lapsed gift may pass to the deceased beneficiary's children.

letters of administration Legal document issued by the court to an administrator authorizing him to act on behalf of the estate of a decedent who left no will.

letter of instruction Informal letter or other writing by which a person provides helpful information to survivors regarding personal matters, property affairs, and preferences as to funeral and body disposition.

letters testamentary Legal document issued by the court to an executor authorizing him to act on behalf of the estate of a decedent who left a will.

life estate Property right limited to the lifetime of its holder. For example, the right to occupy a house or to receive income for life. Upon death of the *life tenant*, the life estate interest terminates.

life insurance trust Trust designed to own a person's life insurance policies so that, upon death, the policy proceeds are not included in the decedent's taxable estate.

living trust Trust established and operative during the grantor's life, and which remains under his control until death. Also called an *inter-vivos trust*.

marital deduction For federal gift and estate tax purposes, a deduction for all property that passes from one spouse to a surviving spouse. To claim the deduction the surviving spouse must be a U.S. citizen.

marital deduction trust Trust designed to receive an amount on behalf of a surviving spouse that qualifies for the marital deduction.

medical power of attorney Power of attorney that appoints and authorizes an agent to make medical decisions on behalf of a person unable to make or communicate such decisions.

minor Person under 18 years of age.

mutual wills Separate wills of two or more persons, with reciprocal provisions in each will in favor of the other person(s).

net taxable estate For federal estate tax purposes, the total value of a decedent's gross estate less allowable deductions, credits, and charitable contributions.

next of kin A decedent's closest living relatives, as defined by state law.

no-contest clause   Will or trust clause reciting that any beneficiary who contests the document forfeits whatever he would have inherited through the document. Also called an *in-terrorem* clause.

non-probate property   Property owned or partially owned by a decedent that does not pass through his probate estate, including assets held in joint ownership, in a living trust, or in financial accounts specifying a named beneficiary.

notary public   Person authorized by state law to witness signatures on documents and sign them attesting to their validity.

nuncupative will   Oral will, declared by the testator before witnesses, and later reduced to writing. Legal in only a few states and under strictly limited circumstances.

nuptial agreement   Written agreement between two persons who are married, or about to marry, which specifies the rights of each spouse in property in the event of divorce or death. Also called a *prenuptial agreement.*

pay-on-death (POD) designation   Bank or other financial account which designates a POD beneficiary to receive the account balance, if any, upon death of the owner. During the owner's life, the POD beneficiary has no rights to the account.

personal property   All property except real property (real estate), including vehicles, household contents, financial accounts, securities, jewelry, pets, and personal effects.

personal representative   Generic term for executor and administrator, used in states that have adopted the Uniform Probate Code and some other states.

petition   Legal document filed with the court requesting specific relief such as appointment of an executor, commencement of probate proceedings, and approval of a decedent's will.

pour-over clause   A clause in a will which transfers property from the decedent's estate to an existing trust. Such a will is called a *pourover will.*

power of attorney   A document by which a person (*principal*), designates another person as his agent or *attorney-in-fact*—that is, to act on the principal's behalf. The scope of the power can be limited or broad.

prenuptial agreement Written agreement between two persons who are married, or about to marry, which specifies the rights of each spouse in property in the event of divorce or death. Also called a *nuptial agreement.*

pretermitted heir Child or other descendant omitted from a testator's will. When a testator's will fails to make provisions for a child, either living at the time the will is signed or born later, state law often provides that such child inherits a share of the testator's estate.

primary beneficiary Person named first in line to receive benefits under a will, trust, financial account or life insurance policy.

probate Court-supervised process in which a decedent's will is approved, an executor is appointed, debts and taxes are paid, heirs are identified, and probate assets are distributed according to the will or, if no will, according to state intestacy laws.

probate court Special state court authorized to supervise the probate administration of decedent's estates.

probate estate Assets owned solely by a person at the time of death.

prudent man theory Theory by which an executor or other fiduciary must invest estate assets as an ordinary, prudent man of intelligence and integrity would purchase in the exercise of reasonable care, judgment, and diligence under the circumstances existing at the time of purchase.

public administrator Person appointed by a probate court to administer a decedent's estate if no relatives, creditors, or will-nominated executor is available to assume the role.

publication Declaration by a testator to witnesses that the document being signed is his will. Although witnesses must know the document is a will, they need not know its content.

qualified domestic trust (QDOT) Trust designed to postpone federal estate tax, when more than the amount of the exemption equivalent is left to a non-U.S. citizen spouse by the deceased spouse.

qualified terminable interest trust (QTIP) Trust designed to qualify for the estate tax marital deduction while leaving mandatory income to a surviving spouse and optionally principal at the discretion of the trustee.

real property Real estate, which includes land and things attached to land such as trees, crops, buildings, fixtures, and stationary mobile homes. Anything not considered real property is called *personal property*.

receipt and release Legal document which an executor, administrator, or trustee will request beneficiaries to sign and deliver before receiving their inheritance, releasing the estate or trust from further liability.

recording Process of filing a deed or other real estate document with the county land records office, thus creating a public record of ownership of the property.

remainderman Person entitled to receive property after the termination of a prior holder's interest. For example, a father might deed his house to his son but reserve a life estate. Upon the father's death, his son (a remainderman) will receive the remainder interest at which time he will own complete title to the house.

residuary beneficiary The will-designated beneficiary who receives any remaining property not specifically left in the will to other beneficiaries.

residuary estate Property remaining in a decedent's probate estate after distribution of all specific bequests. Sometimes called the *residue* of an estate.

revocable Subject to amendment or revocation.

revocable trust Trust that may be altered, amended or revoked by the grantor at any time before his incompetency or death.

right of survivorship Right of a surviving joint owner (joint tenant) to automatically acquire the whole of the jointly owned property upon death of the other joint owner.

self-proving will Will that includes a notarized statement signed by its witnesses, thus making it easier to later prove the will's authenticity.

separate property In community property states, all property owned by a spouse that is not community property, such as property acquired before marriage, property acquired by separate gift or inheritance, and property acquired with separate funds.

settlor Person who establishes a trust. Also called a *grantor* or *trustor*.

simultaneous death clause   Clause in a will that provides for disposition of property in the event there is no evidence as to the priority of the time of death of the testator and another. Also called a *common disaster clause*.

small estate   Probate estate that includes property with value small enough to qualify under state laws governing simplified and expedited transfer procedures.

sole ownership   Ownership of property by one person in such a manner that upon death it passes according to the terms of the owner's will or, if no will, according to state intestacy laws.

specific bequest   Will or trust created gift that specifically identifies property left to a named beneficiary.

special needs trust   Trust designed for a disabled beneficiary which gives the trustee complete discretion to make distributions, giving consideration to other benefits available to the beneficiary outside the trust, such as Social Security benefits.

spendthrift clause   Trust provision that prevents assets from being pledged, assigned, or used as collateral for a loan, the purpose of which is to protect the assets from a spendthrift beneficiary's creditors.

spousal share   Portion of the estate of a deceased spouse that must, under state law, be inherited by the surviving spouse. Also called the *elective share* or *forced share*.

sprinkling trust   Trust designed to give the trustee discretion to distribute part or all of the trust's income among beneficiaries in equal or unequal shares.

standby trust   Unfunded living trust, sometimes signed in conjunction with a durable financial power of attorney, to which property may later be transferred.

stepped-up basis   Taxable value of property either on the date of death or the alternate valuation date six months after death, at the option of the executor.

succession   The act of inheriting a decedent's property under state intestacy laws instead of under a will.

successor trustee   Person who takes over as trustee of a trust after the original trustee becomes incapacitated, resigns, or dies.

summary probate Simplified and abbreviated probate transfer procedure available for *small estates*, as that term is defined by state law.

taking against the will Surviving spouse's right as defined by state law, to elect to receive a state-specified share of the deceased's spouse's estate instead of the share specified in the deceased spouse's will.

taxable estate Decedent's property subject to federal estate tax, including the value of all assets owned at death less certain deductions such as debts, administration expenses, and gifts to qualified charities.

tenancy by the entirety Hybrid from of joint tenancy, available only to spouses, and in which neither spouse (alone) can cause a division or severance of the joint property.

tenancy in common Form of co-ownership in which two or more persons own the same property, in equal or unequal shares, and for which there is no right of survivorship.

testamentary Pertaining to a will. A testamentary document is a writing disposing of property at death, being either a will in fact or in the nature of a will.

testamentary trust Trust created under the terms of a will and thus is only effective through probate administration of the will.

testate The act of dying while leaving a valid will. A person who signs a will is called a *testator*.

Totten trust Bank account held in trust for a designated beneficiary who inherits any money in the account upon death of the owner, without probate proceedings. Similar to a *pay-on-death* account.

transfer-on-death (TOD) designation Designation of a beneficiary to receive a transfer of an asset upon the owner's death and without probate administration. In most states, securities may be registered in TOD form. In a few states, a TOD designation may be used on real estate deeds and motor vehicle titles.

trust Legal arrangement under which one person (the trustee) holds legal title to property (the trust property) to protect and manage it for the benefit of another person (the beneficiary).

trustee Person or financial institution who manages a trust and trust property, including distributing trust income and principal under the terms of a trust agreement.

trustor   Person who establishes a trust. Also called a *grantor* or *settlor*.

undue influence   The act of unduly persuading a person to sign, amend, or revoke a will, trust, or other legal document in a way that he would not have done on his own.

unfunded trust   Trust that is not provided with any property, and to which property may later be transferred. Also called a *standby trust*.

Uniform Anatomical Gift Act   Law that permits the donation of bodies and body parts for the use of science, education, or persons needing specific organs.

Uniform Probate Code (UPC)   Set of laws governing wills, trusts, and probate. Most states have adopted some parts of the UPC, but only 16 states have adopted this law in its entirety.

Uniform Prudent Investors Act   Law that establishes guidelines for executors and trustees to follow when investing an estate's assets.

Uniform Gifts to Minors Act (UGMA)   Law that permits gifts of certain property to be held in the name of a custodian for the benefit of a minor. In most states, now replaced by the more flexible Uniform Transfers to Minors Act.

Uniform Transfers to Minors Act (UTMA)   Law that permits gifts of *any* kind of property to be held by a custodian for the benefit of a minor.

will   Legal document, signed and witnessed as required by state law, in which a competent adult designates beneficiaries of his probate assets, nominates an executor to settle his estate, and names a guardian to protect orphaned minor children, if necessary.

witness   Person who observes another sign a legal document (usually a will, trust, or deed) and then signs it to attest that the person's signature is authentic.

FURTHER READING

Abts, Henry W. *How to Settle Your Living Trust: Swiftly, Easily, and Safely*. New York: McGrawHill, 1999.

———. *The Living Trust: The Failproof Way to Pass Along Your Estate to Your Heirs*. 3rd ed. New York: McGrawHill, 2003.

American Bar Association. *The American Bar Association Guide to Wills and Estates*. 2nd ed. Chicago: American Bar Association, 2004.

Apolinsky, Harold, and Stewart H. Welch III. *J. K. Lasser's New Rules for Estate and Tax Planning*. Rev. ed, Waterville, Me.: Thorndike Press, 2006.

Bove, Alexander A., Jr. *Complete Book of Wills, Estates and Trusts*. 3rd ed. New York: Owl Books, 2005.

Clifford, Denis. *Plan Your Estate*. 7th ed. Berkeley, California: Nolo, 2004.

Hughes, Theodore E., and David Klein. *The Executor's Handbook, Third Edition*. New York: Facts On File, 2007.

Kraemer, Sandy F. *60 Minute Estate Planner: Fast and Easy Illustrated Plans to Save Taxes, Avoid Probate, and Maximize Inheritance*. 3rd ed. New York: Amacom, 2006.

Lynn, Joanne, Joan Harold, and The Center to Improve Care of the Dying. *Handbook for Mortals: Guidance for People Facing Serious Illness*. New York: Oxford University Press, 2001.

Plotnick, Charles K., and Stephan R. Leimberg. *How to Settle an Estate: A Manual for Executors and Trustees*. 3rd ed. New York: Plume, 2002.

Randolph, Mary. *8 Ways to Avoid Probate.* 5th ed. Berkeley, Ca.: Nolo, 2006.

Randolph, Mary. *The Executor's Guide.* 2nd ed. Berkeley, Ca.: Nolo, 2006.

Shotwell, Barbara, and Nancy Randolph Greenway. *Pass It On: A Practical Approach to the Fears and Facts of Planning Your Estate.* New York: Hyperion, 2001.

Strauss, Peter J., and Nancy M. Lederman. *The Complete Retirement Survival Guide: Everything You Need to Know to Safeguard Your Money, Your Health, and Your Independence.* New York: Facts On File, 2003.

INDEX

Page numbers in *italic* indicate figures and tables.